First World War
and Army of Occupation
War Diary
France, Belgium and Germany

1 DIVISION
1 Infantry Brigade
Black Watch (Royal Highlanders)
1st Battalion
4 August 1914 - 31 March 1919

WO95/1263/3

The Naval & Military Press Ltd
www.nmarchive.com
Published in association with The National Archives

Published by

The Naval & Military Press Ltd

Unit 10 Ridgewood Industrial Park,

Uckfield, East Sussex,

TN22 5QE England

Tel: +44 (0) 1825 749494

www.naval-military-press.com

www.nmarchive.com

This diary has been reprinted in facsimile from the original. Any imperfections are inevitably reproduced and the quality may fall short of modern type and cartographic standards.

© Crown Copyright
Images reproduced by permission of The National Archives, London, England, 2015.

Contents

Document type	Place/Title	Date From	Date To
Heading	WO95/1263/3		
Heading	1st Division 1st Battalion The Black Watch (Royal Highlanders Aug-Dec 1914		
Heading	1st Guards Brigade, 1st Division.1st Battalion The Black Watch (Royal Highlanders) August 1914		
War Diary	Aldershot	04/08/1914	29/08/1914
War Diary	Remarks	29/08/1914	31/08/1914
Heading	1st Guards Brigade 1st Division 1st Battalion The Black Watch September 1914		
War Diary		01/09/1914	14/09/1914
Miscellaneous	Le Mortier Monnaie T Teleph. 3 Indre & Loire	03/09/1922	03/09/1922
Miscellaneous			
Heading	1st Guards Brigade. 1st Division No War Diary Exists For This Month 1st Battalion The Black Watch October 1914		
Heading	1st Battalion"The Black Watch." October 1914 Diary deficient. Records Perth have no Copy. See 13/C/70.		
Miscellaneous	Headquarters, Southern Area, Portsmouth,	08/06/1922	08/06/1922
Miscellaneous	Copy of a letter From Captain Campbell Krook, Black Watch.	03/07/1922	03/07/1922
Heading	1st Guards Brigade. 1st Division 1st Battalion The Black Watch November 1914		
War Diary	N Ypres	01/11/1914	18/11/1914
War Diary	Borre	19/11/1914	04/12/1914
Miscellaneous	Appendix "B"		
Miscellaneous	Appendix "A"		
Miscellaneous	Please Note The following two letters refer to memories of the events at the end of October, 1914.		
Miscellaneous	On His Majesty's Service.		
Miscellaneous	Letters from Col Rouen Hamilton Capt Campbell Krook		
Miscellaneous	Ypres	03/07/1922	03/07/1922
Miscellaneous	War Office Whitehall, S. W.	09/06/1922	09/06/1922
Miscellaneous	Copy of a letter from Captain Campbell Krook, Black Watch	03/07/1922	03/07/1922
Diagram etc	Annex to letter of Capt. Campbell Krook Black Watch		
Miscellaneous			
Diagram etc	Annex to letter of Capt. Campbell Krook Black Watch		
Miscellaneous	App. C.	26/11/1914	26/11/1914
Map	Hooge		
Heading	1st Guards Brigade, 1st Division1st Battalion The Black Watch December 1914		
War Diary	Borre	01/12/1914	20/12/1914
War Diary	Bethune	21/12/1914	21/12/1914
War Diary	Cuinchy	21/12/1914	21/12/1914
War Diary	Givenchy	22/12/1914	25/12/1914
War Diary	Cuinchy	25/12/1914	27/12/1914
War Diary	Givenchy	28/12/1914	31/12/1914
Heading	1st Division 1st Brigade1st Battalion Royal Highlanders. Jan-Dec 1915		

Heading	1st Division 1st Brigade War Diary 1st Battalion Royal Highlanders January 1915		
War Diary	Givenchy	01/01/1915	13/01/1915
War Diary	Beuvry	14/01/1915	14/01/1915
War Diary	Bethune	15/01/1915	21/01/1915
War Diary	Beuvry	21/01/1915	25/01/1915
War Diary	Cuinchy	25/01/1915	26/01/1915
War Diary	Annequin	26/01/1915	26/01/1915
War Diary	Bethune	26/01/1915	27/01/1915
War Diary	Beuvry	28/01/1915	28/01/1915
War Diary	Annequin	29/01/1915	30/01/1915
War Diary	Bethune	30/01/1915	31/01/1915
Miscellaneous	Report by Captain W. Green, Commanding, "C" Company 1st. Bn. The Black Watch Appendix "C"	01/02/1915	01/02/1915
Heading	1st Division 1st Brigade War Diary 1st Battalion Royal Highlanders February 1915.		
War Diary	Bethune	01/02/1915	03/02/1915
War Diary	Burbure	04/02/1915	27/02/1915
War Diary	Les Choquaux	27/02/1915	28/02/1915
War Diary	Rue Du Bois	28/02/1915	28/02/1915
Heading	1st Division 1st Brigade War Diary 1st Battalion Royal Highlanders March 1915.		
War Diary	Rue Du Bois	01/03/1915	02/03/1915
War Diary	Le Touret	03/03/1915	03/03/1915
War Diary	Rue Du Bois	04/03/1915	05/03/1915
War Diary	Le Touret	06/03/1915	07/03/1915
War Diary	Rue Du Bois	08/03/1915	10/03/1915
War Diary	Le Touret	11/03/1915	14/03/1915
War Diary	Rue Du Bois	14/03/1915	16/03/1915
War Diary	Le Touret	16/03/1915	17/03/1915
War Diary	Rue Du Bois	18/03/1915	19/03/1915
War Diary	Le Touret	20/03/1915	22/03/1915
War Diary	Hinges	22/03/1915	30/03/1915
War Diary	Rue Du Bois	30/03/1915	31/03/1915
Heading	1st Brigade 1st Black Watch Vol IX 1-30.4.15		
War Diary	Rue Du Bois	01/04/1915	03/04/1915
War Diary	Rue De L'Epinette	03/04/1915	06/04/1915
War Diary	Rue Du Bois	07/04/1915	11/04/1915
War Diary	Rue De L'Epinette	11/04/1915	14/04/1915
War Diary	Mesplaux	15/04/1915	18/04/1915
War Diary	Long Cornet	19/04/1915	22/04/1915
War Diary	Allouagne	23/04/1915	30/04/1915
Heading	1st Division 1st Black Watch Vol X 1-31.5.15		
War Diary	Allouagne	01/05/1915	02/05/1915
War Diary	Le Casan	02/05/1915	02/05/1915
War Diary	Richebourg St Vaast	02/05/1915	03/05/1915
War Diary	Rue Des Berceaux	04/05/1915	08/05/1915
War Diary	Chocolat Menier Corner	08/05/1915	09/05/1915
War Diary	Rue Du Bois Richebourg	09/05/1915	09/05/1915
War Diary	Hinges	09/05/1915	11/05/1915
War Diary	Bethune	12/05/1915	12/05/1915
War Diary	Beuvry	12/05/1915	15/05/1915
War Diary	Sailly-La-Bourse	15/05/1915	19/05/1915
War Diary	Vermelles	19/05/1915	23/05/1915
War Diary	Sailly-La-Bourse	23/05/1915	23/05/1915
War Diary	Noyelles-Lez-Vermelles	24/05/1915	26/05/1915

War Diary	Vermelles	27/05/1915	30/05/1915
War Diary	Sailly-La-Bourse	31/05/1915	31/05/1915
Heading	Ist Division 1st Royal Hrs Vol XI 1-30.6.15		
War Diary	Bethune	01/06/1915	09/06/1915
War Diary	Cuinchy	10/06/1915	16/06/1915
War Diary	Bethune	16/06/1915	18/06/1915
War Diary	Lapugnoy	19/06/1915	23/06/1915
War Diary	Hurionville	24/06/1915	28/06/1915
War Diary	Labeuvriere	29/06/1915	30/06/1915
Heading	1st Division 1st Black Watch Vol XII 1-31.7.15		
War Diary	Labeuvriere	01/07/1915	04/07/1915
War Diary	Noyelles Lez Vermelles	05/07/1915	18/07/1915
War Diary	Annezin	19/07/1915	24/07/1915
War Diary	Annequin	25/07/1915	31/07/1915
Heading	1st Division 1st Royal Hrs Vol XIII August 15		
War Diary	Annequin	01/08/1915	02/08/1915
War Diary	Z. I.	03/08/1915	05/08/1915
War Diary	Annezin	06/08/1915	11/08/1915
War Diary	Noyelles	12/08/1915	14/08/1915
War Diary	Y.3	15/08/1915	17/08/1915
War Diary	Noyelles	18/08/1915	20/08/1915
War Diary	Y.1	21/08/1915	23/08/1915
War Diary	Annezin	24/08/1915	30/08/1915
War Diary	Ferfay	31/08/1915	31/08/1915
Heading	1st Division 1st Brigade War Diary of. 1st Royal Highlanders September 1915		
War Diary	Ferfay	01/09/1915	20/09/1915
War Diary	Le Marquet Wood	21/09/1915	23/09/1915
War Diary	Verquin	24/09/1915	24/09/1915
War Diary	Y. Section	25/09/1915	25/09/1915
War Diary	German Lines	26/09/1915	27/09/1915
War Diary	Y Section	28/09/1915	29/09/1915
War Diary	Left N Deux Les Mines	30/09/1915	30/09/1915
Miscellaneous	1st Brigade Appendix "A"	28/09/1915	28/09/1915
Heading	Ist Division 1st Royal Hrs Vol XV Oct 15		
War Diary	Noeux-Les-Mines	01/10/1915	04/10/1915
War Diary	Near Chalk Pit, Loos	05/10/1915	07/10/1915
War Diary	N Lone Tree	07/10/1915	10/10/1915
War Diary	W of Hulluch	11/10/1915	14/10/1915
War Diary	Le Rutoire	14/10/1915	14/10/1915
War Diary	Sailly La Bourse	14/10/1915	14/10/1915
War Diary	Noeux Les Mines	14/10/1915	14/10/1915
War Diary	Lillers	15/10/1915	27/10/1915
War Diary	La Buissiere	28/10/1915	28/10/1915
War Diary	Huichon	28/10/1915	31/10/1915
War Diary	Lillers	31/10/1915	31/10/1915
Miscellaneous	1st Bn The Black Watch Reference French Map. 36 C N.W.3. 1-10,000 Appendix A	20/10/1915	20/10/1915
Heading	1st Division 1/Royal Highrs Nov 1915 Vol XVI		
War Diary	Lillers	01/11/1915	14/11/1915
War Diary	Mazingarbe	14/11/1915	14/11/1915
War Diary	N of Loos	14/11/1915	17/11/1915
War Diary	Philosophe	17/11/1915	19/11/1915
War Diary	Houchin	19/11/1915	26/11/1915
War Diary	Philosophe	26/11/1915	28/11/1915
War Diary	Nr Hulluch	29/11/1915	30/11/1915

Heading	1st Bde 1/ Roy. Highrs Dec 1915 Vol XVII		
War Diary	Near Hulluch	01/12/1915	02/12/1915
War Diary	Near Lone Tree	02/12/1915	04/12/1915
War Diary	Near Hulluch	05/12/1915	08/12/1915
War Diary	Mazingarbe	08/12/1915	13/12/1915
War Diary	Near Loos	14/12/1915	16/12/1915
War Diary	Philosophe	17/12/1915	19/12/1915
War Diary	Near Loos	20/12/1915	24/12/1915
War Diary	Loos	25/12/1915	25/12/1915
War Diary	Noeux Les	27/12/1915	27/12/1915
War Diary	Mines	28/12/1915	31/12/1915
Heading	1st Division 1st Brigade 1st Battalion Black Watch (R. Highlanders) Jan-Dec 1916		
Heading	1st Brigade.1st Division. 1st Battalion Black Watch (R. Highlanders) January 1916.		
Heading	1st Royal Has Jan Vol XVIII		
War Diary	Hulluch	01/01/1916	03/01/1916
War Diary	Philosophe	04/01/1916	06/01/1916
War Diary	N Hulluch	07/01/1916	12/01/1916
War Diary	Noeux Les Mines	13/01/1916	13/01/1916
War Diary	Allougne	14/01/1916	31/01/1916
Heading	1st Brigade.1st Division 1st Battalion Royal Highlanders (Black Watch) February 1916.		
War Diary	Allouange	01/02/1916	15/02/1916
War Diary	Mazingarbe	16/02/1916	20/02/1916
War Diary	Maroc (Section Left)	21/02/1916	22/02/1916
War Diary	South Maroc	23/02/1916	25/02/1916
War Diary	Maroc (Left Section)	26/02/1916	28/02/1916
War Diary	Les Brebis	29/02/1916	29/02/1916
Heading	1st Brigade 1st Division. 1st Battalion Royal Highlanders (Black Watch) March 1916.		
War Diary	Les Brebis	01/03/1916	08/03/1916
War Diary	Loos Sector	09/03/1916	11/03/1916
War Diary	North Maroc	12/03/1916	14/03/1916
War Diary	Loos Sector	15/03/1916	17/03/1916
War Diary	N Loos	18/03/1916	20/03/1916
War Diary	Les Brebis	21/03/1916	26/03/1916
War Diary	Maroc Section	27/03/1916	29/03/1916
War Diary	South Maroc	30/03/1916	31/03/1916
Heading	1st Brigade 1st Division 1st Battalion Royal Highlanders (Black Watch) April 1916.		
Miscellaneous	In Line I M 2 3 b.O.S. Should Read M. 21 B. O 5. I Think	21/02/1938	21/02/1938
War Diary	South Maroc	01/04/1916	01/04/1916
War Diary	Maroc Sec.	02/04/1916	04/04/1916
War Diary	South Maroc	05/04/1916	07/04/1916
War Diary	Petit Sains	08/04/1916	13/04/1916
War Diary	Loos	14/04/1916	16/04/1916
War Diary	Reserve Loos & O.G.I	17/04/1916	18/04/1916
War Diary	Loos & O.G.I	19/04/1916	19/04/1916
War Diary	Loos	20/04/1916	22/04/1916
War Diary	Loos & O.G.I.	23/04/1916	25/04/1916
War Diary	Les Brebis	26/04/1916	30/04/1916
Heading	1st Brigade 1st Division 1st Battalion Royal Highlanders (Black Watch) May 1916.		
War Diary	Les Brebis	01/05/1916	01/05/1916

War Diary	Maroc Section	02/05/1916	07/05/1916
War Diary	S. Maroc	08/05/1916	12/05/1916
War Diary	Les Brebis	13/05/1916	17/05/1916
War Diary	Calonne	18/05/1916	29/05/1916
War Diary	Bully Grenay	30/05/1916	31/05/1916
Heading	1st Brigade 1st Division 1st Battalion Royal Highlanders (Black Watch) June 1916.		
War Diary	Bully Grenay	01/06/1916	01/06/1916
War Diary	Les Brebis	02/06/1916	09/06/1916
War Diary	Maroc Section	10/06/1916	13/06/1916
War Diary	North Maroc	14/06/1916	17/06/1916
War Diary	Les Brebis	18/06/1916	21/06/1916
War Diary	Calonne Section	22/06/1916	30/06/1916
Heading	1st Bde 1st Div War Diary 1st Battalion Black Watch (R. Highlanders) July 1916.		
War Diary	Calonne Section	01/07/1916	02/07/1916
War Diary	Barlin	03/07/1916	05/07/1916
War Diary	Naours	06/07/1916	06/07/1916
War Diary	Moullins au Bois	07/07/1916	07/07/1916
War Diary	Baizieux	08/07/1916	08/07/1916
War Diary	Albert	09/07/1916	09/07/1916
War Diary	Becourt	10/07/1916	10/07/1916
War Diary	Contalmaison	11/07/1916	13/07/1916
War Diary	Albert	14/07/1916	16/07/1916
War Diary	Becourt	17/07/1916	18/07/1916
War Diary	O.G.2	19/07/1916	19/07/1916
War Diary	Bazentin Wood	20/07/1916	20/07/1916
War Diary	Lozenge Wood	21/07/1916	21/07/1916
War Diary	Shelter Wood	22/07/1916	22/07/1916
War Diary	Bazentin Wood	23/07/1916	24/07/1916
War Diary	Baizieux	25/07/1916	31/07/1916
Miscellaneous	Cover For Branch Memoranda.		
Heading	1st Brigade 1st Division 1st Battalion The Black Watch August 1916		
War Diary	Baizieux	01/08/1916	13/08/1916
War Diary	Becourt	14/08/1916	14/08/1916
War Diary	Bazentin	15/08/1916	18/08/1916
War Diary	Mametz Wood	19/08/1916	19/08/1916
War Diary	Quadrangle Area	20/08/1916	26/08/1916
War Diary	High Wood	27/08/1916	28/08/1916
War Diary	Bazentin Le Grand	29/08/1916	30/08/1916
War Diary	Quadrangle Area	31/08/1916	31/08/1916
Operation(al) Order(s)	Operation Orders By Major G.T. Hunter-Gray, Commanding 1st Bn The Black Watch Appendix No 1	16/08/1916	16/08/1916
Operation(al) Order(s)	Operation Orders By Major G.T. Hunter-Gray, Commanding 1st Bn The Black Watch Appendix 2	17/08/1916	17/08/1916
Miscellaneous	1st Infantry Brigade. Appendix III	18/08/1916	19/08/1916
Heading	1st Brigade 1st Division 1st Battalion Royal Highlanders (Black Watch) September 1916		
War Diary	Quadrangle Area	01/09/1916	01/09/1916
War Diary	High Wood	02/09/1916	03/09/1916
War Diary	Bazentin Le Grand	04/09/1916	04/09/1916
War Diary	Black Wood	05/09/1916	09/09/1916
War Diary	Millencourt	10/09/1916	10/09/1916
War Diary	La Houssoye	11/09/1916	15/09/1916
War Diary	Bresle	16/09/1916	18/09/1916

War Diary	Albert	19/09/1916	19/09/1916
War Diary	Cough Drop	20/09/1916	21/09/1916
War Diary	Matmetz Wood	22/09/1916	24/09/1916
War Diary	Flers Line will 2 Coys at Matmetz Wood	25/09/1916	25/09/1916
War Diary	Matmetz Wood Camp	26/09/1916	27/09/1916
War Diary	Bresle	28/09/1916	30/09/1916
Operation(al) Order(s)	Operation Order by Lieut-Col. J. G. H. Hamilton D.S.O., Commanding 1st Bn The Black Watch Appendix I	02/09/1916	02/09/1916
Miscellaneous	Operation Report Dated 3/9/16. Appendix 2	03/09/1916	03/09/1916
Miscellaneous	Brigade Operation Orders By A. J. Reddie, D.S.O. Brig-Gen. Comdg. 1st Infy Bde. Appendix I	20/09/1916	20/09/1916
Miscellaneous	Operation Orders By Major V. M. Fortune, D.S.O. Commanding 1st Bn The Black Watch Appendix II	20/09/1916	20/09/1916
Miscellaneous	Operation Report :-Dated 21:9:16. For War Diary. Appendix III	21/09/1916	21/09/1916
Miscellaneous	Operation Order by Major V.M. Fortune, D.S.O., Commanding 1st Bn The Black Watch Appendix No. 1	24/09/1916	24/09/1916
Operation(al) Order(s)	Operation Order No.2 By V. M. Fortune D.S.O., Commanding 1st Bn The Black Watch Appendix 2	25/09/1916	25/09/1916
Miscellaneous	Narrative Of Operations On 25th. September, 1916. Appendix 2	27/09/1916	27/09/1916
Heading	1st Brigade 1st Division 1st Battalion Royal Highlanders (Black Watch) October 1916.		
War Diary	Bresle	01/10/1916	02/10/1916
War Diary	Miannay	03/10/1916	31/10/1916
Heading	1st Brigade 1st Division 1st Battalion Royal Highlanders (Black Watch) November 1916.		
War Diary	Hennan Court Wood	01/11/1916	05/11/1916
War Diary	Becourt Camp	06/11/1916	15/11/1916
War Diary	High-Wd	16/11/1916	21/11/1916
War Diary	Mametz Wd	22/11/1916	26/11/1916
War Diary	High Wood	27/11/1916	01/12/1916
Heading	1st Brigade 1st Division 1st Battalion Royal Highlanders (Black Watch) December 1916.		
War Diary	Bazentin Le Petit Camp	01/12/1916	08/12/1916
War Diary	Bazentin Le Petit No 1	09/12/1916	13/12/1916
War Diary	Bazentin Le Petit No 4	13/12/1916	17/12/1916
War Diary	Fricourt Farm	29/12/1916	01/01/1917
Heading	1st Division 1st Infy Bde 1st Battalion The Black Watch. Jan-Dec 1917		
Heading	War Diary 1st. Bn. The Black Watch. 1st. Infantry Brigade. 1st. Division. January 1917.		
War Diary	Fricourt Camp	01/01/1917	09/01/1917
War Diary	Albert	10/01/1917	22/01/1917
War Diary	Warloy	23/01/1917	31/01/1917
Heading	War Diary 1st. Bn. The Black Watch. 1st. Infantry Brigade. 1st. Division. February 1917.		
War Diary	Warloy	01/02/1917	03/02/1917
War Diary	Hamel	04/02/1917	06/02/1917
War Diary	Marley	07/02/1917	07/02/1917
War Diary	Chuignes	08/02/1917	13/02/1917
War Diary	Trenches	14/02/1917	28/02/1917
Heading	War Diary 1st. Bn. The Black Watch. 1st. Infantry Brigade. 1st. Division. March. 1917.		
War Diary	Assevillers	01/03/1917	03/03/1917

War Diary	Chuignolles	04/03/1917	11/03/1917
War Diary	Trenches	12/03/1917	21/03/1917
War Diary	Becquincourt	22/03/1917	29/03/1917
War Diary	Rosieres	29/03/1917	31/03/1917
Heading	War Diary 1st. Bn. The Black Watch. 1st. Infantry Brigade. 1st. Division. April. 1917.		
War Diary	Rosieres	01/04/1917	03/04/1917
War Diary	Curchy	04/04/1917	16/04/1917
War Diary	Chuignes	17/04/1917	30/04/1917
Heading	War Diary 1st. Bn. The Black Watch. 1st. Infantry Brigade. 1st. Division. May. 1917.		
War Diary	Chuignes	01/05/1917	19/05/1917
War Diary	Marcelcave	19/05/1917	26/05/1917
War Diary	Fletre	27/05/1917	31/05/1917
Heading	War Diary (With Appendix),1st. Bn. The Black Watch. 1st. Infantry Brigade. 1st. Division. June. 1917.		
War Diary	Fletre	01/06/1917	11/06/1917
War Diary	Bavinchove	12/06/1917	19/06/1917
War Diary	Wormhoudt	20/06/1917	20/06/1917
War Diary	Zuydcoote	21/06/1917	21/06/1917
War Diary	Oust Dunkerque	22/06/1917	23/06/1917
War Diary	Trenches	24/06/1917	29/06/1917
War Diary	Nieuport Bains	30/06/1917	30/06/1917
Operation(al) Order(s)	1st Battalion The Black Watch Order No. 1. Appendix I	23/06/1917	23/06/1917
Heading	War Diary 1st. Bn. The Black Watch. 1st. Infantry Brigade. 1st. Division. July 1917		
War Diary	Nieuport Bains	01/07/1917	03/07/1917
War Diary	St Idesbald	04/07/1917	17/07/1917
War Diary	Bray Dunes	18/07/1917	18/07/1917
War Diary	Le Clipon	19/07/1917	31/07/1917
Heading	War Diary 1st. Bn. The Black Watch. 1st. Infantry Brigade. 1st. Division. August 1917.		
War Diary	E Clipon Camp	01/08/1917	31/08/1917
Heading	War Diary 1st. Bn. The Black Watch. 1st. Infantry Brigade. 1st. Division. September 1917.		
War Diary	Le Clipon Camp	01/09/1917	30/09/1917
Heading	War Diary 1st. Bn. The Black Watch. 1st. Infantry Brigade. 1st. Division. October. 1917.		
War Diary	Le Clipon Camp	01/10/1917	22/10/1917
War Diary	Le Pringhan	23/10/1917	26/10/1917
War Diary	Herzeele	27/10/1917	31/10/1917
Heading	War Diary (With Appendix). Ist. Bn. The Black Watch 1st. Infantry Brigade. 1st. Division. November. 1917.		
War Diary	Herzeele	01/11/1917	05/11/1917
War Diary	Schools Camp	05/11/1917	06/11/1917
War Diary	Dambre Camp	07/11/1917	12/11/1917
War Diary	Canal Bank	13/11/1917	14/11/1917
War Diary	Irish Farm	15/11/1917	19/11/1917
War Diary	Canal Bank	20/11/1917	27/11/1917
Miscellaneous	Appendix I.	30/11/1917	30/11/1917
Heading	War Diary 1st. Bn. The Black Watch. 1st. Infantry Brigade. 1st. Division. December. 1917.		
War Diary	Pidgeon Camp	01/12/1917	08/12/1917
War Diary	Front Line	09/12/1917	13/12/1917
War Diary	Eikhoek Camp	14/12/1917	31/12/1917

Heading	1st Division 1st Brigade 1st Battalion The Black Watch 1918 Jan-1919 Mar		
War Diary	Line	01/01/1918	31/01/1918
War Diary	Eikhoek Camp	01/02/1918	09/02/1918
War Diary	Hospital. Fm.	11/02/1918	05/03/1918
War Diary	Hospital Fm	05/03/1918	10/03/1918
War Diary	Huddleston Camp	11/03/1918	14/03/1918
War Diary	Support Bn Area	15/03/1918	31/03/1918
War Diary		04/04/1918	28/04/1918
Heading	1st Brigade 1st Division 1st Battalion Royal Highlanders (Black Watch) April 1918.		
War Diary	Ypres-Staden Rly	01/04/1918	03/04/1918
War Diary	Canal Bank	03/04/1918	18/05/1918
War Diary	Noeux-Les-Mines	01/05/1918	28/05/1918
War Diary	Hohenzollern Sector	01/06/1918	05/06/1918
War Diary	Annequin	05/06/1918	13/06/1918
War Diary	Noeux-Les-Mines	13/06/1918	21/06/1918
War Diary	Cambrin Sector	21/06/1918	30/06/1918
War Diary		10/06/1918	19/06/1918
War Diary	Cambrin Sector	01/07/1918	16/07/1918
War Diary	Noeux-Les-Mines	11/07/1918	31/07/1918
Miscellaneous	War Diary	06/07/1918	06/07/1918
Operation(al) Order(s)	1st Battalion The Black Watch. Operation Order No. 1.	06/07/1918	06/07/1918
Miscellaneous	Report On Raid Carried out by "D" Company	08/07/1918	08/07/1918
Miscellaneous	Head Quarters, 1st Infantry Brigade.	08/07/1918	08/07/1918
Miscellaneous	1st Division No. G. 327/45 C.R.A. B.G.C., 1st Inf. Bde.		
Miscellaneous	Dear Anderson	08/07/1918	08/07/1918
Miscellaneous	Operation Orders by Lieut. Colonel ?	01/07/1918	01/07/1918
War Diary	Hohenzollern Left Sub-Sector	31/07/1918	05/08/1918
War Diary	Annequin	05/08/1918	11/08/1918
War Diary	Barlin	11/08/1918	19/08/1918
War Diary	Lisbourg	19/08/1918	31/08/1918
War Diary		31/08/1918	30/09/1918
Miscellaneous	Headquarters Infantry Brigade	03/02/1918	03/02/1918
Miscellaneous	Headquarters 1st Brigade	04/12/1918	04/12/1918
Map	Maps		
Miscellaneous	1st The Black Watch. Operation From 17th To 24th September 1918. Appendix "A"		
Map	3rd Bde		
War Diary		30/09/1918	31/10/1918
War Diary	La Vallee-Mulatre	01/11/1918	06/11/1918
War Diary	Fresnoy-Le-Grand	06/11/1918	23/12/1918
War Diary	Roisdorf	23/12/1918	31/12/1918
War Diary		04/12/1918	04/12/1918
War Diary	Roisdorf Germany	01/01/1919	31/01/1919
War Diary	Roisdorf Germany Ref. Map Sheet Germany 2 L 1/100,000	01/02/1919	28/02/1919
War Diary	Roisdorf Germany Ref. Map Sheet Germany 2 L 1/100,000	01/03/1919	17/03/1919
War Diary	Roisdorf Germany	00/03/1919	31/03/1919
Miscellaneous	Appendix "A"		
Miscellaneous	Special Order Of The Day By Brigadier General L. L. Wheatley, C.M.G., D.S.O., Commanding 1st Infantry Brigade.	25/03/1919	25/03/1919

$$3 \overline{) 1263}$$

3095

1ST DIVISION

1ST BATTALION
THE BLACK WATCH (ROYAL HIGHLANDERS)
AUG - DEC 1914

1st Guards Brigade.
1st Division.

1st BATTALION

THE BLACK WATCH

(Royal Highlanders)

AUGUST 1914

WAR DIARY

INTELLIGENCE SUMMARY

(Erase heading not required.)

Summary of Events and Information

Date		Summary	Remarks
August 4th	3 p.m. July 4th	Order to Mobilize received. Conducting party to depot	
August 5th		No horses. No contractors from Board of Trade except sheep from Rev. Progress normal. Two saddles arrived late owing to obstruction.	
August 6th		30½ Reservists joined from depot. No horses, 2 trailers 3 shoemakers arrived. No boots. Tailors where sent back to T.S. of T. Progress normal	
August 7th		Horses arrived. Head collars all very much too large - delay caused thereby, his one obtained by sewing of flaps known. 305 Reservists joined from depot. Documents completed. No to drafts in much confusion some deficient owing to first men of reservists to arrive or first day, odd cannot verify.	
August 8th		20 Reservists joined from depot	

Army Form C. 2118.

WAR DIARY
or
INTELLIGENCE SUMMARY.
(Erase heading not required.)

1st Bn. The Black Watch Appendix 2

Hour, Date, Place	Summary of Events and Information	Remarks and references to Appendices
1914 Aldershot Aug. 9th	Church Parade. Company Training. (Company returns to complete and some SIGN? documents. Captain returns to complete and some documents.)	Ap)
Aug. 10th	Company Training. One Captain reports to complete	Ap)
" 11th	Brigade route march, etc.; H.M. the King inspected the Brigade. 13 reservists arrived from Depot. Captain Henderson, Lt. Smith, 2/Lt. Houston Boswall, 15 N.C.O's, transfer their or another visit to Ap. 2)	Ap)
" 12th	Company Training. Captains FMB Robertson, 2nd Bn. enrolled for service abroad, appointed to the Bn. by wire. Not to rejoin Bn. and to the Depot in relief of Captain Henderson.	Remarks on mobilization Appendix 1

Army Form C. 2118.

3

WAR DIARY
or
INTELLIGENCE SUMMARY.
(Erase heading not required.)

Hour, Date, Place	Summary of Events and Information	Remarks and references to Appendices
Thursday Aug. 13th	Entrained at Farnborough (S&R) on two trains for Southampton. Considerable delay while Regt: Transport of 2 Bns 9th Brigade was being placed on board our transport "Italian Prince". On entrained completed a great advantage. Sailed about 9 p.m. Fine & calm. Rendered thanks at ten minutes tempest.	
Friday Aug 14th	Rowed through about noon. Landed. On account of the heat did not march to camp above Honfleur till 6 p.m.	Slings are far gentler than those for embarking or clearing horses.
Saturday " 15th	Heavy thunderstorms in night. Heavy rain all day.	No verie ration Honour
Sunday " 16th	Marched at 2.15 a.m. to Havre. Entrained in one train; French staff assisted & have in entraining but it took less than 1½ hrs. Left Havre 18.39. Refreshment at Rouen	

Army Form C. 2118.

4

WAR DIARY
or
INTELLIGENCE SUMMARY.
(Erase heading not required.)

Instructions regarding War Diaries and Intelligence Summaries are contained in F.S. Regs., Part II. and the Staff Manual respectively. Title pages will be prepared in manuscript.

Hour, Date, Place	Summary of Events and Information	Remarks and references to Appendices
Aug. 16 (Contd)	a very small resort. Coffee & wine accommodation & provision of water for the men generally moderate.	
Monday Aug 17	Reached Divisionary Regulating Station 12.15 a.m. Detrained at Le Nouvion about 2.15 a.m. Bivouacked till 7 a.m.	
Tuesday Aug 18 Wednesday " 19 " 20th (21?)	Marched to BOUÉ. rejoined the Brigade & took up billets there. In billets at BOUÉ & Route marching &c.	18. 3 Pte airs to Base
Friday " 21st	Marched 9 miles to billets at CARTIGNIES.	
Saturday " 22nd	Marched 11 miles. Long halt. Marched ½ mile to LIRON FONTAINE and then marched through Maubeuge to night at GRAND RENG - a very Foggy ahead.	

(73989) W4141—463. 400,000. 9/14. H.&J.Ltd. Forms/C. 2118/10.

Army Form C. 2118.

WAR DIARY
or
INTELLIGENCE SUMMARY.
(Erase heading not required.)

Instructions regarding War Diaries and Intelligence Summaries are contained in F.S. Regs., Part II and the Staff Manual respectively. Title pages will be prepared in manuscript.

Hour, Date, Place	Summary of Events and Information	Remarks and references to Appendices
Thursday. Aug. 27th	7 miles on ac [account] and the men under arms for 27 hours. Ordered at 6 p.m. to take up a position between kilometre 19½ & 19¾ on the BEAUMONT-MAUBEUGE road. 3rd Inf. Bde right about TEISSANT.	
Friday. Aug. 28th	About 1½ mile N Enemy artillery engagement visible from [rear?] of the position in the morning between MERBES STE MARIE and MERBES LE CHATEAU. Withdrew before noon and reformed 1st Bde near BETTIGNIES. On road through FEIGNIES to here at LA LONGUE- VILLE.	

Army Form C. 2118

WAR DIARY
or
INTELLIGENCE SUMMARY.
(Erase heading not required.)

6

Hour, Date, Place	Summary of Events and Information	Remarks and references to Appendices
Tuesday, Aug. 25th	Marched by LIMON FONTAINE to billets at DOMPIERRE. Very hot, most of they march of 7 miles.	
Wednesday, Aug. 26th	Marched to GRAND FAYT and occupied position when to D. R. B. de had front retired upon, fell were taken into MARQUILLES by the German artillery but on then aid they advance died away and the French on our right appeared to have occupied the hills overlooking that town. Very heavy artillery fire in the direction of LANDRECIES all day. Marched in afternoon to billets at PETIT CAMBRESIS.	

WAR DIARY or INTELLIGENCE SUMMARY

Army Form C. 2118.

Hour, Date, Place	Summary of Events and Information	Remarks and references to Appendices
Thursday. Aug. 27th	Battalion ordered to occupy position hastily prepared, covering ETREUX, to cover retirement of the rest of the 1st Bde. in support duty between the French (a part of our 2nd Bde) on right and 2nd Bde. on left about WASSIGNY. A cavalry patrol of about 12 (believe the 1st Cockstream Guards) old of OISY into the position which be evacuated. Thought attack. Firing has been heard about BERGUES and BOUE. Two companies 1st SCOTS Guards blocked the roads etc	

WAR DIARY
or
INTELLIGENCE SUMMARY.
(Erase heading not required.)

Army Form C. 2118.

Hour, Date, Place	Summary of Events and Information	Remarks and references to Appendices
Aug 27th (contd)	approaching ETREUX from the E. but if was evident that the enemy villages lay to the SE, and on reaching the exposed portion of the road to GUISE W. of LA NEUVILLE to the 2 companies 1st Scots Guards came under sharp artillery rifle fire but supported by the 118th By R.F.A/Mouspa packard succeeded in withdrawing with a loss of 7 R+F slightly wounded 3 missing (one probably killed). Bivouac at TOUQUEUSE	
Friday. Aug 28th	Marched 25 miles to St GOBAIN Men were together but very much [tired]	

Army Form C. 2118.

9

WAR DIARY
or
INTELLIGENCE SUMMARY.
(Erase heading not required.)

Instructions regarding War Diaries and Intelligence Summaries are contained in F. S. Regs., Part II. and the Staff Manual respectively. Title pages will be prepared in manuscript.

Hour, Date, Place	Summary of Events and Information	Remarks and references to Appendices
Aug 28th (cont'd)	exhausted. Bivouacked.	
Saturday, Aug 29th	Rest.	
REMARKS.	A Lyddite Cordite much wanted for H.Q. and to officers, also reserve better food to keep them fit. The weight of the men's equipment is excessive. A large increase in the O.R.'s of the W.P. feet (which should be carried on the man) is desirable.	
Sunday, Aug 30th	Marched 2-30 a.m. through forest of ST GOBAIN via SERTVAUX & BRANCOURT and reached our bivouac on N edge of	

Army Form C. 2118

WAR DIARY
or
INTELLIGENCE SUMMARY.
(Erase heading not required.)

Instructions regarding War Diaries and Intelligence Summaries are contained in F.S. Regs., Part II. and the Staff Manual respectively. Title pages will be prepared in manuscript.

Hour, Date, Place	Summary of Events and Information	Remarks and references to Appendices
Aug 30th (contd)	ALLEMANT about 1 p.m. Coldstream & an officers billeted in LA MOTTE Chateau. Very comfortable quarters.	
Sunday, Aug 31st	Marched 5.30 a.m. through SOISSONS and bivouacked at MISSY AUX BOIS.	

1st Guards Brigade.

1st Division.

1st BATTALION

THE BLACK WATCH

SEPTEMBER 1 9 1 4

Army Form C. 2118

1st Bn the Black Watch

WAR DIARY
or
INTELLIGENCE SUMMARY.
(Erase heading not required.)

Hour, Date, Place	Summary of Events and Information	Remarks and references to Appendices
Tuesday Sept 1st 1914	Marched about 9am. Battn forming Rear guard. Cavalry reported a German column had crossed the Aisne R. some 10 miles to the N.W. but they did not interfere with our retirement. Reached VILLARS COTTERETS after a march of some miles. Through forest about 1 p.m. where we halted for dinner. We heard heavy firing to N. on reaching village which transferred to the Cavalry Bde also 4th Guards Bde. A Coy held to hold N end of village reinforced soon after by Remainder of Battn. Rear guard fortunately not attacked and retirement	

Army Form C. 2118

WAR DIARY
or
INTELLIGENCE SUMMARY.
(Erase heading not required.)

Instructions regarding War Diaries and Intelligence Summaries are contained in F. S. Regs, Part II. and the Staff Manual respectively. Title pages will be prepared in manuscript.

Hour, Date, Place	Summary of Events and Information	Remarks and references to Appendices
Wednesday, Sept 2nd	Effected though not without crossed OURCQ R at LA FERTE MILON and bivouacked on heights on S. side of R. C. Coy. M.G. sent down to guard bridge to cover retirement of Gd Bde at night	
Thursday, Sept 3rd	Marched at 7 am - long(?) & fast and bad track on first then on main road to VARREDDES. Muddy talk of road. Bivouacked at CHAMBRY	
	Marched about 3am via GERMINY by the Marne about of LA FERTE, billeted at JOUARRE. Very hot day.	

WAR DIARY
or
INTELLIGENCE SUMMARY.
(Erase heading not required.)

Army Form C. 2118.

Hour, Date, Place	Summary of Events and Information	Remarks and references to Appendices
Friday, Sept 4th	Marched early to COULOMMIERES, reaching the town 9 a.m. Spent most of the morning in an ettie-enacting numbers of wire thrown on to canal bank about midday, when we had dinner and washed. In the evening Batta. found Bde. outposts flanking section of Headquarters Bath (as did Bde. H.Q. A Coy post on JOUARRE road was attempted to be rushed by a patrol of Uhlans. They captured 5 who only arrived one to escape. In the evening Cavalry had a scrap with Germans just N of COULOMMIERES	

WAR DIARY
or
INTELLIGENCE SUMMARY.

(Erase heading not required.)

Army Form C. 2118.

Instructions regarding War Diaries and Intelligence Summaries are contained in F.S. Regs., Part II. and the Staff Manual respectively. Title pages will be prepared in manuscript.

Hour, Date, Place	Summary of Events and Information	Remarks and references to Appendices
Saturday, Sept 5.	Marched via MAUPERTHUS & NESTLES, where we bivouacked. First reinforcements arrived under Lt. Macnaghten. Cameron Highrs joined Bde. ffpany Munster Fuseliers joined 1st Bde 1st Div, in fact whole 1st Expeditionary force now concentrated.	
Sunday, Sept 6.	Retirement ended and offensive assumed. Moved E through ROZOY toward VOINSLES. Coldstream and Brigade? 1.7.9. as advanced guard fired with considered opposition and retired. Battn took up position covering the retirement and came under considerable amount of shell fire and were	

WAR DIARY
or
INTELLIGENCE SUMMARY.
(Erase heading not required.)

Army Form C. 2118.

Hour, Date, Place	Summary of Events and Information	Remarks and references to Appendices
Sept. 6 (cont'd)	Ready to leave only 5 moralle. Enemy retired in afternoon. 'Both' found a gn. guard and advanced across country to LA GLOISE FARM where we bivouacked.	
Monday, Sept. 7.	Marched at 5 am via LA BOISSERITE - CHATEAU-GRANGE MESNIL. AMELIS. CHEVNEU to CHOISY not intercepted near NANCY from Germans reported retiring hastily before us.	
Tuesday, Sept 8.	Marched early in POULIGNY-JOLLY-LE-ARRIEL Both, as advanced guard. A leading heights above BELLOT B Coy came under piece fire. Found BELLOT occupied by French cavalry who had suffered severely from shell fire and had not pressed in. But seized they found on N. side of valley. Both pushed on A & D Coys to seize ridge N. of BELLOT – SABLONNIÈRES road. B Coy pushed forward	

Forms/C.2118/10

(9 29 6) W 4141—463 100,000 9/14 H W V

Army Form C. 2118.

WAR DIARY
or
INTELLIGENCE SUMMARY.
(Erase heading not required.)

Instructions regarding War Diaries and Intelligence Summaries are contained in F.S. Regs., Part II. and the Staff Manual respectively. Title pages will be prepared in manuscript.

Hour, Date, Place	Summary of Events and Information	Remarks and references to Appendices
Sept. 8th (Cont'd)	along SABLONNIERES which was then occupied by a Jaeger Battn. B. Coy came under heavy rifle fire on ridge overlooking village while we reinforced by C Coy & 1 Coy's 1/9th Alex Battn. M.G. then Capt. Daigue and 2/Lt. Wilson were killed and Capt. Dunnmore wounded and 25 casualties occurred. Village cleared and E.O. Germans captured. M.G. gave good execution. Advance continued some 5 miles to HONDEVILLERS where we bivouaced. Lieut. Holt and 20 Reinforcement joined.	
Wednesday, Sept. 9th	Marched early and crossed Marne R. at NOGENT. Thence by CHARLY-SUR-MARNE to	

Army Form C. 2118.

WAR DIARY
or
INTELLIGENCE SUMMARY.
(Erase heading not required.)

Hour, Date, Place	Summary of Events and Information	Remarks and references to Appendices
	LANOUETTE Farm, where we bivouacked.	
Thursday, Sept 10th	Marched early via LE THUVET - LUCY LE BOCAGE, TORCY, COURCHAMP. 2nd Bde when in leading, became heavily engaged about and 1st Bde were brought up to support. Advanced in direction of LATILLY in artillery formation (?) Movement had gone and we bivouacked in LATILLY.	
Friday, Sept 11th	Marched hurriedly about 5 a.m. Batt. as advance guard to TROONY, where we billeted. 2 Coys (A & G) on outpost.	
Saturday, Sept 12th	Marched to BAZOUCHES, which we reached after rain in the rain and bivouacked in a large farm. Route via FERE-EN-TARDENOIS and MONT NOTRE DAME. L'Allun left week.	

WAR DIARY
or
INTELLIGENCE SUMMARY.

(Erase heading not required.)

Army Form C. 2118.

Hour, Date, Place	Summary of Events and Information	Remarks and references to Appendices
Sunday, Sept. 13th	Marched via VAUXCERE-LONGUEVAL & crossed AISNE R. at BOURG. 2nd Bde were leading and on their becoming engaged in the direction of MOULINS 1st Bde were sent up in support and Battn. and Company L Zouaves at PAISSY. to occupy PAISSY Ridge. Regulars this and had to advance. Found Company of Zouaves at PAISSY. Blocked there in caves, with outposts on Ridge above. 2nd Bde took over outpost line later.	
Monday, Sept. 14th	1st Bde advanced guard to C.E. Stream Gds leading - Second by 1.9th 4.5"(?) fd.Bs Scouts. Marched early in the morning hurriedly and moved through MOULINS and VENDRESSE on to northern extremity of VENDRESSE ridge where Brigade order for attack was	

WAR DIARY or INTELLIGENCE SUMMARY

Army Form C. 2118

Hour, Date, Place	Summary of Events and Information	Remarks and references to Appendices
Sept 14th (cont'd)	arrived. Coldstream Gds left Bn at VENDRESSE and moved independently up to Troyon leaving to the Sucrerie. A wet morning & mist. Kept further given as the Sucrerie (factory) was moved up (ooooo to no. Attack) Soon came under artillery and rifle fire and artillery formation were broken at with Stationary line. As attack moved up VENDRESSE plateau 79th moved to the West to meet a German attack moving down BEAULNE ridge. Leading Coys of Battn moved to E of Factory (A & C Coys) and advanced up to CHEMIN DES DAMES. D Coy was sent to support 79th. B Coy held in reserve. Later on 2nd Bde came up to Troyon Valley on our Right & side	

WAR DIARY
or
INTELLIGENCE SUMMARY.
(Erase heading not required.)

Army Form C. 2118.

Hour, Date, Place	Summary of Events and Information	Remarks and references to Appendices
Sept 14th (Contd)	Pushed back German attack on BEAULNE ridge - 19th and D. Coy of own assisting, by flanking fire, 116th Battery who brought into action where track to Factory debouches on VENDRESSE plateau and B. Coy was sent to escort the Battery. The Company remained under heavy shell fire and long range rifle fire until about 11 p.m., seeing that the units of the 13th Brigade were returning from the junction of CHEMIN DES DAMES with Troyon Valley and 79th returning into CHIVY valley. 2nd Guards also last TROYON valley. Scots Guards who had occupied St. Etienne & VENDRESSE plateau, also retired from the	

WAR DIARY or INTELLIGENCE SUMMARY.

(Erase heading not required.)

Army Form C. 2118

Hour, Date, Place	Summary of Events and Information	Remarks and references to Appendices
Sept. 11th continued	crest. The plateau was then momentarily unoccupied, but was collecting men to take them back to re-occupy the position against Colonel Grant Duff was mortally wounded. Units from the Regiments being collected the plateau was generally again occupied from its southern extremity up to near Troyon road and the Gloucester Regt. being sent to held southern extremity and below a counter attack if necessary. The M.G. section had earlier moved	

WAR DIARY
INTELLIGENCE SUMMARY
(Erase heading not required.)

Gunning on the S.W. extremity of ridge and together with 9th made a weak attempt in spitting a second attack made by Germans turn the CHIVY valley on night of 3rd Bde. About 1 pm all that were left of the Battn only about 150 of B Coy's & 1 plr of A+C Coys were drawn up and occupied a position on VENDRESSE plateau just NE of where VENDRESSE - TROYON road debouches on to plateau. This position they held till night. Left alone the remnants of other Coys D from direction of CHIVY valley. A+C from direction of road of TROYON valley & Dr G detachment regained. Rest of A+C Coys with Capt. Green Lieut Jolliffe + R.F.C. airscrews men occupied a position on the CHEMIN des DAMES all day and only fell back at nightfall. 3rd Bde. somewhere through CHIVY in the afternoon relieved pressure on us. Dug in at night. A wet and beastly night & have english with a small party, intending for Pioneers rest, and some Gloucesters found had got behind German lines in the direction of CERNY and managed to work their way back into TROYON valley after dark. (Casualties were Officers killed 2 Colonel A Grant McC wounded, Captain H.F.S. Anning, Lieut A.V. Holt, Lieut R.C. Anstruther, Lieut L. Renouf, Lieut N. Boyd-Lieut P.K. Campbell (slightly). Missing Major A. Colonel Murray Lieut L.R. Cumming (also reported killed). Lieut Don Rank File killed

chez Monsieur le Vicomte de la Panouse

LE MORTIER
MONNAIE TÉLÉPH. 3
INDRE & LOIRE

Sept. 3 1922

My dear Edmonds,

Mr Vivian Law
Mrs Adrian Grant-Duff, the
widow of my brother whom
killed in action has drawn
my attention to the footnote
on Page 19 of the Official
History of the war —

I think the enclosed

Before 1912 there was practically no coordination between the various government departments of this country ximimkaxxx for the eventuality of war. Even the Admiralty & the War Office made their plans separately. But one or two far reaching minds had seen the extreme danger of this state of things in our modern world,& had begun to attempt some sort of cooperation. In January 1911 a subcommittee on coordination was appointed under the Imperial Defence Committee,& when in August of the same year the risk of war with Germany over the Agadir incident revealed our complete unpreparedness the Goverment realised its enormous improtance.

Sir Charles Ottley,the secretary of the Committee of Imperial Defence, was secretary of this committee & Colonel Grant Duff,who had been among the foremost in pressing for this inquiry,was the assistant secretary. It was on him that the bulk of the work fell. It was he who, with infinite patience,designed the framework of the War Book into which were fitted the full instructions for each Goverment Office for the action to be taken by them on the outbreak of war concerning every foreseen contingency,such as:

"Mobilisation of Naval centres & signal Stations,Protection of vulnerable points,Harbour traffic,certain preliminary stages of Navy & Army mobilisation,censorship,control of aliens,treatment of enemy merchantmen in port,Trading with the enemy,Goverment War Insurance

---

X It should moreover be noted that all the provisions of the "book" are defensive,& that it moight in Col.Grant Duff's opinion,have been better to use the word"ddefence" instead of "war" as the whole object of the work was protective.

of Shipping & Cargoes, Control of Railways, & many other similiar mea-
-sures, down to such internal arrangements as the suspension of cer-
-tain acts if found necessary.

The first Edition of the War Book was completed by Colonel Grant Duff
in May 1912, from the material supplied to him by nine Goverment
Departments [One excellent result of the Coordination Committee was
that most, if not all, the Deparments drew up War Books for internal
office use - setting out the precise action to be taken, & assigning
the responsibility, & indicating where everything & everybody were to
be found] Colonel Grant Duff also edited the second edition dated
18 June 1913 in which eleven Departments were represented, & which
extended the system to all parts of the British Empire. The War Book
was finally brought up to date just before the war by his successor,
Colonel Longridge.

Credit for the War Book has been given by Mr Lloyd George to Sir
Maurice Hankey, who after succeeding Sir Charles Ottley in 1912 as
Secretary of the C.I.D. was responsible for all the work of the secre-
-tariat, but, as mentioned in the Official History of the War (Naval
Operations: Corbett) Chap.1, it was Colonel Grant Duff who was respon-
-sible for its design. It was he who saw that the various parts
really fitted into each other, & did most of the work which saved this
country from chaos in Aug.1914 by the extraordinary smoothness &
success with which all his arrangements worked out.

[†] Note It was for the War Book that he was given his C.B. 1913

[marginal note: omit if too long.]

1st Guards Brigade.
1st Division.

NO WAR DIARY EXISTS FOR THIS MONTH

1st BATTALION

THE BLACK WATCH

OCTOBER 1914

1st Battalion "The Black Watch."

1914.

~~August to~~ October ~~to January~~   Diary deficient.

Records Perth have no copy.

See 13/C/70.

Letters from
Col. Rowen Hamilton
Capt Campbell Krook

Headquarters,
Southern Area,
Portsmouth,

8th June, 1922.

Dear Colonel,

Reference your letter.

My memory of the events at the end of October, 1914, is not extraordinarily clear, and I have not since then refreshed it in any way by perusing war diaries, records, etc.

I would suggest that General Corkran, late Commandant, Senior Officers' School, be also consulted, as he was Brigade Major, 1st Brigade, at the time, and would verify, no doubt, some of the following statements.

I was Adjutant, 1st Bn. The Black Watch, at the time, and was generally at Battalion Headquarters. I never saw or heard of such a message as the one referred to in your letter being sent. I think it is very unlikely that it was sent, as the earliest intimation I had of the situation on the right of the 1st Brigade was the arrival of elements of "B" and "C" Companies (the Companies attached to Coldstream Guards on the right of the 1st Brigade line), via Brigade Headquarters, and some time after the penetration by the Bosche had occurred.

At this time, the remainder of the Battalion was on the left of the 1st Brigade, near POLYGON WOOD, holding a part of the line. There may have been a Company in reserve at the time, which could have been used for counter-attack, but I think not.

The two Companies "B" and "C" with the Coldstream Guards on the right, were not under your command, and it is therefore improbable that Major Murray, who was commanding 1st Battalion at that time, with Headquarters and two Companies on the left of 1st Brigade, would have been in charge of any counter-attack, or would be likely to have written the message, and I have no recollection of any operations being contemplated or undertaken by the Battalion in the vicinity of the Menin Road after we had moved to Polygon Wood.

General Corkran (if the records do not disclose the facts) could probably say whether any counter-attack was ordered and who carried it out.

From the reports of the Officers of "C" Company, both now killed, Nolan and Macneil, who were with "C" Company (on left of Coldstream Guards), the Bosche certainly arrived from right flank and right rear, and I fancy Scots Guards were on the left of "C" Company. It is quite possible that a message of this sort might have been sent a few days earlier when the 1st Brigade were operating from Gheluvelt eastwards, or later on when Scots Guards were holding the right of 1st Brigade front near Veldhoek, though I don't recollect it.

I hope this is of some use.

Yours
Guy Rowan-Hamilton

YPRES, 29th October 1914.

Copy of a letter from Captain Campbell Krook, Black Watch.

Elizabelis Tela 3 ds 9,
Riga,
Latvia.
3-7-22.

My dear Wavell,

Very many thanks for your letter. Owing to my having changed my address your letter only reached me yesterday. I think that Edmonds' explanation is probably the correct one. The break through occurred on the right of the Coldstream line somewhere in the region of B Company, Black Watch.

Whether it was actually at the point held by B Company or not no one knows.

The line was then rolled up as follows:- B Company, 1st Black Watch, Nos.1, 2 & 3 Companies Coldstream with Battalion Headquarters. This left No.4 Company, Coldstream and C Company 1st Black Watch.

We held out until about 11 a.m. when the trench was finally captured by Germans who came out of a wood immediately in rear of the trenches. There was an interval of about 160 from my left and the first detached post of the Scots Guards. It is therefore probable that more Germans pushed on through the wood and came out also behind the Scots Guards.

I am quite certain that Murray could not have sent such a message for the reasons stated by Edmonds.

The enclosed rough sketch, from memory, shows what happened.

Our line should be shown somewhat on the Menin side of the cross roads - but when B Company trench was taken and 1, 2 & 3 Coldstream, the Boche were able to fire into our trenches from behind as well as in front.

Gibbs (commanding No.4 Coldstream) and I sent out a couple of sections to line up where I have placed an X on the sketch in order to prevent the Boche getting into the wood - anyhow without our knowing it. All these men were wiped out without our getting any messenger back - so that we did not know that they were in the wood though we knew that they were working that way.

McNeil told me that he had seen some troops in the woods - supposed to be Gloucesters and we got a <u>verbal</u> message that 2 platoons of the Gloucesters were coming to our assistance and wanted instructions as to where to come. I sent out McNeil to bring them up but he never returned. The wood was very thick and only about 12 yards behind the trench. An attempt was made 3 times from G on sketch to take the refused portion of my trench but it was repulsed each time.

Steady firing was kept up from the German line in front and the sudden burst of Germans from the wood in rear was quite unexpected as we did not know that they had got so far round and also hoped for the Gloucesters from the wood. The same probably applies to the Scots Guards only they were told Black Watch coming up.

I am getting along fairly well here at present and making progress but not much money as yet. They are very difficult and tricky people to deal with.

I flew to Danzig and back the other day in a German monoplane, 3 hours flying each way and quite comfortable.

It will be interesting to see how Collins & Co. manage the Irish rebels. Does'nt everyone boil with rage about Sir Henry Wilson's murder. One fine feature was the bravery of the police and also the attitude of the public at the time. As regards this country, 1½ million inhabitants, it seems to be impossible that it can live without Russia - the prosperity of the place depends practically entirely on the hinterland with the result that trade is very restricted and they have no money and no resources to speak of. Have you ever been here? I suppose the 1st Battalion is at Borden with A.G.W. in command - is it?

        Best of luck,

           Yours ever,

              A.D. Campbell Krook.

1st Guards Brigade.
1st Division.

1st BATTALION

THE BLACK WATCH

NOVEMBER 1914

Appendices attached:-
    Reports on Operations 2nd & 11th November
    Extraxts from letterfrom C in C.
    Map.

WAR DIARY
or
INTELLIGENCE SUMMARY

(Erase heading not required.)

Army Form C. 2118

Hour, Date, Place	Summary of Events and Information	Remarks and References to Appendices
November 1st., M. Ypres	Lt. Col. C.E. Stewart arrived from Marseilles and took over Command of the Battⁿ. Capt Amory Bnt & Lt Pearse. 60 rank & file arrived from S⁺ Nazaire.	
November 2nd.		
11 a.m.	120th Regiment (French) advance through our lines to attack but were heavy Shrapnel attack drove away Germans attack along MENIN road about	
1.30 p.m	1300 yards to our right and carry services held by 8/H Brigade on our right. Under orders from Brigadier Gen Fitzclarence the 1st/Bde Reserve – A, B, C Coys of the Battⁿ under Capt Amory make counter attack which though only 120 men and supported by machine guns successfully stops German advance. Capt Fortunes Bttⁿ on left was specially commended by Brigadier. Three companies occupied trenches TCA vacated by troops & held them until relieved on the	see App A.
4.15 p.m	night of Batt. guards until relieved from sd 13th at dusk. 79 Casualties. Officers 3rd & Wounded Lieut R.F.D. Polton (3058⁰) Wounded Capt P.S. Amory, Bnt & V & ? Pearse. Rank & file Killed 5. Wounded 34 Missing 21.	

● Army Form C. 2118

WAR DIARY
or
INTELLIGENCE SUMMARY
(Erase heading not required.)

Instructions regarding War Diaries and Intelligence Summaries are contained in F. S. Regs., Part II. and the Staff Manual respectively. Title pages will be prepared in manuscript.

Hour, Date, Place	Summary of Events and Information	Remarks and References to Appendices
November 3rd. Ns Ypres.	Batt'n Headquarters moved. had broken shelled. Weather fine day but damp underfoot. Casualty Killed Rank & File One	
November 4th. 2 a.m.	Heavy firing on our right. Shelling not quite so heavy during day. Weather some rain.	
November 5th.	Very heavy shelling all day. At dusk a good deal of rifle fire on our right. Our losses were all from shell fire during the day. Casualties Rank & File Wounded. 2nd Lt T. Graham (3rd B'n) Rank & File Killed 1. Wounded 19. Weather fine, mist in evening	

Army Form C. 2118

WAR DIARY
or
INTELLIGENCE SUMMARY

(Erase heading not required.)

Instructions regarding War Diaries and Intelligence Summaries are contained in F. S. Regs., Part II. and the Staff Manual respectively. Title pages will be prepared in manuscript.

Hour, Date, Place	Summary of Events and Information	Remarks and References to Appendices
November 6th. Nr Ypres.	Heavy shelling from 8 a.m. until dusk. Casualties Killed Rank & File One. Wounded (attached died) Rank & File One. Weather very foggy early and in evening.	12
November 7th. Nr Ypres.	Heavy Shelling from 7.30 a.m. until dusk. Lieutenant J.W.L. Sport with reinforcement of 32 men arrives from SOUTHAMPTON. Casualties Rank and File Wounded Two.	
November 8th. Nr Ypres.	Very heavy shell fire. About 2.30pm Germans break through trenches held by Zouaves immediately N. of MENIN road and fire through trench. Occupied by Royal North Lancashire. A. & B. Coys of the Batt. under Captain V.M. Fortune re-occupy the 2 N. Lancs trench at 3.45 p.m. and hold line between 1/ Scots Guards and MENIN road. Germans in trench 40 yards to their right front. Our 2 machine guns so done & during night enfilade this trench.	
November 9th Nr Ypres	Killed from here this rifles sent up to # 1st Bde JPQR. Casualties on 8th Wounded Rank & File 8	

Army Form C. 2118

WAR DIARY
or
INTELLIGENCE SUMMARY
(Erase heading not required.)

Instructions regarding War Diaries and Intelligence Summaries are contained in F. S. Regs., Part II. and the Staff Manual respectively. Title pages will be prepared in manuscript.

Hour, Date, Place	Summary of Events and Information	Remarks and References to Appendices
November 9th Nr Ypres	Heavy shelling all day. At night the 1st K.O. & 2nd Lancashire Regt relieve A, B Coys in trenches & they form Bde reserve again, arriving at hd qrs about 11.40 p.m. with two machine guns which go down to D Coy in front trench on left. Q Cameron Highlanders for night 9/10th. Casualties Rank & file 5 killed, 5 wounded. Weather Fine	
November 10th	Heavy shelling all day — especially on D Coy's trench. Casualties Rank & File. 3 killed, 12 wounded. Weather Foggy.	
November 11th 7 – 9.30 a.m	Heavier shelling yet experienced from 7 a.m to 9.30 a.m. About 9.30 a.m the Prussian Guard having got within 50 yards of trenches on right of D Coy break through in mass. D Coys right in swung round & German attack curved round to Bde head quarter's post where C Coy hold Defensive post under Lieut F. Anderson. C Coy got them in cuffilade & there German attack split up into parties	A/p B.

WAR DIARY
or
INTELLIGENCE SUMMARY
(Erase heading not required.)

Army Form C. 2118

Hour, Date, Place	Summary of Events and Information	Remarks and References to Appendices
Nov 11th Continued. 10 a.m.	of 100 duel of 50 men. One party advance to Bn headquarters but are held up there – a few succeed in getting into wood behind. The Colonels of the Black Watch & Camerons told on to the farm area.	
12.45 p.m.	About 12.45 p.m. a mixed force of the Black Watch, Camerons and 3 coys Northamptons advance from wood 150 yards behind and eventually clear ground as far as Lieut Anderson's post held by him & 6 C Coy. with the greatest gallantry.	App B.
3.30 p.m.	During the evening all farmers in the area were rounded up and Copraced.	

Casualties. Officers Killed 2nd Lieut A.S. Lawson. Wounded Lt Col E. Stewart Comdg, Capt & Adjt G.A. Rowan-Hamilton, Capt E.C. West, Lieut J. Anderson, Murray, Lieut F.M. S. West, 2nd Lieut M. McNeil. Other Ranks Killed 18. Wounded 52. Missing 49.

WAR DIARY
or
INTELLIGENCE SUMMARY

Army Form C. 2118.

(Erase heading not required.)

Hour, Date, Place	Summary of Events and Information	Remarks and References to Appendices
Nov. 11th – 12th	At 2 a.m. 2nd Grenadiers & 1st Irish Guards under General Fitzclarence VC advanced to retake trenches of the 1st Brigade. Captain Jenkins, CSM Gray, 2341 Pte A. Mitchell all of the Black Watch acting as guides. Gen Fitzclarence was shot & the O.C. 5th Bde decided that attack should not take place. Casualties. C Coy relieved from Fort by Northamptonshire Regt. H.Q. Black Watch now in farm late H.Q. of Black Watch & Camerons.	
12th	Quiet day. Practically no shelling	
13th	Relieved by Camerons after dusk after sometime. Quiet day & went into bivouac on North side of road opposite HOOGE CHATEAU.	
14th	Crossed road into hard ground HOOGE CHATEAU when 1st Brigade dug themselves into dug outs. Capt. M Thomson (Argyll & Sutherland Hldrs) & 2 m/Lt M'Bain & 2nd Lt joined with NCOs & men. Two drafts in all partly from Mgg @ parts to 1st Reinforcements of the 2nd Bn.	
15th – 16th	Quiet day. 1st Brigade left at 1 a.m. – avoided YPRES by walking round the town along railway line we met POPERINGHE ROAD – head halted just on the YPRES side of VLAMERTINGHE & marched to WESTOUTRE – when we billeted for night	
16th	1st Brigade marched to billets in BORRE the vicinity – the battalion being billeted in 3 farms about ½ mile S W of	
17th	BORRE village	
18th	Quiet day. Battalion commenced to reorganize & refit.	

Army Form C. 2118.

WAR DIARY
or
INTELLIGENCE SUMMARY
(Erase heading not required.)

Instructions regarding War Diaries and Intelligence Summaries are contained in F. S. Regs., Part II. and the Staff Manual respectively. Title pages will be prepared in manuscript.

Hour, Date, Place	Summary of Events and Information	Remarks and References to Appendices
19 November. BORRE	Lt Col Stewart returns from hospital at BOULOGNE and resumes command of the Battn. Capt W.T. Kerr joins from Staff duty at HAVRE and takes over command of B Coy. Weather frost. Some snow.	
20 November. BORRE.	Reftusyk Maj Gen Landon, Commdg 1st Divn visits Battn HdQrs. Orders permitting officers 96 hrs leave to go home come out. Capt Fortune goes on leave. Lieut J.N.O. Ryecroft acts adjt. Weather. Sharp frost.	
21 November. "	Reftusyk Arm inspection. Lieut G.M. Richmond, Reserve of Officers, joins from 3rd Battn and takes temporary command of A Coy. Weather Sharp frost.	
22 November. "	Divine Service. Orders received to enrol 2nd Coy Divn Cyclists for 46 hrs (Viz 1st & 3rd B des which officers conveyed). Lieut W.H.C. Edwards (who had been sick) & 2nd 2nd Lieut S.C. Huddleston with draft of 35 other ranks (mostly men who had been wounded) rejoin from HAVRE. Lt/Col. St David Hamilton 9 Lt Edwards takes over C Coy, 2nd Lt Huddleston joins D Coy. Weather. Sharp frost.	
23 November. "	Reftusyk Major! St David Henderson Commdg RFC, 250 Reftusyk Major! St David Henderson Commdg 1st Divn inspects billets. B Coy moves into new billets, 2nd Lt A McAdam to B Coy, 2nd Lt J Muller to A Coy Orders received that 2 NCO's per Bn may be granted 120 hrs leave. Weather Cloudy. frost.	
24 November. "	Reftusyk C Coy route marching	
25 November. "	Majr Gen! H.C. Landon Commdg 1st Brde visits belgn.	

Army Form C. 2.

WAR DIARY
or
INTELLIGENCE SUMMARY
(Erase heading not required.)

Instructions regarding War Diaries and Intelligence Summaries are contained in F. S. Regs., Part II. and the Staff Manual respectively. Title pages will be prepared in manuscript.

Hour, Date, Place		Summary of Events and Information	Remarks and References to Appendices
26 Nov.	BORRE	In billets. Refitting.	
27 Nov.	"	"	
28 Nov.	"	Capt. Sir E. Stewart Richardson, (discharged of wounds received at Alwin in London) rejoined.	
		Lt. Col. Sir John Trevor, Commdg. Brit. Expeditionary Force, inspected the Battalion and thanked them for their services up to date in the war.	
29 Nov.	"	Divine Service. Draft 2nd Lieut. J.H. Willett, 3rd Bn., and 280 other ranks arrived from M.G.C.	App C.
30 Nov.	"	In billets. Refitting.	
1. December	"	"	
2. December	"	In billets. Bttn. in readiness to move in 2½ hrs from 8 a.m.	
3. December	"	H.M. the KING sees battalion. Draft 2nd Lt. W. Stirling, 3rd Seaforth Highlanders and 150 other ranks arrive from M.G.C.	
4 December	"	In billets. Training and refitting.	

Appendix "B"
14.
Nov.11th.

Owing to the heavy shelling a great amount of trench in "B" Coys. line was destroyed. As it stopped about 9-30a.m. their look out discovered the Prussian Guard just beginning to cross the wire entanglement while the trenches on their right were unoccupied by our troops. 2/Lieut. McNeil kept in front of the trench and opened fire with his revolver but was hit and fell back in the trench. The few men of "A" Coy. with him fired a few shots and seeing their right flank surrounded ran down the trench and joined "D" Coy. whom Captain West had formed up in prolongation of the line of the Liverpool Regiment almost at right angles to his own original line and on the S. edge of the ZONNEBEKE race course wood. The Germans drove the left and centre of this party into the wood and swept up until they came under the fire of "C" Coy. at Lieut. Anderson's point d'appie 380 yards from S&W. corner of ZONNEBEKE wood. This caused their front line to split up keeping over 150 yards on either side of the supporting work.

Some 200 came over the dug out where Lieut. Sprot with 45 men of "A" & "B" Coys. were and rushed them before they got into their firing trench and about 9-50a.m. some 50 German's had reached the farm 60 yards behind in which were The Black Watch and Cameron Headquarters. Lieut-Colonel Stewart followed by two of the headquarter men occupied the fire trench in the garden of the farm. Lieut-Colonel. McEwan of the Camerons had two or three others in a dug out. The other German's went off to the right rear towards the N. part of NONNE BOSSCHEN wood where at least 300 more of them had swept round.

Captain and Adjutant G&B&Rowan-Hamilton rallied a mixed line of British in the prxxixx Southern portion of this wood where Captain Fortune and 2/Lieut. A&S&Lawson (who had been at Brigade Headquarters) had previously formed up a number of stragglers along the Eastern edge of the lower part of NONNE wood. The few German's in the Battalion Headquarters farm made no attempt to follow their comrades after two had been shot by No.1008 Cpl. Redpath and the farm was shelled with shrapnel by both sides. About 11-15a.m. Captain Rowan-Hamilton ran out along the 60 yards which separated the South portion of the NONNE BOSSCHEN wood from Battalion Headquarters intending to bring forward the mixed force he had, but was wounded.

Lieut-Colonel Stewart who had been slightly wounded then ordered the two N.C.O's and two R.F.A. telephone operators with him to go back to the wood and reported to the Brigadier how weakly the farm was held. Before this however the Brigadier had ordered the whole of the Force including 3 Coys. of the Northamptonshire Regiment to advance past the farm to "C"Coys. supporting work. The farm was re-occupied by 1-30p.m. The Northamptonshire eventually with the Oxfordshire L.I. advanced t to our supporting work.

The Colonel and other Officer's having become casualties the command of the Battalion developed temporarily on Captain Fortune who was the sole Officer left except Lieut & Quarter-master W&Fowler i/c of the 1st.& 2nd. line transport.

Appendix "A"
1914.
Nov.2.

The counter attack was made by throwing forward each Coy. separately, as quickly as possible. Captain Fortune with 2 Platoons went forward just at 1 p.m. and got within 200 yards of the main road by which the German's main attack advanced. Captain Amery with "B" & "C" Coys. joined him in 10 minutes time, extending line to the left but lost severely when going through a gap in the hedge on which a German Machine Gun was trained. Lieut. Nolan also led his Platoon on the left of "C" Coy. very boldly forward.

The German Machine Gun caught this last Platoon, mortally wounding Lieut. Nolan and carrying about 15 casualties, but the German forward movement stopped. Captain Fortune succeeded in prolonging the line facing S.E. on the left of the Scots Guards.

Captain Amery was badly hit in three places and 2/Lieut. Rennie was severely wounded but the rest of "B" & "C" Coys. rejoined the ½ of "A" Coy. in the gap near the main MENIN Road.

No. 313 Cpl. Culpin "C" Coy. was especially proinent for good leadership. No. 1008 Cpl. Redpath "C" Coy. took forward those men of "B" Coy. who were left without a leader on the extreme left after the fall of Lieut. Nolan.

The whole German attack fell back except for snipers who still occupied some houses in VELD HOEK and some advanced pits dug by the Zouaves two days previously.

After dark "A", "B", & "C" Coys. under Captain Fortune (about 75 men in all) were withdrawn and a new line was taken up somewhat in rear of the original one.

....

Please note

The following two letters refer to memories of the events at the end of October, 1914.

On His Majesty's Service.

Letters from

Col Rowen Hamilton.
Captain Campbell Krook

Letters from
Col Rowen Hamilton
Capt Campbell Krook

Elizabetes Iela 3. as 9.
Riga
Latvia.

"Ypres"
29 Oct 1914
Letter from Capt Campbell Kirosk
"Black Watch"

3. 7. 22.

My dear Wavell,

Very many thanks for your letter. Owing to my having changed my address your letter only reached me yesterday.

I think that Edmonds explanation of the incident is probably the correct one.

The break through occurred on the right of the Coldstream line somewhere in the region of B Coy 1st B.W.

Whether it was actually at the point held by "B" Coy or not no one knows.

The line was then rolled up as follows "B" Coy 1st B.W. No 1. 2 & 3 Coys Coldstream with Bn. H.Q. This left No 4 Coy Coldstream and "C" Coy 1st B.W.

We held on until about 11 am when the trench was finally captured by Germans who came out of a wood immediately in

rear of the trenches. There was an interval
of about 160 yards my left and the
first detached post of the Scots Guards.
It is therefore probable that more Germans
pushed on through the wood and came out
also behind the Scots Guards.
I am quite certain that Murray could
not have sent such a message for the
reasons stated by Edmonds.
The enclosed rough sketch, from memory, shows
what happened
Our line should be shown somewhat on the MENIN
side of the cross roads — But when B Coy
trench was taken and 1, 2 & 3 Coldstream, the
Boche were able to fire into our trenches
from behind as well as in front
Gibbs (cmdg No 4 Coldstream) & I sent out
a couple of sections to line up when I

have placed an X on the sketch in order to prevent the Boche getting into the wood - anyhow without our knowing it. All these men were wiped out without our getting any messages back - so that we didn't know that they were in the wood though we knew that they were working that way.

McNeil told me that he had seen some troops in the woods - supposed to be Gloucesters and we got a verbal message that 2 platoons of the Gloucesters were coming to our assistance and wanted instructions as to where to come. I sent out McNeil to bring them up but he never returned. The wood was very thick & only about 12 yards behind the trench.

An attempt was made 3 times from G on sketch to take the repeated portion of my trench but it was repulsed each time.

Steady firing was kept up from the German line in front and the sudden burst of Germans from the wood in rear was quite unexpected as we did not know that they had got so far round. & also hoped for the Gloucesters from the wood.

The same probably applies to the Scots Guards only they were told Black Watch coming up.

I am getting along fairly well here at present
& making progress but not much money as
yet. They are very difficult and tricky
people to deal with.
I flew to Danzig & back the other day in a
German monoplane 3 hours flying each way
& quite comfortable.
It will be interesting to see how Collins & Co
manage the rebel irish rebels. Doesn't everyone boil
with rage about Sir Henry Wilson's murder. One
fine feature was the bravery of the police and
also the attitude of the public at the time.
As regards this country, 1½ million inhabitants
it seems to me impossible that it can live
without Russia – the prosperity of the place
depends practically entirely on the hinterland
with the result that trade is very restricted
& they have no money & no resources to
speak of. Have you ever been here.
I suppose the 1st Bn. is at Bordon with
A.E.W. in command – is it?
      Best of luck
              Yrs ever
              A O Lumley Kroek

War Office,
Whitehall,
S.W.

June 9. 1922

Dear Edmunds

I enclose a letter from Rowan Hamilton who was adjt of the 1st Bn on Oct. 29. I have written to Krook, but as he is in Riga or Russia it

May be some time before I get any reply.

A.P. Wavell

YPRES, 29th October 1914.

Copy of a letter from Captain Campbell Krook, Black Watch.

Elizabelis Tela 3 ds 9,
Riga,
Latvia.
3-7-22.

My dear Wavell,

Very many thanks for your letter. Owing to my having changed my address your letter only reached me yesterday. I think that Edmonds' explanation is probably the correct one. The break through occurred on the right of the Coldstream line somewhere in the region of B Company, Black Watch.

Whether it was actually at the point held by B Company or not no one knows.

The line was then rolled up as follows:- B Company, 1st Black Watch, Nos.1, 2 & 3 Companies Coldstream with Battalion Headquarters. This left No.4 Company, Coldstream and C Company 1st Black Watch.

We held out until about 11 a.m. when the trench was finally captured by Germans who came out of a wood immediately in rear of the trenches. There was an interval of about 160 from my left and the first detached post of the Scots Guards. It is therefore probable that more Germans pushed on through the wood and came out also behind the Scots Guards.

I am quite certain that Murray could not have sent such a message for the reasons stated by Edmonds.

The enclosed rough sketch, from memory, shows what happened.

Our line should be shown somewhat on the Menin side of the cross roads - but when B Company trench was taken and 1, 2 & 3 Coldstream, the Boche were able to fire into our trenches from behind as well as in front.

Gibbs (commanding No.4 Coldstream) and I sent out a couple of sections to line up where I have placed an X on the sketch in order to prevent the Boche getting into the wood - anyhow without our knowing it. All these men were wiped out

Annex to letter of
Capt. Campbell Kerr
Black Watch

YPRES
29 Oct 1914

without our getting any messenger back - so that we did not know that they were in the wood though we knew that they were working that way.

McNeil told me that he had seen some troops in the woods - supposed to be Gloucesters and we got a verbal message that 2 platoons of the Gloucesters were coming to our assistance and wanted instructions as to where to come. I sent out McNeil to bring them up but he never returned. The wood was very thick and only about 12 yards behind the trench. An attempt was made 3 times from G on sketch to take the refused portion of my trench but it was repulsed each time.

Steady firing was kept up from the German line in front and the sudden burst of Germans from the wood in rear was quite unexpected as we did not know that they had got so far round and also hoped for the Gloucesters from the wood. The same probably applies to the Scots Guards only they were told Black Watch coming up.

I am getting along fairly well here at present and making progress but not much money as yet. They are very difficult and tricky people to deal with.

I flew to Danzig and back the other day in a German monoplane, 3 hours flying each way and quite comfortable.

It will be interesting to see how Collins & Co. manage the Irish rebels. Does'nt everyone boil with rage about Sir Henry Wilson's murder. One fine feature was the bravery of the police and also the attitude of the public at the time. As regards this country, 1½ million inhabitants, it seems to be impossible that it can live without Russia - the prosperity of the place depends practically entirely on the hinterland with the result that trade is very restricted and they have no money and no resources to speak of. Have you ever been here? I suppose the 1st Battalion is at Borden with A.G.W. in command - is it?

        Best of luck,

            Yours ever,

                A.D. Campbell Krook.

YPRES
29 Oct. 1914

Annex to letter and
Capt Campwell Krook
Black Watch.

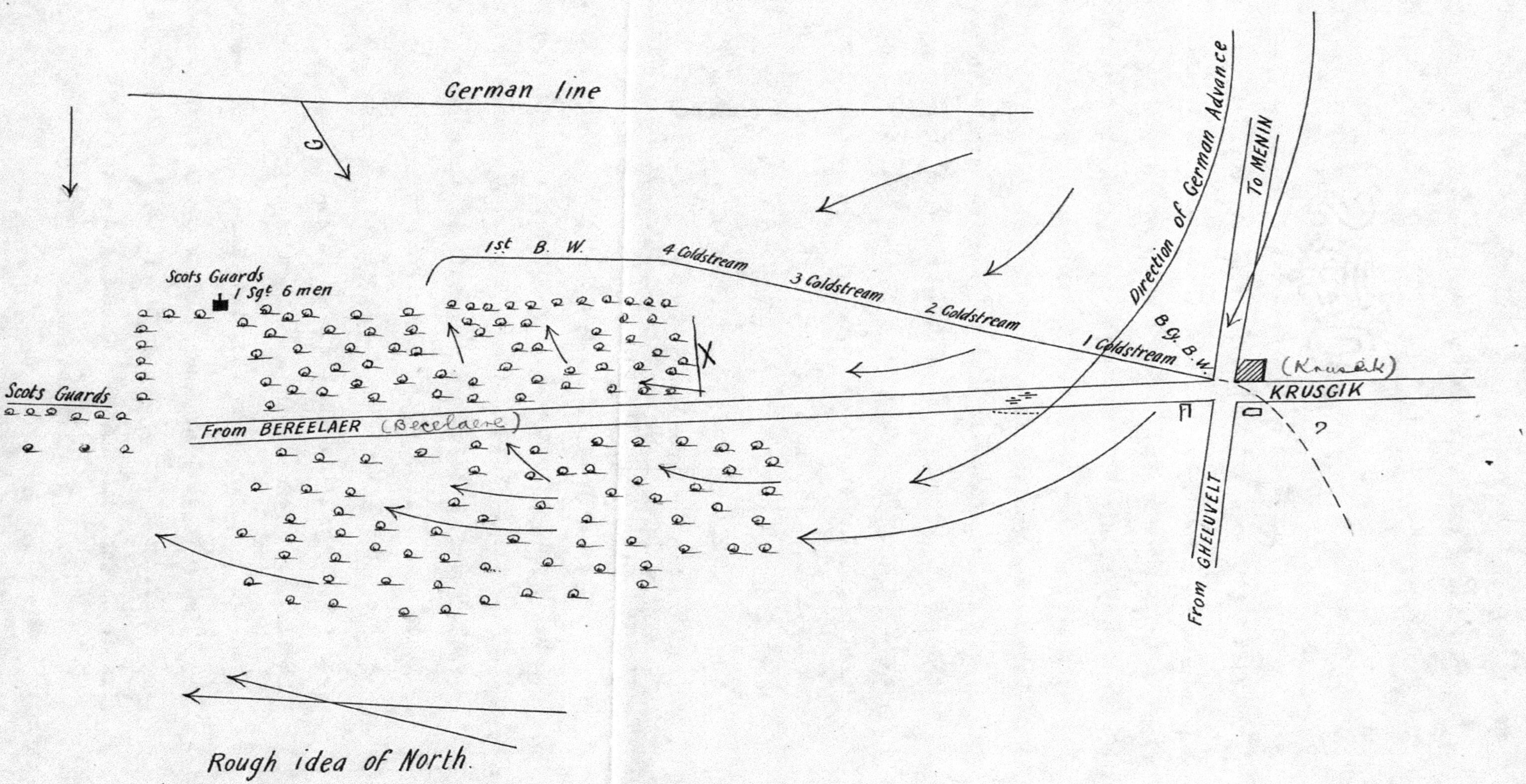
German line
G
1st B. W.
4 Coldstream
3 Coldstream
2 Coldstream
1 Coldstream
B. G. B. W.
Direction of German Advance
To MENIN
(Kruseik)
KRUSGIK
?
From GHELUVELT
Scots Guards
1 Sgt 6 men
Scots Guards
X
From BEREELAER (Becelaere)
Rough idea of North.

YPRES
29 Oct. 1914

● Annex to letter and
Capt. Campwell Krook.
Black Watch.

KRUSGIK

TO MENIN

From CHELUVELT

Direction of German Advance

Bg. B.W.
1 Coldstream
2 Coldstream
3 Coldstream
4 Coldstream
1st. B.W

German line

Scots Guards
1 Sgt 6 men

From BEREELAER

Scots Guards

Rough idea of North

App. C.

Extracts taken from the speech made by Field Marshall Sir John French,
Commander-in-Chief of the British Army In-the-Field.

Black Watch, you have suffered great losses on which I condole with you-
you have suffered also great hardships.

I condole with you on the loss of your gallant Colonel -
Colonel Grant Duff- who fell as I am certain he would have wished to
have fallen- in the fore front of battle.

The Black Watch - a name we know so well, have always
played a distinguished part in the battles of our country.

You have many well known honours on your colours of which
you are naturally proud very proud - but, you will feel as proud, of the
of the honours, which will be added to your colours after this campaign.

At the battle of the MARNE - you distinguished yourself -
they say that the Jaeger of the German Guard ceased to exist after that
battle - " I expect they did".

You have followed your Officer's and stuck to the line
against treble your numbers, in a manner deserving the highest praise.

I as Commander-in-Chief of this Force thank you, but that is
a small matter, your country thank's you - and is proud of you.

The Russians have won great victories, and we have just received news of another great Russian victory, but you, by holding back
the Germans, have won great victories as well, as, if you had not done this,
the Russians could not have achieved their successess.

I am very glad of this opportunity of addressing and thank-
ing you personally for your splendid work.

In-the-Field. 26.11.14.

Taken down from memory immediately after parade

1st Guards Brigade.
1st Division.

1st BATTALION

THE BLACK WATCH

DECEMBER 1914

Army Form C.

WAR DIARY
or
INTELLIGENCE SUMMARY.
(Erase heading not required.)

Instructions regarding War Diaries and Intelligence Summaries are contained in F. S. Regs., Part II. and the Staff Manual respectively. Title pages will be prepared in manuscript.

Place	Date	Hour	Summary of Events and Information	Remarks and references to Appendices
BORRE	1st December		Copied from previous month	
"	2nd "		In Billets re-fitting.	
"	3rd "		In billets. Brigade in readiness to move for 24 hours from 8 a.m. H.M. The King sees battalion. Draft 2nd Lt.W.Stirling,3rd Seaforth Highlanders and 150 other ranks arrive.from NIGG.	
"	4th "		In billets. Training and re-fitting.	
			(continued on next page)	

Army Form C.

WAR DIARY
or
INTELLIGENCE SUMMARY
(Erase heading not required.)

Instructions regarding War Diaries and Intelligence Summaries are contained in F. S. Regs., Part II. and the Staff Manual respectively. Title pages will be prepared in manuscript.

Hour, Date, Place		Summary of Events and Information	Remarks and References to Appendices
5. December	BORRE	In billets - Training & refitting	
6. Dec	"	Divine Service. German aeroplane over HAZEBROUCK at 9 a.m. drops 2 bombs	
7. Dec	"	Capt. V. m. Fortune appointed adjutant (dated 4 Dec)	
8. Dec	"	In billets. Route march	
9.	"	" Training	
10.	"	" "	
11.	"	" "	
12.	"	" Divine Service. H.M. Queen Alexandra's presents arrive	
13.	"	by special messenger.	
14.	"	In billets Training & 1st Bde held in readiness as Reserve	
15.	"	" " Training &c	

WAR DIARY
or
INTELLIGENCE SUMMARY
(Erase heading not required.)

Army Form C.

Instructions regarding War Diaries and Intelligence Summaries are contained in F. S. Regs., Part II. and the Staff Manual respectively. Title pages will be prepared in manuscript.

Hour, Date, Place	Summary of Events and Information	Remarks and References to Appendices
1914		
16. December BORRE.	In billets. Training, refitting.	
17 " "	" " " Division under orders to move at 2 hrs	
18 " "	In billets Training. 2nd Lieut W. Stanbuig 3rd Seaforth High'rs attached, sent down sick.	
19 " "	In billets. Training & refitting.	
20 " 5 p.m. dine of March	B'dn marches 5 p.m. via MERVILLE	
21 " 2.30 a.m. BETHUNE	Arr. BETHUNE at 2.30 a.m. – 23 miles march. Owing to extent inoculation and boots only received the previous day a large number (119) fall out. Billet in tobacco factory	
12.40 p.m.	Bn marches to PONT FIXE, & CUINCHY. Battalion with London Scottish in 2nd line.	
2.45 p.m. CUINCHY	The 3 leading coys attack & carry GIVENCHY-LEZ-LA-BASSEE Batt'n to billets in CUINCHY. Casualties 2 wounded. Weather wet & stormy.	

WAR DIARY
or
INTELLIGENCE SUMMARY
(Erase heading not required.)

Army Form C.

Instructions regarding War Diaries and Intelligence Summaries are contained in F. S. Regs., Part II. and the Staff Manual respectively. Title pages will be prepared in manuscript.

Hour, Date, Place	Summary of Events and Information	Remarks and References to Appendices
1914		
December 22nd GIVENCHY. 7.30 p.m	Captain L.P. Evans reports from R. & C. Industry and takes command of A. Coy. Battn taken over trenches held by Coldstream Guards and 1/Oxfordshire Regt in old strip in left round GIVENCHY. Casualties men 5 wounded	
23rd GIVENCHY.	D. + A. Coy trenches on left pushed forward. Some sniping and shelling. 4401 Sgt Henderson very splendid work in bringing wounded under fire Casualties men 1 killed 9 wounded	
24th "	Shelter trenches & other things in reserve fire many wounded Coldstream Guards, R.Mounster Fus, & & Canadian Officers Hallett listen 2nd Lieut A. McAndrew killed, Capt. N. Thomson. Q & S. Hughes (coy q) wounded men nil.	
25	Colonel distributes Their Majesty's Christmas Cards at daybreak	
CUINCHY 9 pm	Relieved by 1/Coldstream Guards, 1/Scots Guards, 1/Cameroons about 6.30 p.m and march back to CUINCHY. Draft 40 arriving from Base. Casualties men 1 killed 5 wounded	

WAR DIARY
or
INTELLIGENCE SUMMARY

(Erase heading not required.)

Army Form C.

Instructions regarding War Diaries and Intelligence Summaries are contained in F. S. Regs., Part II. and the Staff Manual respectively. Title pages will be prepared in manuscript.

Hour, Date, Place	Summary of Events and Information	Remarks and References to Appendices
1914		
December 26. CUINCHY	HRH Princess Mary's gift received. Dug outs arranged.	
" 27. "	Batt" working near ANNEQUIN	
" 28. GIVENCHY	Relieve 1/Coldstream Gds, 1/Scots Gds, 1/Cameron, London Scottish in GIVENCHY Trenches in evening and attached for duty to 2nd Inf Bde.	12 —
	Casualties. Men. 1 wounded.	
" 29. "	Trench farm bombed by Minnen Werfer in morning and part of house and trench knocked in.	
	Casualties Officers. Capt W.T. Kerr — wounded slightly. Men 1 killed 1 wounded.	
" 30. "	London Scottish relieve 2 Coys (B.C.) Coys from 1st and man Reserve at PONT FIXE. Men 2 killed 3 wounded	

WAR DIARY
or
INTELLIGENCE SUMMARY

(Erase heading not required.)

Army Form C. 2

Instructions regarding War Diaries and Intelligence Summaries are contained in F. S. Regs., Part II. and the Staff Manual respectively. Title pages will be prepared in manuscript.

Hour, Date, Place	Summary of Events and Information	Remarks and References to Appendices
1914		
December 31. GIVENCHY.	3.30 p.m. Observation post lost by a Regiment S. of canal	
	A + D Coys of the Regiment relieved by B and C. – the former going to PONT FIXE to form reserve.	
	12. m.n. In trenches. L/Cpl. McLeod stays the Gdns of the Saul at midnight.	
	Casualties. Men 1 Killed 4 wounded.	
	Wind S.E. Weather Some rain.	

1ST DIVISION
1ST BRIGADE

1ST BATTALION
ROYAL HIGHLANDERS.
JAN - DEC 1915

1st Division.
1st Brigade

WAR DIARY

1st Battalion ROYAL HIGHLANDERS

JANUARY

1915

WAR DIARY
or
INTELLIGENCE SUMMARY
(Erase heading not required.)

Army Form C. 2118

Hour, Date, Place	Summary of Events and Information	Remarks and References to Appendices
1915		
January 1. GIVENCHY	1st Bde headquarters both at CUINCHY. Bat'n once more with 1st Bde (held by three sections) at French farm. B and C Coy relieve A + D in [illegible] Main Trench & Sections. Trenches and soakers as Casualties. Men 2 wounded. Weather Damp. Some shelling at [illegible]	
2. "		
3. "	Brigadier (OC Gen C. Gordon M.V.O.) visits trenches. Reconnoitred French ¼ [illegible]. Twelve Northamptonshire and Sussex regiments in trenches on our right. Very showery. [Col Robinson Q.S.O.] 1st Divn visits trenches. French farm (held by London Scottish) Shelled.	
4. "	Lieut R.P. Austwick, rejoins and takes over command D Coy. 2nd Lt C.W. Murray Menzies joins and posted to B. Coy. Casualties. Other ranks 1 wounded. Col Scanlon CRE plans redoubt. 3 Platoon D take over wagon section Trench Pen London Scottish. B Coy and ¼ D to billets. A Coy takes over Main Trench [illegible]. Casualties. Other ranks 1 wounded. Saps forward begun. Showery.	
5. "	1st Divn Saps and new French worked on. Read in summary Canadian Divn arrive, A wounded. Brigadier visits Trenches. Major Gen'l C. At Divn sends congratulatory [illegible] on good work by A + C Coys at New Cut. Capt W. Green rejoins and takes command of C Coy who for tonight with B Coy to trenches. Showery.	
6. "	Casualties Other ranks 1 wounded	

WAR DIARY
or
INTELLIGENCE SUMMARY

(Erase heading not required.)

Army Form C. 2118

1915. Hour, Date, Place	Summary of Events and Information	Remarks and References to Appendices
January 7. GIVENCHY.	In trenches. Casualties Other ranks. 1 wounded.	
" 8.	Brigadier visits trenches. Heavy shelling on right 12.30pm to 1pm. Major J.H. Hamilton D.S.O joins and takes over duties of 2nd in Command. Capt. P.Q.M Shewe joins with draft of 73 men from. Capt. Shewe takes over Command D Coy. C Coy relieve A in main trench. Their strength wooden account for 2 German snipers. Casualties O.R. 2 wounded. Weather wet.	
" 9. ... 1.15pm GIVENCHY	Heavy British gun and rifle fire. Casualties O.R. 5 wounded Weather very stormy & wet.	
" 10. " 12.50pm	Bombardment by our artillery followed by 10 min burst of fire from our trenches.	
" 2 pm	Bombardment by our artillery on right. 2nd Brigade attack. S of Canal. A Coy relieve D in trench trench. Casualties O.R. 2 killed. 1 wounded	

Army Form C. 2118

WAR DIARY
or
INTELLIGENCE SUMMARY
(Erase heading not required.)

Instructions regarding War Diaries and Intelligence Summaries are contained in F. S. Regs, Part II. and the Staff Manual respectively. Title pages will be prepared in manuscript.

Hour, Date, Place	Summary of Events and Information	Remarks and References to Appendices
1915		
January 11 GIVENCHY	Meerut Cavalry Brigade in on left evacuate forward Trenches on account of water, and occupy Support Trenches. Weather Stormy on our left. Casualties O.R. 3 wounded	
12 "	During night the Central Trenches more short at one again in during patrol wounding 1 NCO. 1st Dival Cyclists take over left New Cut from 2 platoons B.Co. Casualties O.R. 1 killed 1 wounded	1, 2
13 "	3rd Brigade relieve all Battalion except The Regiment in trenches. B Co back to New Cut via Dival Cyclists. Casualties O.R. 3 wounded	
10pm 14 BEUVRY	8 Warr Borderers relieve Battalion in Trenches. March to billets in BEUVRY. Casualties O.R. 1 wounded	

Army Form C. 2118

WAR DIARY
or
INTELLIGENCE SUMMARY
(Erase heading not required.)

Instructions regarding War Diaries and Intelligence Summaries are contained in F. S. Regs., Part II. and the Staff Manual respectively. Title pages will be prepared in manuscript.

Hour, Date, Place	Summary of Events and Information	Remarks and References to Appendices
1915. January 15. BETHUNE	To billet in tobacco factory where also 1/Cameron.	
" 16	Recd drafts of 2/Lt Rutland (A Coy), R. Mackenzie (D Coy), J.G Scott 3rd Bn (C Coy) join.	
" 17	Afternoon In billets Rifles recd Reft	
6 pm	Divine Service. G.O.C 1st Div'n instructions postponed. In state of readiness to move at 2 hours notice for 24 hours. Recd the Div'n intimation of remaining in [ ].	
" 18	G.O.C 1st Div'n inspection for billets. Refit. Cause of difficulties in D Coy. A and D Coys segregated. Any genuine staff unit suspected B.Y.C. Coys C. & D Coys to Lachen.	
" 19	Draft 90 arrive.	

Army Form C. 2118

WAR DIARY
or
INTELLIGENCE SUMMARY
(Erase heading not required.)

Instructions regarding War Diaries and Intelligence Summaries are contained in F. S. Regs., Part II. and the Staff Manual respectively. Title pages will be prepared in manuscript.

Hour, Date, Place	Summary of Events and Information	Remarks and References to Appendices
1915.		
January 20 Cuinchy/BETHUNE	C, D Coys in trenches Refit – trench throwing practice	
	Captain W.T. Rees sick with after fort.	
" 21. BETHUNE	Major General Munro gave 1st Corps criticism Battalion	
2 p.m.	Marching out	
3.15 p.m.	To billets in BEUVRY. In brigade reserve	
" 22 BEUVRY	Billets Brigade Reserve	
" 23	C Coy under Capt Green returns for duty in neighbourhood of GIVENCHY to 3rd Bde. Remainder of Bn in reserve at b/m under 2nd I R Brigade.	
	1 platoon D Coy for dressing duty at PONT FIXE with 3rd Bde.	
" 24	7 a.m. D Coy platoon returns. Divine Service	

WAR DIARY
or
INTELLIGENCE SUMMARY
(Erase heading not required.)

Army Form C. 2118

Instructions regarding War Diaries and Intelligence Summaries are contained in F. S. Regs., Part II. and the Staff Manual respectively. Title pages will be prepared in manuscript.

Hour, Date, Place	Summary of Events and Information	Remarks and References to Appendices
1915.		
Jan. 25. BEUVRY 8.45 a.m.	Orders to move at once. CAMERON in enemy attacking CUINCHY	
9.45 a.m.	March off. (less C Coy or BK CUINCHY)	
10 a.m.	Report 1st Bde Hdqrs. 3 Coys up to CUINCHY	
CUINCHY 11.30 a.m.	Arrive CUINCHY. Orders for joint attack with K.R.R.; Lt.Col Stewart in charge of all troops in left counter attack – area N of CUINCHY. Changes to railway embankment. Attack to take place at 1 noon. – D and B Coys front line + supports, A Coy reserve.	Appendix ___
	Machine guns on left flank with troy/Cameron.	
	[crossed out line]	
1 p.m.	D + B Coys advance with one platoon each in firing line – coming almost at once under heavy rifle + shell fire from the embankment on left and of frontal fire. Both front platoons were reinforced and made progress.	
2 p.m.	B Casualties being very heavy. Col Simmance was sent back to ask for reinforcements. One platoon from reserve C Coy was conducted up to firing line. Sergeance Capt Shine D Coy was had been wounded in the head early in the day. Col Simmance led forward men by Mr Huddlestone wounded early and his Company was taken over by Mr Miller.	
3 p.m.	Advance made mostly by crawling. Ammo sent up via communication trench. Sent up a second reinforcing platoon under Lieut Miller together.	

79
3298

WAR DIARY
or
INTELLIGENCE SUMMARY
(Erase heading not required.)

Army Form C. 2118

Instructions regarding War Diaries and Intelligence Summaries are contained in F. S. Regs., Part II. and the Staff Manual respectively. Title pages will be prepared in manuscript.

Hour, Date, Place	Summary of Events and Information	Remarks and References to Appendices
1915 Jan. 25 CUINCHY 3.15 p.m.	Then banking party reports to Major Romilly, 1/Scots Guards, at the Keep, the danger that it cannot work from his right of the trench held of the Germans so the platoon ships in along the Communication trench known as Old Kent Road and links up with French trench believed by Lieuten Scott-Ker as 2nd Lieutenant Sir Faulkner Cauvey S. G. was wounded in the heel and up to this had continued to push the C's forward but now ordered back by a dressing station and the command of B with 1 platoon A devolved on that Scout. Lieut. Buril was killed about	
3.45 p.m.	leaving his forward platoon which was 210 yards beyond the Twicks but it machinegun then acted under orders originally listed by the Germans. Lieut Richmond who was the only officer left with 3 Co as Lieut Huddleston was killed about now by direct fronted fire when pressing forward the right of our line.	
4 p.m.		
4.55 p.m.	Until dark the line now about 120 strong made some progress by crawling forward until their left was nearly 100 yards beyond Old Kent and their right within 100 yards of the Keep opposite Brickworks occupied by the Germans	

WAR DIARY
or
INTELLIGENCE SUMMARY
(Erase heading not required.)

Army Form C. 2118

Hour, Date, Place	Summary of Events and Information	Remarks and References to Appendices
1915		
Jan 25. CUINCHY 5 pm	The 1 Bn received orders to hold this line until the R Sussex Regt delivered an attack through them by night. The first attack by the Sussex did not succeed in re-establishing the old line from the Keep to the Brig bridge	
Jan 26 CUINCHY 3.30 am	At 3.45 am the O.C. R Sussex reported that his 1 Bn had established itself from the Keep to the railway embankment.	App. C.
" 4 am	The front line of the 1 Bn was withdrawn and all 3 coys returned	
" ANNEQUIN 6 am	to billets at ANNEQUIN. The operations of C Coy at GIVENCHY are given in Appendix C. - for this the F.O. Genl Commdg 2nd Bde sent an expressed mention of their good work and looked for the names of certain officers, N.C.O.s & men. Total Casualties of the 4 Companies on the 25/26th were Killed Officers 2nd Lieut K Blunt (2nd Bn), 2nd Lieut S.C Stoddlestone (3rd Bn). Wounded Capt P.g.m Secure, Lieut R.S. Quarterley, 2nd Lieut (W Bruney-Menzies (also missing) 2nd 2nd Lieut J.H Willett (2nd Bn). Other ranks Killed 48. Wounded 150, Missing 7.	App. C.

… Army Form C. 2118

WAR DIARY
or
INTELLIGENCE SUMMARY
(Erase heading not required.)

Instructions regarding War Diaries and Intelligence Summaries are contained in F. S. Regs., Part II. and the Staff Manual respectively. Title pages will be prepared in manuscript.

Hour, Date, Place		Summary of Events and Information	Remarks and References to Appendices
1915			
January 26	ANNEQUIN 8:30 pm	March to billets at BETHUNE	
	BETHUNE 10.0 pm	In billets BETHUNE. The trace of 2nd about railway near ga. in Clearing hospitals	
27		Capt W Green and C. Cy return from 3rd Bde. V3? Genl Butler sends in a not favourable	Cf. App. C.
		account of their recapture of houses and village trench at GIVENCHY on 25th inst	
	9.15 pm	Stand by for an hour in readiness to move.	
28	BEUVRY 7.15 pm	Received orders to leave at once for BEUVRY where to billets vice 1/Cameron H/Flanders	
		attached to 2nd Bde	
29	ANNEQUIN 11. a.m.	Orders to march received 10.30 a.m. In BEUVRY 10 a.m. and to billets in ANNEQUIN	
		Stand by, one company at 5 minutes notice.	
30	" 6.30 pm	Stand by until 6.30 pm when relieved by 3rd Bn Coldstream Guards to billets	
	BETHUNE 6. pm	In BETHUNE (Ecole Militaire) when 1st Bde	
31	"	Attached again to 2nd Bde. In reserve at 3/4 hour notice. Divine Service.	

(signed) Allerred. Colonel
E... / Lt Col...

Appendix "C".   Report by Captain W.Green, Commanding, "C" Company,

1st. Bn. The Black Watch.
....

GIVENCHY.-   On morning of January, 25th. "C" Company distributed as follows-

2 Platoons in GIVENCHY in cellars in close support of VILLIAGE trench. (Lieut. W.H.C.Edwards.)
2 Platoons in reserve about 300x S.of PONT FIXE with myself.

At 7-25 a.m. the Germans commenced to shell GIVENCHY & CUINCHY. At about 7-45 a.m. when it was obvious that the bombardment was serious I march on GIVENCHY with the 2 reserve Platoons, followed by about 50 of the Welch Regiment also in reserve S.of PONT FIXE. On arrival at GIVENCHY I found the 2 Platoons which were in support of VILLIAGE Trench and several of the Welch who had been holding VILLIAGE Trench on the road N. of the keep. There were Germans at the church "C" Company after remaining N.of the keep for about 15 minutes moved round W.of the keep and worked forward along a trench to the corner of the barbed wire round the keep. From there I sent forward 3 Platoons Lieut. Edwards, 2/Lieut.Shand, 2/Lieut. Scott, each prolonging the line to his right and coming on the left flank of the Germans. The remaining Platoon I kept in support either of the 3 Platoons or of the Welch, should the Germans advance further down the road from the church to the keep.

The 3 leading Platoons chased the Germans from the village. Lieut. Edwards with an Officer and some of the Welch retook the bit of trench which had been lost, when I had to report that the trench was retaken I brought up the reserve Platoon.The 2 other Platoons I also brought up to the trench. The company was afterwards collected and took over about 200 yards of VILLIAGE Trench on the right of the Welch. which it held until relieved on the 27th.

1-2-15.   (sd) W.Green, Captain., Commanding,

"C" Company, 1st. Bn. The Black Watch.

1st Division.
1st Brigade

WAR DIARY

1st Battalion ROYAL HIGHLANDERS

Febuary

1915.

Army Form C. 2118.

WAR DIARY
or
INTELLIGENCE SUMMARY

(Erase heading not required.)

Instructions regarding War Diaries and Intelligence Summaries are contained in F. S. Regs., Part II. and the Staff Manual respectively. Title pages will be prepared in manuscript.

Hour, Date, Place		Summary of Events and Information	Remarks and References to Appendices
1915			
February, 1st	BETHUNE.	Attached to 2nd Brigade in billets in readiness to turn out at 15 minutes notice – Divisional Reserve.	
" 2nd	"	Billets. 2nd Lieut R Macfarlane with draft 38 other ranks arrives.	
" 3rd	"	2nd Lieut L.J.S Sotheby 3/Argyll & Sutherland Highlanders and draft 60 other ranks arrive	
" 4th	BURBURE	March off at 10 a.m. via CHOQUES to BURBURE – 10 miles – where billeted. Once more with 1st Brigade. Major J.T.C. Murray rejoins Battalion and 2nd Lieut. J & Murdoch 2nd Batt" joins	
" 5	"	Field Training.	
" 6	"	Training. Lecture by Major General Haking C.B. Commdg 1st Division	
" 7	"	Training Divine Service Training	
" 8	"	Training	
" 9	"	Training	
" 10	"	Training 2nd Lieut C.W. Murray-Menzies body found and buried at CUINCHY [by] 4th Guards Brigade.] He was reported wounded and missing on the night 25/26 December January.	

WAR DIARY
or
INTELLIGENCE SUMMARY
(Erase heading not required.)

Army Form C. 2118

Instructions regarding War Diaries and Intelligence Summaries are contained in F. S. Regs., Part II. and the Staff Manual respectively. Title pages will be prepared in manuscript.

Hour, Date, Place	Summary of Events and Information	Remarks and References to Appendices
1915		
February 11th BURBURE	Training	
12th "	2nd Lieut S. B. Meravglees, 4th A & S Highlanders arrives.	
13th "	Too wet for divine Service. Training	
14th "	"	
15-16 "	Training 2nd Lt J B S Haddow, draft of 99 other ranks arrive	
16th "	Major J T C Murray, Sergt J Hart no 407 killed by the premature explosion of fuse when at experimental bomb throwing. [Sgt Hart buried in BURBURE graveyard] Casualties Killed Officer 1. Other ranks 1.	
17th "	Training Major J T C Murray's funeral in LILLERS.	
18th "	Training draft of 110 Rycroft temporarily attached for duty as acting adjutant.	
19th "	Training Route march.	
20th "	Capt & Adjt W M Fortune promoted B't Major and Capt F Anderson awarded the Military Cross for their gallantry and good work on the 2nd & 11th Nov respectively (who was wounded on the AISNE)	
21st "	Divine Service. Lieut L F Hay arrives with draft of 65 other ranks.	

Army Form C. 2118.

WAR DIARY
or
INTELLIGENCE SUMMARY.
(Erase heading not required.)

Instructions regarding War Diaries and Intelligence Summaries are contained in F.S. Regs., Part II and the Staff Manual respectively. Title pages will be prepared in manuscript.

Hour, Date, Place	Summary of Events and Information	Remarks and references to Appendices
1915.		
February 22nd BURBURE	Training.	
" 23rd "	drum Rynoff rejoins got 1st Div?	
" 24th "	Capt & 9 Chalmers returns (wounded in Oct) and takes over duties of m.g. officer. 1st Guards Bde. Draft of other ranks arrive.	
" 25th "	Maj General Sir Charles Munro KCB inspects Battalion in marching order. Strength 18 officers 902 other ranks. He made an exceedingly complimentary speech to the Battalion.	
" 26th "	Training and filling up trenches	
" 27 6pm "	Bde leaves BURBURE at 1pm for HINGES. Battalion goes on to LES arriving CHOQUAUX	
LES CHOQUAUX	CHOQUAUX where arrive about 6pm (13 miles). and into billets. Lieut PK Campbell who had been wounded in October arrives with draft of 30 other ranks. (3 offr)	
28. 3pm LES CHOQUAUX	leave 3pm — Have teas at LE TOURET	
6.30pm RUE DU BOIS	Relieve 2/3 Gurkhas and City of London Journoured (c=j) in trenches from RUE DU BOIS to roadway village. A, B, C Coys in trenches, D Coy reserve right — Left (LAHORE Div?) and 1/Cameron Hy[ld]rs on our right. After SB? Seaforth High= on our Strength of B[attalio]n 21 officers 932 other ranks.	

R.A Stewart Lt Colonel Comm[an]d[in]g 1/ The Black Watch

1st Division.
1st Brigade

W A R   D I A R Y

1st Battalion ROYAL HIGHLANDERS

March

1915.

Army Form C. 2118.

WAR DIARY
or
INTELLIGENCE SUMMARY.
(Erase heading not required.)

Instructions regarding War Diaries and Intelligence Summaries are contained in F.S. Regs., Part II and the Staff Manual respectively. Title pages will be prepared in manuscript.

Hour, Date, Place	Summary of Events and Information	Remarks and references to Appendices
1915 March 1st RUE du BOIS	In trenches. Lt Col C.E. Stewart temporarily in command of 1st Guards Brigade as Brig. General H.C. Lowther C.V.O, C.M.G, D.S.O ill. Major J.G.H. Hamilton D.S.O in Command of Batt during Col Stewart's absence. Accurate sniping by batt of 111th Jaegers in front. B Thunder & snow in afternoon. Casualties: killed 3 wounded. Weather: Thunder & snow in afternoon. Wind W.	
2nd " "	Patrols early up to German wire. Bomilly Batt relieve Delurn Dawn Bat on our left. 5th Gor Yankshums Rifles 1/Coldstream Guards relieve "B" in evening "3rd" to billets LE TOURET on Bde Reserve at 1 hours notice at end of RUE du BOIS. Very fine. Weather: V fine. Wind W.	
7.30pm LE TOURET		
3rd. 6.15 a.m LE TOURET	Heavy shelling by French S of CUINCHY 3 cop moved to billets in LE TOURET still in Bde Reserve. Report that Major Jon G. S. Murray, missing since 14 Sept is a prisoner of war at SOLTAU, HANOVER. Casualties: Other ranks 1 wounded. Weather: Rain. Wind W.	
4th RUE du BOIS 7.30pm	Battalion relieve 1/Coldstream Guards in evening in same trenches. Weather fine. Wind W.	

WAR DIARY
or
INTELLIGENCE SUMMARY
(Erase heading not required.)

Army Form C. 2118.

Hour, Date, Place	Summary of Events and Information	Remarks and References to Appendices
1915. March 5. RUE du BOIS	Sniping at both sides. B⁹ General back so L⁹ Col Stewart back to command Bⁿ Casualties Other ranks 5 wounded. [Wind W. high. Weather Some showers]	
" 6. "	At 12 noon German howitzer artillery gave us 30 rounds high explosive. Snipers on both sides. Our snipers we but does no real damage. 1/Coldstream Guards relieve Bⁿ 2 Telescopic Sights rifles to do effect. 1/ wounded. at night 2nd Lieut JH Gordon and 1 wounded from the O.C. STOMER from Mining Group reported to have been heard in centre of our line.	
LE TOURET	To billets at LE TOURET about 9 p.m. Casualties Other ranks 3 killed 5 wounded. Weather Very wet 2nd Lieut T.Style (Sulby) and Brigade reserve at ½ hour notice. 22 other ranks burnt Casualties Other ranks 1 wounded	
" 8. RUE du BOIS	In evening relieve 1/Coldstream Guards. 2nd Lt P.K Campbell (3rd Bⁿ) to hospital sick. Weather V. cold, sharp frost, then snow. Wind NNE	
" 9. "	Some shelling. Capt W.T Kidd rejoin from being sick. Enquiry 2nd F.R.M. Purves and 42 Other ranks. Casualties Other ranks 1 killed. Wind NE. Weather fine, Very cold, a little snow.	

Army Form C. 2118

WAR DIARY
or
INTELLIGENCE SUMMARY
(Erase heading not required.)

Instructions regarding War Diaries and Intelligence Summaries are contained in F.S. Regs., Part II. and the Staff Manual respectively. Title pages will be prepared in manuscript.

Hour, Date, Place	Summary of Events and Information	Remarks and References to Appendices
1915.		
March 10th. 7.30 a.m. RUE du BOIS	Heavy shelling by British N. + S. commences 7.30am. British attacks at NEUVE CHAPELLE and GIVENCHY.] Battⁿ given rapid burst of fire at fixed hours. [MEERUT Divⁿ through NEUVECHAPELLE] Casualties Other ranks 6 wounded. Wind E. Weather, grey misty.	
11th.	Shelling to north and about 2 p.m. at Bois du BIEZ.	
7.30 p.m.	1/ Gordons Guards relieve battalion Divisional.	
9.30 p.m. LE TOURET	To Wagon reserve at 1/2 hours notice in LE TOURET Casualties Officer 2nd Lieut J.M. Garden Wounded. Other ranks Killed 1. Wounded 5. Wind E. Weather grey.	
12th. 5.45 a.m. " "	British shelled up to 8.15am by German field guns. 1 cook killed & 1 cooker damaged. 8 a.m. fire from German counterattack. Major Hamilton DSO to 1st Divⁿ h.d.q^{rs} at LE HAMEL as liaison officer for day. Weather foggy. Casualties O.R. 1 crossed Killed. Weather foggy.	
13th "	35th reported to B^{de} reserve. Draft 53 O.R. arrive. Weather very fine.	

Army Form C. 2118

WAR DIARY
or
INTELLIGENCE SUMMARY
(Erase heading not required.)

Instructions regarding War Diaries and Intelligence Summaries are contained in F. S. Regs., Part II. and the Staff Manual respectively. Title pages will be prepared in manuscript.

Hour, Date, Place	Summary of Events and Information	Remarks and References to Appendices
1915		
March 14. LE TOURET	2nd battⁿ a mile away billetted at LA COUTURE	
7.30pm RUE du BOIS	Relieve 1/Coldstream Guards in front line which advanced by 60 yards at night. Wind W. Weather very fine	
" 15. RUE du BOIS.	In breastworks. Casualties O.R. 5 wounded. Wind W. Weather very fine	
" 16. 12 noon "	Headquarters shelled	
7.30pm LE TOURET	Relieved by 1/Coldstream Guards 7 to 16 de reserve at 1/2 hrs notice at LE TOURET. Casualties Other ranks. Killed 1. Weather fine.	
" 17. "	Bⁿ in reserve.	
" 18. RUE du BOIS.	At night relieve 1/Coldstream Guards. Weather fog.	
" 19. " "	Casualties O.R. wounded 1.	
" 20. LE TOURET	1/Coldstream Guards relieve Bⁿ at night. Casualties O.R. Wounded 2. Weather sharp frost early, very fine	

Army Form C. 2118

WAR DIARY
or
INTELLIGENCE SUMMARY
(Erase heading not required.)

Instructions regarding War Diaries and Intelligence Summaries are contained in F. S. Regs., Part II. and the Staff Manual respectively. Title pages will be prepared in manuscript.

Hour, Date, Place	Summary of Events and Information	Remarks and References to Appendices
1915		
March 21. LE TOURET.	Bde reserve. 2nd Lieut RM Pinnes (3rd Bn) goes to hospital. A recovery of bad ear. Wind S. Weather Rayfine	
" 22. LE TOURET 11.59 pm. HINGES	A man wounded in working party. Remar of Bn relieved by 2/KRR (part of 2nd Bde) and march to HINGES. Where billetted. 1st Bde = Divl Reserve. Casualties O.R. Wounded 1.	
" 23. HINGES.	Rest of Bde in BETHUNE. Divl reserve.	
" 24. "	Divl reserve. Rest of Bde move to LOCON & vicinity. 2nd Lieut Wallen gazetted to Battalion. Minor Holdous to Bomb course at St Venant.	
" 25. "	Divl Reserve. [Capt Kidor & 2nd Lieut Wenlen to 9th & 13th Liverpool Regts] to instruct.	
" 26 "	Div Reserve.	
" 27 "	Divisional Reserve. 2nd Lieut Strand to instruct 9th Bn Liverpool Regt in Indirect Wenlen also Sick.	

Army Form C. 2118.

WAR DIARY
or
INTELLIGENCE SUMMARY.
(Erase heading not required.)

Instructions regarding War Diaries and Intelligence Summaries are contained in F.S. Regs., Part II and the Staff Manual respectively. Title pages will be prepared in manuscript.

Hour, Date, Place	Summary of Events and Information	Remarks and references to Appendices
1915 March, 28th. HINGES.	Divisional Reserve. Divine Service. Capt W.T. Ridd and 2nd Lieut Ghani return from instructing 9th Batt" Liverpool Regiment.	
" 29th. HINGES.	Divisional Reserve.	
" 30th 6.15pm HINGES.	March off Brigade RUE du BOIS.	
" 10pm RUE du BOIS	B.C.D Coys take over line D1.2 from 2/K.R.R (2nd Bde) A Coy in Bn reserve. London Scottish on right, 1/Cameron Highlanders on left. Batteries 113, 114 in area. Remove some shelters in fort breastwork in our left. 1 Mountain gun. Major Matthews 4 other officers 24 N.C.Os from 16th,19th, 20th Coys of London Regt attached for 1 day instruction. Weather V. fine, Sharp frost at night. Wind ENE.	
" 31st. RUE du BOIS	Adjt 18th Conn. of London Reg' (Capt Norman) comes round for instruction. 2nd Lt Gray to hospital 2nd Lieut Wankers returns from hospital 6 other Officers, 6 N.C.O.s replace others of 18,19,20 London Regt. In 24 hours instruction. A Coy relieves B in centre section. Bomb mortar fired by us "Pip Squeak" German 12 pr (?) gun fairly active with good results. Casualties Other ranks 2 wounded (g.s.) Weather V. fine. Wind first SE, rapid. Wind E. (Signed) N.S.N. LtCol Comm'd'g 1/The Black Watch.	

9.E.
5 sheets

131/5255

1st Brigade.

1st Black Watch.

Vol ix. 1 — 30.4.15.

WAR DIARY
or
INTELLIGENCE SUMMARY

(Erase heading not required.)

Army Form C. 2118.

Hour, Date, Place	Summary of Events and Information	Remarks and References to Appendices
1915		
April 1. RUE du BOIS.	In breastworks D1 (no 2). 2 officers 2 sergts 6th City of London Bde replace 6 officers, 6 sergts attached for instruction. B Coy relieve C in centre subsection. Draft 13 other ranks arrive. Strength of Battalion 25 officers 952 other ranks. Casualties Other ranks 1 killed. [Wind N.E. Weather V. fine]	
" 2. " "	"Pip Squeak" Guns & m. gun active, otherwise quiet. 2 officers, 2 sgts late 19th Regt London NK leave. B Coy 21st Bn London Regt attached for instruction. Casualties Other ranks 4 wounded. [Wind W. Weather fine, rain in evening]	
" 3. 4.30 a.m. " "	Small demonstration at 4.30 a.m. – short burst of rifle fire. Lt Col Tomkin and Capt & Adjt Kennedy 21st Bn London Regt visit breastwork.	
" 7.15 pm RUE de l'EPINETTE	Change places with London Scottish and occupy D1 (G). D Coy in breastworks, C in Indian Village, A & B in RUE de l'EPINETTE in Bn reserve. [Wind S.W. Weather V Showery, rain at night]	

Army Form C. 2118.

WAR DIARY
or
INTELLIGENCE SUMMARY
(Erase heading not required.)

Instructions regarding War Diaries and Intelligence Summaries are contained in F. S. Regs., Part II and the Staff Manual respectively. Title pages will be prepared in manuscript.

Hour, Date, Place	Summary of Events and Information	Remarks and References to Appendices
1915 April 4. RUE de l'EPINETTE.	Voluntary Divine Service at headquarters. Working party at night 51 other ranks. Draft of 2 other ranks arrive. Casualties Officers Wounded 2nd Lieut. Muirhead. Other ranks Wounded 1. Wind W. Weather Showery	
" 5. 8 p.m. " " "	B Coy relieves D in front breastwork. A returns C in Indian Village. Casualties Wounded O.R. 3. Wind W. Weather, Very wet.	
" 6. 8 p.m. " " "	B Coy 21st-13th London Reg't relieves 3 platoons B Coy in front trench. 2nd draw A Coy rejoin from hospital. Casualties Wounded O.R. 1. Wind S.S.E. Weather First in morning. Some rain thereafter.	
" 7. 7 a.m. " " "	Lt. Col Tomlin visits his Coy 21st London Reg't.	
8 p.m. RUE du BOIS.	Change places with London Scottish and 1 Platoon C with B Coy 21st London Reg't; D, A Companies occupy D 1 (2). Some shelling. Casualties Nil. Wind W.S.W. Weather Some Showers	
" 8. RUE du BOIS.	Brigadier with Brigadier 6th London Brigade visit breastworks. B Coy billets shelled. C Coy returns A in left subsection, B Coy 21st London Reg't hold our Right Subsection. Casualties Wounded. O.R. 3. Wind W. Weather Showers	

Army Form C. 2118.

WAR DIARY
or
INTELLIGENCE SUMMARY
(Erase heading not required.)

Instructions regarding War Diaries and Intelligence Summaries are contained in F. S. Regs., Part II. and the Staff Manual respectively. Title pages will be prepared in manuscript.

Hour, Date, Place	Summary of Events and Information	Remarks and References to Appendices
1915. April, 9 Rue du BOIS	Lt Col Lord Herbert Scott and Capt & Adjt Thornhill 23rd Bn London Regt up. A Coy reserve. B 21st Bn London Regt in right subsection. Casualties Killed Other ranks 1. Wounded Officers Capt W T Kredz, Other ranks 1. Wind NW. Weather Hail Showers.	
„ 10.	B. Coy 21st Bn London Regt returns to their battalion. Draft 1 O R arrives. Casualties. Wounded. O.R. 1. Wind NNW Weather Some Showers.	
„ 11. 2.am	Machine gun and no 5 post open fire on German working party	
6.pm	nos 5 post shelled and bombed	
8.15pm Rue a l'EPINETTE	Take over D1 (?) from London Scottish. B Coy 23rd Bn London Regt attached to A & D in these reserve. C Coy take over trenches in B Indian Village. instructions — also headquarters (died of wounds) Casualties. Killed Officers 2nd Lieut R T MacKenzie, Other ranks 2. Wounded. Other ranks 9. Wind N. Weather V fine.	
„ 12.	Quiet day. Left hand H Scott 23rd Bn London Regt much improved. Draft 1 O R arrives. Wind W Weather V fine	

Army Form C. 2118.

WAR DIARY
or
INTELLIGENCE SUMMARY
(Erase heading not required.)

Instructions regarding War Diaries and Intelligence Summaries are contained in F. S. Regs., Part II. and the Staff Manual respectively. Title pages will be prepared in manuscript.

Hour, Date, Place	Summary of Events and Information	Remarks and References to Appendices
1915.		
April 13. RUE de l'EPINETTE	Some shelling by German howitzers. A (g returns C in Hantworle, B relieves D in Imotian Village. Draft 2. O.R arrive. Wind W. Weather V fine	
" 14. " " "	13" Jun Hon C. H.D. Willoughby Connell (in Jordon B.C.) reports (in antworle. B Coy 23rd county London Regt with 1 platoon A Cy taken over trenchwork from A Cy who to Batt? Reserve. Draft 6. OR arrive. Shelling of routes to trenches. Causalities Killed O.R.1. Wounded. O.R.1. Wind NW weather Heavy showers. Some hail.	
" 15. 8.30pm " " "	2/1cm R.Welsh Fusiliers take over D1(i) Battalion to Divisional Reserve	
9.30pm MESPLAUX	To billets at MESPLAUX and LES FACONS Wind N. Weather Miserly fine V. first.	
" 16. MESPLAUX.	Divisional Reserve.	
" 17. "	"	Seemed by G.O.C 1st Div? G! LOCON.
" 18. "	"	Divine Service for 2 top and headquarters.
" 19. LONG CORNET.	More billets to LONG CORNET.	

Army Form C. 2118.

WAR DIARY
or
INTELLIGENCE SUMMARY
(Erase heading not required.)

Instructions regarding War Diaries and Intelligence Summaries are contained in F. S. Regs., Part II. and the Staff Manual respectively. Title pages will be prepared in manuscript.

Hour, Date, Place	Summary of Events and Information	Remarks and References to Appendices
1915		
April 20. LONG CORNET	Divisional Reserve.	
" 21. "	" "	
" 22. "	" "	
" 23. ALLOUAGNE	Leave LONG CORNET at 9am, join London Scottish at PONT d'HINGES and march via CROQUES to ALLOUAGNE (10 miles) where arrive 12 noon. In Corps Reserve. Divisional Reserve.	
" 24. "	Come into 1st Corps Reserve. 1st Guards Bde headquarters move from CORNET MALO to VENDIN-LEZ-BETHUNE. Draft 3 sgts, 3 cpls, 71 other ranks arrive.	
" 25. "	Come into 1st Army Reserve. Divine Service.	
" 26. "	1st Army Reserve. Battalion games in afternoon.	
" 27. "	" " " " Battalion games. Draft 11 other ranks arrive.	
" 28. "	" " " "	
" 29. "	" " " " 2nd draft H West transferred from HAC joins	
" 30. "	" " " "	

(Signed) [illegible]
Comdg 1/ The [illegible]

121/5556

1st Division

1st Black Watch.

Vol X — 1-31.5.15

Army Form C. 2118.

WAR DIARY
or
INTELLIGENCE SUMMARY.
(Erase heading not required.)

Instructions regarding War Diaries and Intelligence Summaries are contained in F.S. Regs., Part II. and the Staff Manual respectively. Title pages will be prepared in manuscript.

Hour, Date, Place		Summary of Events and Information	Remarks and references to Appendices
1915.			
May 1.	ALLOUAGNE.	1st Army Reserve. Strength 24 Officers, 981 other ranks	
9.30 a.m.	2. "	March 9.30 a.m.	
1.15 p.m.	" LE CAZAN	Midday halt.	
5 p.m.	" RICHEBOURG St VAAST	1st Guards Bde Reserve. March Hamilton Reserve 9th Bn Liverpool Regt B Cos in dug outs.	
" 3.	RICHEBOURG St VAAST.	Our guns bombard certain points at 6.30 p.m.	
10 p.m.	" 4. RUE des BERCEAUX	Relieve 1/Cameron Highlanders in front line "D.2" from CHOCOLAT MENIER corner to CINDER Track. Wind W. Weather Fine, Thunderstorm in evening.	
" 5.	"	V Battery R.H.A. established at 53rd Headquarters. B.Coy Sn Thurfer Counts 2nd & 6th visit D.2. Casualties O.R. 4 wounded. Wind W. Weather Very fine.	
" 6.	"	Brigadier shown points in German line from "Ritz" Casualties O.R. 1 killed Wind N. Weather fine early, rain fair.	
7 p.m.	" 7.	Issue Orders for tomorrow attack which postponed at 7 p.m. for 24 hours. Casualties O.R. 1 killed, 6 wounded. Wind N. Weather Very fine, rain in evening.	
" 8.	"	Major F.M.B. Robertson arrives and posted to A Coy. (2nd Brigade)	
11.15 p.m.	CHOCOLAT MENIER CORNER.	All companies relieved by Northamptonshire Regt and bivouac at CHOCOLAT MENIER Corner in baintarbs. Casualties O.R. 2 wounded. Wind E. Weather Very fine.	

Army Form C. 2118.

WAR DIARY
INTELLIGENCE SUMMARY.
(Erase heading not required.)

Instructions regarding War Diaries and Intelligence Summaries are contained in F.S. Regs., Part II. and the Staff Manual respectively. Title pages will be prepared in manuscript.

Hour, Date, Place	Summary of Events and Information	Remarks and references to Appendices
1915 May 9. 4 a.m. CHOCOLAT MENIER CORNER.	In bivouac. Battalion fighting strength Officers 22. Other Ranks 807. Machine Guns 4. The 1st Bde were in Divl Reserve. The objective of the 2nd Bde was from Pt (Q 2) to (V.1) inclusive, that of the 3rd (V.1) exclusive to the Orchard (Reference VIOLAINES map 1:10.000). Our pack animals were our bivouac. Our S.A.A. carts near MESPLAUX - 3 mess contact but reserve ammn & depots were formed near 4 in the breastwork. At 4 a.m. our artillery began to register.	
5 a.m. to 5.30 a.m.	Artillery bombardment and wire cutting. The enemy's artillery replied. a few high explosive shells were fired at our corner, wounding 1 man.	
5.30 a.m. to 5.40 a.m. Near RUE du BOIS RICHEBOURG	Intense bombardment. The attacking assaulting Battns of the 2nd Bde left their trenches. We moved into trenches D, C, A & B successively "A" & "D" Coys occupying A and "B" & "C" B line with their left on the	
6.15 a.m.	CINDER TRACK, their right opposite (R.1.) between the 2nd & 3rd Bde assaults. All our conference in position was successful.	
7 a.m.	Lieut Edwards was killed before turn by a bullet built in B line.	
7.40 a.m.	All ammunition brought up from pack animals which sent back to 1st echelon near MESPLAUX.	

Army Form C. 2118.

WAR DIARY
INTELLIGENCE SUMMARY.
(Erase heading not required.)

Instructions regarding War Diaries and Intelligence Summaries are contained in F.S. Regs., Part II and the Staff Manual respectively. Title pages will be prepared in manuscript.

Hour, Date, Place	Summary of Events and Information	Remarks and references to Appendices
1915 Rue du Bois / Richebourg		
7.55 a.m.	Orders for 3 coys of this Battalion to occupy A trenchworks from opposite ALBERT road to CINDER TRACK. 1 coy with 2 coy 1/Coldstream Guards in B line. All to be prepared to meet counter attack.	
8.50 a.m.	A, B, D Coys in front line (A), C and 2 coy 1/Coldstream Gds in 2nd line (B).	
9.45 a.m.	Owing to casualties in front line 2 platoons of C Coy reinforce front line (A) at 12.45 p.m.	
11.5 a.m.	Orders received that a second assault to be delivered by 2nd and 3rd brigades who are to gain their original first objective and entrench line (Q2) to Orchard. The Battalion and Cameron Highlanders to withdraw to C (third) line, 1/Coldstream and 1/Scots Gds to D (fourth) line. After assault two companies each of Battalion and Camerons to move up at once to A and two companies each to B line. Withdraw 2 platoons of C Coy back to B line.	
11.10 a.m.	Hour for commencement of bombardment altered from 12 noon to 2 p.m.	
11.25 a.m.	Battalion back in Third (C) line.	
12.10 p.m.		
12.45 p.m.	Hour for commencement of bombardment altered from 2 p.m. to 4 p.m.	
1.20 p.m.	Brigadier interviews Company Officers with reference to alteration in battalions for assault.	

Army Form C. 2118.

WAR DIARY
INTELLIGENCE SUMMARY.
(Erase heading not required.)

Instructions regarding War Diaries and Intelligence Summaries are contained in F. S. Regs., Part II and the Staff Manual respectively. Title pages will be prepared in manuscript.

Hour, Date, Place	Summary of Events and Information	Remarks and references to Appendices
1915.		
2.20pm 9 May RUE du BOIS, RICHEBOURG	Commanding Officer takes Coy Commanders forward, points out objectives and direction for assault to each Coy.	Reference VIOLAINES map 1:10,000.
2.45pm	Operation Order received. The Black Watch and 1/Camerons, (with 3rd Bn Be) on their left to repeat assault. The Black Watch to occupy trench from A (first line) to a line C. Assault to be delivered at points (R2) to (R6) inclusive. 2nd B2e in line C. Assault to be delivered by the 2nd Battalion under similar conditions to those detailed in Divnl Orders. Bombardment commences 3.20pm, Assault to be delivered at 4pm. Intensive bombardment to last 15 mins. Objective first B= Second line of German trench (R3) to (R1) Camerons responsible for communication trench running 5 from (R5). Machine guns under Batt"Commanders. 1/Coldstream & 1/Scots Guards to occupy B line (second line), London Scottish in C line. All these three battalions to be in readiness to a deliver a counter stroke in case A line occupied by the enemy. The Black Watch to endeavour to clear Germans 2nd line towards (Q2). A line will be occupied from Guides Trace from left to (R2) or (Q2) whichever can be gained on the right. This line to be held whether 3rd Brigade is successful or not. Orders for packs to be removed for assault.	
3pm		

WAR DIARY
INTELLIGENCE SUMMARY.
(Erase heading not required.)

Army Form C. 2118.

Instructions regarding War Diaries and Intelligence Summaries are contained in F.S. Regs., Part II. and the Staff Manual respectively. Title pages will be prepared in manuscript.

Hour, Date, Place	Summary of Events and Information	Remarks and references to Appendices
1915		
9 May (RUE du BOIS, RICHEBOURG)		Ref VIOLAINES map 1:10,000.
3.25 p.m.	Battalion in position that lies facing (R2) to (R6). A Cy supported by D on right, D supported by C on left. Two machine guns in centre and two in centre of D. Cy. Left Platn. of A Cy to march on a tree midway between (R2) and (R6).	
3.37 p.m.	Enemy's breastwork opposite (R2) blown down. Sent The two left machine guns more chars opposite it. They open fire on enemy's communication trench by the Royal Irish Lancashire Regt.	
3.50 p.m.	O.C. 1/Cameron Highlanders reports that his Battalion is blocked and cannot possibly get his men ready to move at 3.57. Heavy hostile shelling. Orders received from Brigade headquarters that The Black Watch are to carry on assault as ordered and the Camerons to follow at once when ready.	
3.55 p.m.		
3.57 p.m.	A and D Coys cross parapet, followed at 50 yds by 2nd line of 2 platoons of B and C Coy. 2 platoons of Camerons and 1 Coy Camerons followed by 2 platoons advance with our 2nd line. Pipers play at 150 yards from enemy's trench except one in 2nd line (L/Cpl Stewart) who plays the whole way. On right up to 1st left's platoon Cpl D Ripley. Finds gap in wire and dashes on.	
3.59 p.m.	Parapet at 3.59 p.m. and diverts men. The other three platoons A Coy hardly lose a man until 30 yards from the	

WAR DIARY
or
INTELLIGENCE SUMMARY.
(Erase heading not required.)

Army Form C. 2118.

Hour, Date, Place	Summary of Events and Information	Remarks and references to Appendices
1915 May 9. 4.5 p.m. { Rue du Bois { RICHEBOURG	2nd Lieut Shand and some men tried to rush the guns but were cut or killed but one gun was disabled by a shot into the lock mechanism fired by Pte Monson. Sgt Onan then took charge of the platoon of C. Cy. 2nd Lieut Gray's platoon was on the left of Sgt Onan but he was hit whilst on the parapet by a bullet from the 2nd line. On the extreme left 2nd Lieut Scott with his platoon of C apparently broke right through the first German line. As soon the left of the Batt'n was unsupported owing to machine gun fire having stopped the Cy of Cameroons the third line of an attack had also gone forward — the remaining 2 platoons of C. Cy. leaving the whole of A line from the London Div'n to oppose between (R2) and (R6) held by the last 2 platoons of B. Cy. and the 2 machine guns of the Battalion. The Germans who were in the first trenchwork ran down a communication trench from (R2) and met their reinforcements coming up caused much confusion so that our men coaxed fire into the mass. However some worked up through our men and began to Harris trenches. 2nd Lieut Warlin sent a pigeon message	

Army Form C. 2118.

WAR DIARY
or
INTELLIGENCE SUMMARY.
(Erase heading not required.)

Instructions regarding War Diaries and Intelligence Summaries are contained in F.S. Regs., Part II. and the Staff Manual respectively. Title pages will be prepared in manuscript.

Hour, Date, Place	Summary of Events and Information	Remarks and references to Appendices
1915 9. May. RUE du Bois RICHEBOURG	by J.P. Spink saying that machine gun fire might be opened on both flanks. Immediately afterwards a message was received asking for supports. The taking of our first objective was reported and a request sent that the Supporting Battalion might be pushed forward at once. On the right 2nd Lieut Sotheby's platoon, owing to the mowing through the gap in the German wire was checked to the right of A Coy and found the wire uncut and could not get through.	
4.6 p.m.	A message received from 1/B.W. that all supports were to be pushed forward which was sent on immediately to the Coys.	
4.10 p.m.	Message from our front line "Send supports quickly." Can trust a battalion	
4.19 p.m.	Message received that 2 Coys 1/North Lancashire Reg.t are to support at once. Prepare to move supports and machine guns with them. The two	
4.29 p.m.	Companies filed into our front of A breastwork from the left.	
4.25 p.m.	Message from 1/B.de. Two more Companies L.N. Lancs were to follow first two	
4.26 p.m.	Message from our line in German Breastwork "Tell machine guns to watch our flanks."	

Army Form C. 2118.

WAR DIARY
or
INTELLIGENCE SUMMARY.
(Erase heading not required.)

Hour, Date, Place	Summary of Events and Information	Remarks and references to Appendices
9 May RUE du BOIS RICHEBOURG		
4.30 pm	Report to 1st Bde that the first two companies X. H Davies almost ready to go forward to L.N. Davis	
4.32 pm	Message from 2nd Bde "Cancel order to support assault & remain in fire trench"	
4.36 pm	Message from 1st-13th to Cameron's "You have to stand fast"	
4.42 pm	Message from 1st-13th "Attacking troops are to be withdrawn under cover of artillery fire to trenches/cover. State this message was acknowledged by 2nd Seaforths. Gave orders for the men to retire when fired down to the extreme left and all began to fall back.	
5.14 pm	Message that the Batty was to withdraw to B line and later that the machine guns were also to be retired	

WAR DIARY or INTELLIGENCE SUMMARY

Army Form C. 2118.

Hour, Date, Place	Summary of Events and Information	Remarks and references to Appendices
1915 May 9. Rue du BOIS RICHEBOURG 4 a.m.	Enemy's wire in spite of heavy rifle fire Major J. M. B. Robertson was hurt by a bullet 50 yards away. Wire apparently the enemy could not depress their machine guns so as to fire at our men. The wire was not cut near the German (R B) second line and 3rd and 4th platoons of A Coy so they crowded through a gap cut as their left and reached the top of the German parapet 1/2 a minute before 4 p.m. nearly. One platoon of B Coy under 2nd draw Wallace with them. The total distance in fairly 300 yards and was covered, obstacles & all in about 2 minutes. 2nd draw Lyle's party on the right reached the second trench without opposition where they could not fire nor be fired at. They breached a trench running to the right and then own trench to the left. (They were eventually all shot out of action by bombs on their own side. Our men with three bombs with them.) 2nd draw Wallace and Wallace secured themselves on both flanks to the Company Officer by flag "Joy and" but the Supplies were there shot in the arm On the left D Coy mostly came through the same gap in the wire as A & B., their right platoon under 2nd draw Shand found themselves opposite two machine guns which however could not fire at them on the parapet	

WAR DIARY
or
INTELLIGENCE SUMMARY.
(Erase heading not required.)

Army Form C. 2118.

Hour, Date, Place	Summary of Events and Information	Remarks and references to Appendices
1915		
6.15 p.m. May 9. Rue du Bois Richebourg	All companies withdrawn to B line and then sent by platoons down Rue du Bois to LE TOURET where ordered to go to the billets at HINGES.	
11.50 p.m. HINGES.	In billets at HINGES. Casualties Officers Killed Lieut W H C Edwards. Wounded Maj Thos Reardon, Capt W Green, 2nd Lieut T F Mandola, Wounded & missing 2nd Lts A Newton, A Shroud, A Gray, J Wallace, Missing 2nd Lt JJ Scott, T Boyle, G Bone, H West - Other ranks Killed 55, Died of wounds 6, Wounded 241, Wounded & missing 6, Missing 153. Total Casualties Officers 14, Other ranks 461.	
May 10. HINGES.	Battalion fighting strength today Queen Bees 8 other ranks 354. In Divisional Reserve. Congratulations to the Bn. on it's gallant behaviour from Wynne Gen Sir D Haig. Wind NE. Wr. otherwise fine.	
" 11 "	Divl Reserve. HRH the Prince of Wales visits Headquarters. Major Gen R Haking CB over to convey congratulations to the Battalion on it's gallant behaviour on the 9th. From Major Gen Sir C Monro Comdg 1st Corps and Gen Sir D Haig Gen Comdg 1st Army. Draft of 52 other ranks under Lt J Robinson joined.	
10.20 a.m. 12 BETHUNE BEUVRY	March from HINGES in rear of Bde and arrive in billets at BETHUNE 12 noon when Lieut. Colonel Lt Gen Sir C Monro addresses BGS on their fine behaviour on the 9th.	
2.30 p.m. BEUVRY	To billets in BEUVRY. 2nd visit from HRH the Prince of Wales. Divisional Reserve. Draft of 76 OR under 2nd Lt D Cooke, 2nd Lt arrived 2nd Lt Cooke takes over D Coy	

WAR DIARY
or
INTELLIGENCE SUMMARY
(Erase heading not required.)

Army Form C. 2118.

Hour, Date, Place		Summary of Events and Information	Remarks and References to Appendices
1915.			
May. 13	BEUVRY	In Brigade Reserve. Capt J. of Chalmer who 13th Machine Gun Officer reports for duty and takes command of C.Coy. Orders for relief of Bde in CUINCHY Section by 12/1st (London) Bde. The Comm'dy Officer letter from Lt.Col. 9th Queen D.S.O. Comm'dy 2/Royal Sussex asking for 10 Comm'dy 3 men thanks and admiration to the Batt'n for conduct on 9th.	
May. 14	"	In Divisional Reserve. 156 Division transferred to "Baxter Force" which consists of 19th and 47th (late London) Divisions.	
4.30 pm May. 15.	"	March off from BEUVRY when 9th Liverpool Reg't take over billets.	
5 p.m	SAILLY-LA-BOURSE	In Bde reserve. Bde relieves 58th (French) Division in trenches in front of VERMELLES.	
		Letters from Major L R Philips DSO Comm'dy 2nd 13th KRRC asking that the thanks of his "Bn" might be conveyed to Officers and their admiration and good wishes to our Men.	
May. 16	SAILLY-LA-BOURSE	Divnl Reserve. Brigade Reserve. Wind N. Weather Very fine.	
" 17 " "	"	Bde. Reserve. Wind N.W. Weather Much rain.	
" 18 " "	"	Bde Reserve. Following five officers join and posted: Capt. R.E. Forrester (from wounded and sick) to D.Coy, Lt F.R.C. Anderson (from wounded rejoining) to A.Coy, 2nd Lt J.W. Gardeur (from wounded rejoining) to C.Coy, 2nd Lt H.U. Hayes (first appointment) to C.Coy, 2nd Lt H.M. Ritchie (first appointment) to D.Coy. Sent No 10 to RICHEBOURG to identify bodies and prop. Wind WNW. Weather Damp and foggy.	

Army Form C. 2118.

WAR DIARY
or
INTELLIGENCE SUMMARY.
(*Erase heading not required.*)

Instructions regarding War Diaries and Intelligence Summaries are contained in F.S. Regs., Part II. and the Staff Manual respectively. Title pages will be prepared in manuscript.

Hour, Date, Place	Summary of Events and Information	Remarks and references to Appendices
1915		
7.30pm May 19. SAILLY LA BOURSE	Marched off by platoons to relieve 1/Cameron Highlanders.	
10.45pm VERMELLES	B, D, C Coys take over Y.3 Section in front of VERMELLES – A Coy and 1 Coy 1/Cameron Highlanders in Support. Old trenches built trenches – all good. Wind NW. Weather some rain.	
May 20. VERMELLES	"R" Squad on — sight of front trench about 10 a.m. Our machine guns fire by notes from 10.7 p.m. at intervals until 12 m.n. Whilst artillery fire at certain good junctions. The 1st Divn are relieved to 1st Corps from Bethune Line today. Casualty O.R. 1 Killed.	
" 21 "	A good deal of shelling on all our front – chiefly H.E howitzers 4.5 inch. Our left machine gun open fire on German working party on front of first HOHENZOLLERN at 11.30 a.m. – range 500 – with good result. Capt Inskip & G/ Kenions Highlanders wounded – Capt Grieve in left Support trench. Casualties O.R. 3 Killed 11 wounded. Wind N. Weather Trench fine.	

WAR DIARY
or
INTELLIGENCE SUMMARY.
(Erase heading not required.)

Army Form C. 2118.

Instructions regarding War Diaries and Intelligence Summaries are contained in F.S. Regs., Part II and the Staff Manual respectively. Title pages will be prepared in manuscript.

Hour, Date, Place	Summary of Events and Information	Remarks and references to Appendices
1915		
May 22. VERMELLES	2nd Lieut. B. Coy trench blown in by two shells about 4.30 p.m. C and 2nd Lieut R.G. Horne, [name] M Gunn (3 d by [name] (31st)) [name] (3½), slightly wounded with draft of 156 other ranks. Officer patrol as previous 2nd Lieut Horne [name] Gunn A Cy, [name] to C, posted to D. J. Heavy bombardment by shells towards S. of the midnight. Casualty O.R. 1 wounded. Wind E. Weather fine. Temperature at midnight 41°.	
" 23. VERMELLES	51st Battery RFA in position behind us & october to 117th.	
10.10 am. SAILLY-LA-BOURSE	Relieved by 1/Cameron Highlanders. A and D Cos march from Trench in to T D.S.O. Billeted in VERMELLES in reserve to Y1 and Y3 (1/Scots Guards and 1/Cameron Highlanders). Headquarters, B, C Cos to SAILLY-LA-BOURSE in brigade reserve. Casualty O.R. 1 wounded. Wind NE. Weather V. fine.	
12.5 pm - 24 NOYELLES-LEZ-VERMELLES	Headquarters B, C Cos move up to NOYELLES-LEZ-VERMELLES	
6.30 pm	Six shells into village Casualty O.R. 1 wounded Wind NE. Weather V. fine.	

Army Form C. 2118.

WAR DIARY
or
INTELLIGENCE SUMMARY.
(Erase heading not required.)

Instructions regarding War Diaries and Intelligence Summaries are contained in F.S. Regs., Part II and the Staff Manual respectively. Title pages will be prepared in manuscript.

Hour, Date, Place		Summary of Events and Information	Remarks and references to Appendices
1915	May 25 - NOELLES les - VERMELLES	Brigade Reserve. Major H H Sutherland (invalided from 2nd Batt") (to Clay). 2nd Lieuts N D MacLeod, Capt R G Leggatt & 2/Lt J Gordon (3rd Bn"), J L Paton (3rd Bn") join.	
	" 26. " "	Bde Reserve. Capt J G Chalmer rejoins Bde Staff as Machine Gun Officer. 2nd Lieut G Mitchell + 5 other ranks to mortar class at CHOQUES.	
9.30pm	" 27 VERMELLES	Relieve / Cameron H'ldrs / in Section Y3. A and D Coys in front trench with 1½ platoons each of B +C Coys. Capt C O.R. join Wind ENE. Weather grey, cold.	
	" 28 "	Some shelling in front trench. Draft 2nd Lieut P B Whyte (3rd Bn") and 83 O R join. Casualty O R 1 wounded. Wind E. Weather fine, cold.	

Army Form C. 2118.

WAR DIARY
or
INTELLIGENCE SUMMARY.
(Erase heading not required.)

Instructions regarding War Diaries and Intelligence Summaries are contained in F.S. Regs., Part II. and the Staff Manual respectively. Title pages will be prepared in manuscript.

Hour, Date, Place	Summary of Events and Information	Remarks and references to Appendices
1915		
May 29. VERMELLES	2nd Bde on our left relieved 1st Gloster Regt in Z 1 redoubts	
7.45 pm	1/4 attached 1st Bde. Only 1 Platoon from B + C Coy hors du Combat kenel with A + D Coy. Mines blown up at CUINCHY Wind WNW Weather V fine	
" 30. VERMELLES	Quiet day Wind NW Weather V fine	
11.30 pm " 31 SAILLY-la-BOURSE	1 Cameron Highlanders relieve 1/5th wao to Bde Reserve in SAILLY-la-BOURSE. Wind E. Weather Very fine	

A.Stewart McNeil
Lieut Colonel
Comdg 1/[?] Highland Batt'n

121/6013

1st Division

1st Royal H'rs

Vol XI 1 — 30.6.15.

Army Form C. 2118.

WAR DIARY
or
INTELLIGENCE SUMMARY
(Erase heading not required.)

Instructions regarding War Diaries and Intelligence Summaries are contained in F. S. Regs., Part II. and the Staff Manual respectively. Title pages will be prepared in manuscript.

Hour, Date, Place	Summary of Events and Information	Remarks and References to Appendices
1915.		
9p.m. June 1. BETHUNE	Relieved in billets at SAILLY-LA-BOURSE by 15th & 5th London Regiment and proceeded to billets in FAUBOURG D'ARRAS, BETHUNE. 2/Lt Stewart away on eight days leave. Strength Officers 26 Other ranks 835.	
" 2.	Corps Reserve	
" 3.	"	
" 4.	"	
" 5.	Draft 29 Other ranks arrives	
" 6.	"	
" 7.	" Draft D.I. Murray Menzies joins & General Sir Charles Munro Commdg 1st Corps inspects and addresses the Battalion.	
" 8.	Corps Reserve.	
" 9.	2/Lt Stewart Rexels from leave.	
7.30 p.m. " 10. CUINCHY	Relieve 2nd & 3rd R. Munster Fusiliers in A.3 in front of CUINCHY, left bank Canal with Canadian Division north of it. 1/Scots Guards on our right. B.C Companies in front line, A in support, D in reserve. 1 Coy 1/Intelligence Guards also in reserve. Wind W. Weather Grey, Thunderstorm at night	

79/3228

Army Form C. 2118.

WAR DIARY
or
INTELLIGENCE SUMMARY
(Erase heading not required.)

Instructions regarding War Diaries and Intelligence Summaries are contained in F. S. Regs., Part II. and the Staff Manual respectively. Title pages will be prepared in manuscript.

Hour, Date, Place	Summary of Events and Information	Remarks and References to Appendices
1915. June 11. CUINCHY. 4.3.	Some shelling. Casualties Other Ranks 2 wounded. Wind. W. Weather grey, damp.	
" 12. 4.3.	A good deal of shelling. 'Pip Squeak' and heavy howitzer h.e (57?) Casualties Other Ranks 1 killed, 7 wounded. Wind W. Weather fair.	
" 13. 4.3.	Bombardment by our artillery along our front and N of canal. A, D Companies relieve B, C in front line - B to support, C in reserve 1/Coldstream Guards relieve 1/Scots Guards on our left. 1 Cpy Scots Guards in reserve to 4.3. Casualty Other Ranks 1 wounded. Wind N. Weather very fine.	
" 14. 4.3.	Bombardment by our siege artillery from 9 a.m until dusk. Casualties Other Ranks 3 wounded. Wind N. Weather very fine.	
" 15. 4.3.	Intense bombardment by our artillery. On North of Canal assault by Canadian Division, 7th Division, 51st Bde at 6 p.m. On our left Canadians get well through. Captain R. Fonralles Conway D Cpy shot through the head 6.20 p.m. Casualties Officers 1 killed, Other Ranks 4 wounded. Wind. N. Weather very fine.	

Army Form C. 2118.

WAR DIARY
or
INTELLIGENCE SUMMARY
(Erase heading not required.)

Instructions regarding War Diaries and Intelligence Summaries are contained in F. S. Regs., Part II. and the Staff Manual respectively. Title pages will be prepared in manuscript.

Hour, Date, Place	Summary of Events and Information	Remarks and References to Appendices
1915. June 16. CUINCHY	Much shelling by enemy. Relieved in trenches at 6.30 p.m by 1st Bn Northamptonshire Regt	
9 p.m. BETHUNE	Arrive in billets in Chemin de la Gare, BETHUNE at 9 p.m. In Corps Reserve. Casualties, Other Ranks. 5 Killed, 10 wounded. Wind N. Weather very fine	
" 17. "	Corps Reserve. Six Distinguished Conduct Medals awarded to NCOs and Men of Battalion for 9th May.	
" 18. "	Corps Reserve - 1 hour notice.	
" 19. LAPUGNOY.	March 7 miles to LAPUGNOY where billeted vice 1/K.R.R. London Scottish also billeted in same village. Corps Reserve.	
" 20. "	Divine Service. Corps Reserve. 8th Bn The Black Watch at BURBURE 4 miles away	
" 21. "	Corps Reserve. Lt Gen Sir Charles Monro Commdg 1st Corps rides through. 2nd Lieut P. Macfarlane invalided to England. 2nd Lieut M. Gunn temporary machine gun officer.	

Army Form C. 2118

WAR DIARY
or
INTELLIGENCE SUMMARY.
(Erase heading not required.)

Instructions regarding War Diaries and Intelligence
Summaries are contained in F. S. Regs., Part II.
and the Staff Manual respectively. Title pages
will be prepared in manuscript.

Hour, Date, Place		Summary of Events and Information	Remarks and references to Appendices
LAPUGNOY	June 22	Corps reserve.	
"	23	" March to RUITBURE where Staff & 4th Royal Highlanders.	
" 24 HURIONVILLE		March to billets in HURIONVILLE whence also London Scottish. Corps Reserve.	
"	25	Corps reserve. Draft 51 O.R. arrive.	
"	26	"	
"	27	" Divine Service. Lt/Genl Lomax cmg. Bde over to L/Col Stewart Cmg temporarily in command of 1st Guards Bde, Major J.G. Hamilton D.S.O. in command of Battalion.	
"	28	" Corps Reserve.	
" 29 LABEUVRIERE		Divisional Reserve. March to billets in LABEUVRIERE	
"	30	" Strength Battalion Officers 25. Other ranks 845.	

A Stewart Lieut Colonel
Commdg 1st Bn
The Black Watch.

12.E
3 sheets

121/6292

1st Division

1st Black Watch

Vol XII 1 — 31.7.15.

Army Form C. 2118.

WAR DIARY
or
INTELLIGENCE SUMMARY.
(Erase heading not required.)

Instructions regarding War Diaries and Intelligence Summaries are contained in F.S. Regs., Part II and the Staff Manual respectively. Title pages will be prepared in manuscript.

Hour, Date, Place	Summary of Events and Information	Remarks and references to Appendices
1915. July 1. LABEUVRIERE	Divisional Reserve. Strength of Battalion:- Officers 25 Other ranks 836.	
" 2. "	"	
" 3. "	Draft 79 other ranks arrive.	
" 4. "	Divine Service.	
" 5. NOYELLES les VERMELLES	Brigade Reserve. Relieve 2/R. Munster Fusiliers at 10.30 p.m. 1st Guards Bde takes over Section Y of trenches from 3rd Bde Brigade. Major Hamilton DSO on leave so Major H F Sutherland DSO in command as Lt Col Stewart CMG still commanding Brigade.	
" 6. " "	Brigade reserve.	

Army Form C. 2118.

WAR DIARY
or
INTELLIGENCE SUMMARY.
(Erase heading not required.)

Instructions regarding War Diaries and Intelligence Summaries are contained in F.S. Regs., Part II. and the Staff Manual respectively. Title pages will be prepared in manuscript.

Hour, Date, Place	Summary of Events and Information	Remarks and references to Appendices
1915		
July 7th NOYELLES LES VERMELLES	Brigade Reserve	
" 8th "	Brigade Reserve	
" 9th "	Relieved Cameron in g 2	
" 10th "	g 2	
" 11th "	g 2	
" 12th "	Relieved K.R.R. in g 3. Lieut Luttrell relieved in g 2.	Major HAMILTON D.S.O. took command of Regt: Lt. STEWART sick.
" 13th NOYELLES LES VERMELLES	Relieved 5 Cameron to billets NOYELLES	
" 14th "	Brigade Reserve	
" 15th "	Brigade Reserve	
" 16th "	Relieved Cameron in g 3	
" 17th "	g 3	1 casualtie I.O.R. wounded.
" 18th "	g 3	Ken Finn
ANNEZIN 19th 8.30.p.m.	Relieved by 2nd Sussex Regt. g 3. 10th billets in ANNEZIN. 2nd Lt. J.W. GARDEN wounded. Divisional Reserve.	

Army Form C. 2118.

WAR DIARY
or
INTELLIGENCE SUMMARY.
(Erase heading not required.)

Instructions regarding War Diaries and Intelligence Summaries are contained in F. S. Regs., Part II. and the Staff Manual respectively. Title pages will be prepared in manuscript.

Hour, Date, Place	Summary of Events and Information	Remarks and references to Appendices
1915		
20th July ANNEZIN	Divisional Reserve	
21st "	"	
22nd "	Accident with trench mortar team 2nd Lt S. Mitchell + 2 O.R. killed 3 wounded	
23rd "	Divisional Reserve. 2nd Lt P.K. Campbell joined.	
24th "	Divisional Reserve. 1st Brigade Horse Show shown. 2nd Lt J.L. PATON joined.	
25th ANNEQUIN	Relieved 2nd MUNSTER Fusiliers 3.30 p.m. 2nd Lt N.M. RITCHIE to Hospital. Brigade Reserve	
26th "	Brigade Reserve	
27 "	Brigade Reserve	
28 "	Relieved comuners at 5.30 h.m. to Z.1.	
29 "	Z.1.	
30 "	Z.1. draft of 1 Sergt. 2 cnpl. + 42 other ranks arrived. 2nd Lt Satterly posted to 2nd Bn.	
31 ANNEQUIN	Relieved by Camerons to billets ANNEQUIN 6.30 p.m. 2nd Lt J.M. MOIR joined from 3rd H.L.I.	

(73989) W4141—463. 400,000. 9/14. H.&J.Ltd. Forms/C. 2118/10.

121/6753

Lethoy
13. E.
2 sheet

1st 5 Division

1st Royal H'd
70th xxxl

August 15

Army Form C. 2118.

WAR DIARY
or
INTELLIGENCE SUMMARY.

(Erase heading not required.)

Instructions regarding War Diaries and Intelligence Summaries are contained in F. S. Regs., Part II. and the Staff Manual respectively. Title pages will be prepared in manuscript.

Place	Date Augt 1915	Hour	Summary of Events and Information	Remarks and references to Appendices
ANNEQUIN	1st		Brigade Reserve.	
"	2nd		2nd Lt K. GUNN joined	
Z.1.	3rd		Relieved Cameron 6 h.m.	
Z.1.	4th		"	
Z.1.	5th		"	
ANNEZIN	6th		Relieved by North Lancs 7 h.m. Divisional Reserve. 2 7th Lt Ricketts from hospital	
"	7th		Draft O.R. 35 arrived.	
"	8th		"	
"	9th		"	
"	10th		"	
"	11th		2nd Lt R.S. WHYTE appointed bn transport	
NOYELLES	12th		Relieved 2nd Munster Fusiliers Brigade Reserve	
"	13th		"	
"	14th		"	
Y.3	15th		Relieved Cameron 5 h.m.	
"	16th		"	
"	17th		"	

Army Form C. 2118.

WAR DIARY
or
INTELLIGENCE SUMMARY.
(Erase heading not required.)

Instructions regarding War Diaries and Intelligence Summaries are contained in F. S. Regs., Part II. and the Staff Manual respectively. Title pages will be prepared in manuscript.

Place	Date August	Hour	Summary of Events and Information	Remarks and references to Appendices
NOYELLES	18th		Brigade Reserve	
"	19th		"	
"	20th		"	
Y. 1.	21st		Relieved 1st Grenadier Guards 5 A.m.	
"	22nd		2nd Lt A. FRASER & W. FRASER joined	
"	23rd		4. O.R. killed 1 wounded night 23/24 strong	
ANNEZIN	24th		3rd General Reserve. Relieved by NORTH HANTS 7 A.m. 2nd Lt C.S. Erskine Wrest joined	
"	25th		"	
"	26th		"	
"	27th		"	
"	28th		H. Q. Inspection & general	
"	29th		"	
"	30th		"	
FERFAY	31st		" 2 3 7/k 103½ O.R. 2nd 2 OR to annex 6.10 P.m.	

John McKenzie Lt Col
Commanding 1st R Black Watch

1st Dorsons
1st Brigade.

WAR DIARY

OF

1st Royal Highlanders

SEPTEMBER

1915.

Army Form C. 2118

WAR DIARY
or
INTELLIGENCE SUMMARY.
(Erase heading not required.)

Instructions regarding War Diaries and Intelligence Summaries are contained in F. S. Regs., Part II. and the Staff Manual respectively. Title pages will be prepared in manuscript.

Place	Date	Hour	Summary of Events and Information	Remarks and references to Appendices
FERFAY	Sept 1915 1st to 20th inst		2. Brigade Reserve. Training. The following officers joined in Coy to Coy:- 3rd Left 2nd Lieut B.F. YOUNG joined. 12th Left 2nd Lt R. GUNN & subalt of Instruction St VENANT. 13th Left 2nd Lt A. FRASER & 4th Gunn subalt MISDUES. 20th Left 2nd Lt R. GUNN joined from St VENANT.	
LE MARQUIST 2nd Wood	21st		Left FERFAY at 9.2 a.m. + bivouac in wood. Long waiting.	
"	22nd		Training. Many Rumors of move.	
"	23rd		Move to VERQUIN 9.30 h.m. Very wet morning + night.	
VERQUIN	24th		Band billets at 7.15 a.m. Move off to Y section at 6.45 h.m. 1st line transport left in area H.	
Y section	25th		Moved to Jerman tranches. Tranches killed 3 [2nd Lieut R.B. WHYTE, 2nd Lt. J.M. Moore Sn. Younger] Wounded 3 [Captn R.C. ANDERSON (died of wounds), Capt. D. COOKE, Capt. W.E. HAY]. 2nd Lt R. GUNN. Missing] [Lt H.T.G. ROBERTSON. O.R. killed 48. Wounded 127. Missing 36. Wounded + missing 1.	2nd Lt W. Buhl who was attached from Cadet School, Gozee
[illegible]	26th		C + D Coys attack S end of HULLUCH at 12 noon under orders of 3rd Brigade. 4 13 Coys hold trench at 35-89. Maj. Lieut. Capellen wounded. [Capt. P.E. CAMPBELL killed. 2nd Lt. W. FRASER, 2nd Lt N.W. RITCHIE] O.R. killed 12. wounded 23. missing 5.	

2353 Wt. W2514/1454 700,000 5/15 D.D.&L. A.D.S.S./Forms/C. 2118.

WAR DIARY
or
INTELLIGENCE SUMMARY
(Erase heading not required.)

Army Form C. 2118.

Instructions regarding War Diaries and Intelligence Summaries are contained in F. S. Regs., Part II. and the Staff Manual respectively. Title pages will be prepared in manuscript.

Hour, Date, Place	Summary of Events and Information	Remarks and References to Appendices
27th Sept. German Lines	Men back to our old 2nd line = Y sector at 9 a.m. in Brigade Reserve. D Coy remained at Talus [?] front 92. Casualties O.R. Wounded 2.	
28th Sept. Y sector	None — Brigade known committee O.R. I.M. Col. C.E. STEWART C.M.G returns to Command.	
29th Sept. Y sector	Brigade known & 3rd Brigade Casualties O.R. Killed 2. Wounded 5. Lt. R.H. HUTCHESON + 1300 O.R. join.	
30th Sept. NOEUX LES MINES	Leave Y sector 12.10 a.m. arr. at LES BRESSIS 3 a.m. arr. at NOEUX LES MINES at 11.00 a.m. Major H H Sutherland DSO goes to command 10th Br Gloster Reg. Major 7 [?] V.M Jordan acting 2nd major 1st Bde.	

(Signed) E Sherwood
Lt Col Comdg 1st Bn Black Watch
30th Sept 1915 (Commanding)

Appendix "A"
COPY.

1st Brigade.

On 25th September, The Black Watch less "A" Company working party with R.E. were in Brigade Reserve. At about 6. a.m. "A" Company moved out as a working party with the Cameron Highlanders & at 7-30 a.m. reached their objective and entrenched at Points 25, 89 as directed.

About 10-30 a.m. as 2nd Brigade appeared to be held up on right Black Watch were ordered to rush forward 1 Coy, "B" with their right on BOIS CARRE with orders to gain first German Trench and then swing to their right, owing to heavy enfilade fire from right only half this company reached the first German Line where they established themselves forming a protective flank.

At about 2 p.m. remainder of Battalion "C" & "A" Coy's pushed up the HULLUCH Road with intention of attacking the German Trenches in flank. On reaching German Lines, as Germans had surrendered these two companies advanced with 3rd Brigade & took up position in the New German Work at point 76 sending parties to hold jumps at 35, 89 & 52. These positions were maintained during the night.

At 10-30 a.m. on 26th Black Watch received orders orders to attack S. end of HULLUCH in conjunction with 3rd Brigade with their left on point 44. This attack was postponed from 11 a.m. to 12 noon. The attack failed to reach its objective and these two companies established themselves in T head at point 92 where they remained till left T head was relieved on night of 27th.

At about 11 a.m. on the 27th the remainder of Battalion withdrew to German 2nd Line near point 60 & at 9-30 p.m. to British old 1th Line with 1 Company still holding right of T head at 92.

In the Field,   J. M. Hamilton   Lieut-Colonel,
28th September,1915.   Commanding 1st Bn The Black Watch.

121/737

1st/5 Division

1st Royal Wts
total
Oct 15

15-E
8 sheets

HULLUCH
13/10/15

Army Form C. 2118.

WAR DIARY
or
INTELLIGENCE SUMMARY

(Erase heading not required.)

Instructions regarding War Diaries and Intelligence Summaries are contained in F. S. Regs., Part II. and the Staff Manual respectively. Title pages will be prepared in manuscript.

Hour, Date, Place	Summary of Events and Information	Remarks and References to Appendices
1915 October 1. Nœux-Les-Mines.	Strength :- 20 officers, 636 other ranks. Regt.	
" 2. " "	Regt.	
" 3. " "	Divine Service.	
" 4. " "	Regt.	
" 5. 11.55pm Near Chalk Pit, Loos	Take over partially completed trenches from 9th Bn Glosters. 3rd Bde (1/Glosters) on our right, London Scottish on our left. C and D Coys occupy front trenches. Some heavy shelling. Continue digging. Other casualties — Casualties 2 killed 4 wounded. 1 died of wounds. Wind W. Weather fine.	
" 6. Near Chalk pit, Loos	trench shelling.	
" 7. 9pm " "	Relieved by 9th Liverpools and march back except A Coy who deploy with Inniskillen 8th Bn. Much trench destroyed in afternoon. Casualties 3 killed; 3 wounded	
" 10pm N° Lone Tree	Into Old 1st German line near LONE TREE.	
" 8. 4am " "	A Coy return from digging	
" 8.30pm " "	Dav" digging. German counter attack on hill 70 repulsed. 2nd Lieuts R.F. Thomson (A coy) W. Urquhart (B coy) J. McScott (C) J.C. Murray (D coy) join. Casualties Other Ranks 2 killed 3 wounded. Wind SSE, Weather Gray	

Army Form C. 2118.

WAR DIARY
INTELLIGENCE SUMMARY
(Erase heading not required.)

Instructions regarding War Diaries and Intelligence Summaries are contained in F. S. Regs., Part II. and the Staff Manual respectively. Title pages will be prepared in manuscript.

Hour, Date, Place	Summary of Events and Information	Remarks and References to Appendices
1915		
October 9. 9.30am to LONETREE	Battⁿ returns from digging 3.30am	
8 pm	Battⁿ digging. Casualties, Other Ranks – 2 wounded. Wind NNE. Weather good	
10. 3 am	Digging parties return. Casualties Other Ranks 4.O.R. 1 missing. Wind E. Weather Grey, then fine.	
11. 6.30 am W. of HULLUCH	Companies move into new positions west of Hulluch. C. Cy occupy front line, relieving 10th Gloster. Casualties Other ranks 1 wounded. Wind E. Weather Fine.	
" 12.	Captain Dumsdon commdg A Cy sick. B Cy relieve half C and B&C in front line and A and D in res currently line? 60 yds behind. Major Hamilton DSO, 2nd Lieuts Thomson, Inglehart, Murray Scott moved to join 1st line transport 2nd Lieut R Alexander (B Cy) join 9 trps 10th 1st line transport Casualties Other Ranks 1 killed, 4 wounded. Wind SW. Weather very fine.	

(9 26 6) W 257—976 103,000 1/12 H W V 79/3208

Army Form C. 2118.

WAR DIARY
or
INTELLIGENCE SUMMARY
(Erase heading not required.)

Instructions regarding War Diaries and Intelligence Summaries are contained in F. S. Regs., Part II. and the Staff Manual respectively. Title pages will be prepared in manuscript.

Hour, Date, Place	Summary of Events and Information	Remarks and References to Appendices
1915. October, 13 6 a.m. to 1 p.m. War G HULLUCH. 1 p.m.	Wire cutting and preliminary bombardment by our artillery. — 3 Brigades RFA firing HE at 4750. Gun discharge. For details of attack vide Appendix A attached. All three officers of C Coy were killed, and all three of B wounded. The fighting strength of the Battalion was 14 Officers 536 other ranks. The total breadth of the objective was 500 yards. The casualties were Killed Officers 2nd Lieuts. Paton, Fraser, Ballantyne, Hutchison and Hayes (since reported killed) Other ranks. Wounded Lieut Menzies, 2nd Lieuts Hare, Mercer, Laurie and Young. Total casualties. Other ranks 163. Missing Other ranks. 10 officers 229 other ranks. Wind SSW. Weather very fine.	Appendix A.

Army Form C. 2118.

WAR DIARY
or
INTELLIGENCE SUMMARY
(Erase heading not required.)

Instructions regarding War Diaries and Intelligence Summaries are contained in F. S. Regs, Part II. and the Staff Manual respectively. Title pages will be prepared in manuscript.

Hour, Date, Place	Summary of Events and Information	Remarks and References to Appendices
1915.		
October, 14. 12.20am W. of HULLUCH	The Battalion brought back to 1st Brown line were try told Captain Pero, Reime attached 1/Cameron Highlanders gave valuable assistance in cheering our wounded.	
3.30 p.m " "	The 15th County of London Regiment relieve the Bah's who march	
6.15 p.m LE RUTOIRE	up to LE RUTOIRE where we leave at 6.15 p.m and	
8.p.m SAILLY la BOURSE	march to SAILLY LA BOURSE where tea served. Thence to	
10 p.m NOEUX les MINES	Station at NOEUX les MINES where entrain and leave 11.20 p.m	
	Casualties Other ranks 4 wounded. Wind SW Weather Fine.	
October 15. LILLERS	Arrive LILLERS 12.20 a.m and billetted in West end of town. Draft 21 Other ranks arrives. Wind N. Weather Foggy.	
" 16 "	Refitting	

WAR DIARY
or
INTELLIGENCE SUMMARY
(Erase heading not required.)

Army Form C. 2118.

Hour, Date, Place		Summary of Events and Information	Remarks and References to Appendices
1915.			
October 17.	LILLERS	Divine Service.	
" 18	"	Training.	
" 19	"	Training. Lieut W.D. McL Stewart (1st 2nd Bn), 2nd Lt I D Bierson (11th Bn) join	
" 20	"	Training	
" 21	"	"	
" 22	"	"	
" 23	"	Battalion Boxing Tournament	
" 24	"	Divine Service	
" 25	"	Training	
" 26	"	Training	
" 27	"	Brigade Boxing Tournament	

Army Form C. 2118.

WAR DIARY
or
INTELLIGENCE SUMMARY
(Erase heading not required.)

Instructions regarding War Diaries and Intelligence Summaries are contained in F. S. Regs., Part II. and the Staff Manual respectively. Title pages will be prepared in manuscript.

Hour, Date, Place	Summary of Events and Information	Remarks and References to Appendices
1915.		
October 28. LA BUSSIERE.	A Company under Capt W. McL Stewart, 2nd Lieut Murray Morgan, 2nd Lt I D Barron & ? R. Alexander and 202 Other ranks proceeded to LAPUGNOY LABUISSIERE where representatives of the 1st Divn were inspected by H.M the King. They rejoined the Battalion in HUICHON. The Battalion proceeded by rail to NOEUX les MINES and by road to HUICHON - to billets. Captain J L Willcocks (B Coy) and 2nd Lt G C Moira (D Coy) joined. Captain D Lumsden rejoined from hospital.	
" 29. HUICHON.	Training. 2nd Lt J Kelly (D Coy) joined - promoted from 11th Hussars.	
" 30. "	" 2nd Lt T B Anderson (B Coy) joined - promoted from 8th R B.	
" 31. 9.10 a.m. 1 p.m LILLERS.	March off from HUICHON to billets in LILLERS. Draft 3 Sgts, 2 Cpls, 73 Ptes from Strength of Batt? 25 officers (including 2 sick in country), 627 other Ranks (includes 33 employed away on staff duties, 2 sick in country)	

R A Alexander Colonel
Comdg 1st B?
1st Wilson ?

Appendix A.

1st Bn The Black Watch.
Reference Trench Map 36.C.N.W.3. 1:10,000.

Near Hulluch 1 to 1-50 pm	Gas discharge. 1000 P. Smoke Grenades were thrown out every six yards at given intervals up to 1-55.
1-55 pm.	The sections told off in 4 platoons for wirecutting made gaps in our own wire.
2 pm.	Two platoons each of B & C Coys went forward extended to about 4 paces interval. Each platoon had with it its wirecutting section and 12 men carrying 2 units Bombs.

The objective of the Battalion was from Cross Roads H.19.A.76 to H.13.C.47. — exactly 500 yards.

This front had been allotted as follows:—

B Coy (supported by A) From H.19.A.67. to H.13.C.41 with special orders for the capture of the point H.19.A.77.

C Coy (supported by D) From H.13.C.41 to H.13.C.47 with special orders for the capture of the point H.13.C.42.

Bombing Officer & a special party were told off for Sap running from our lines to H.13.C.45.

A Machine Gun was placed on either flank of the Battalion & two opened covering fire from behind headquarters which was 200 yards behind the centre of C Coy.

After deducting bombers & wirers entirely detached from the Battalion the strength was
14 Officers 536 Other Ranks.

2-3 pm.	The leading platoons reached German wire and finding it uncut, proceeded to try & cut it or lift the stakes. Some bombs were hurled at them but fell short. However 2 German Machine Guns posted 30 yards on either flank of ruins of Estaminet at Cross Roads H.19.A.76. did much execution chiefly amongst the 2 supporting platoons of B Coy which came forward with picks & shovels. Owing to the smoke at this time it was difficult to ascertain exactly what was happening. With the supporting platoons telephone instruments went forward as in the smoke it was thought we had got into the German trench.
2-30 pm.	There were heavy casualties amongst the bombers up sap leading to H.13.C.45. & the 2 remaining men Cpl Kerr & L/Cpl Lovejoy blocked the sap, closed to a small square work in the sap 40 yards from the German trench. Two German Machine Guns were in position near H.13.C.42. which prevented C Coy making further progress with the wire.
2-45 pm.	A & D Coys both sent up supporting platoons to assist with
3-10 pm.	fire and at 3.15 pm. D Coy sent other two platoons

	who were much harried by Machine Gun fire.
	B sent forward a second and afterwards a third
4 pm	Again the right platoon of B (the right Coy) was reported wrongly, to have got in. More bombs were sent up but never reached the front companies
4·45 pm	Lieut Mercer collected some Northampton bombers who assisted our party (now one man) in the cap towards H.13.c.45. The left platoon of C Coy was now said to have got into the trench about H.13.c.45 but had only got into the wire.
6 pm	There were now 58 men of the Battalion still in the British front trench & two companies of the Northamptons
7·25 pm	Instructions received to hold present position until further orders but a few men had crawled back from the wire. Every Officer of the Battalion who had left our trench had become a casualty.
8·25 pm	There were 138 men collected in the front British trench
8·50 pm	A patrol of 6 men under 2nd Lieut Mercer, reconnoitred the sunken road leading to the right of our objective, as it was rumoured that some men of the Berkshires had reached the Cross Road Estaminet. The rumours proved unfounded and all the patrol were killed or wounded.
11·45 pm	Orders came for the delivery of an attack on the same objective by the 2nd Bde and for the Battalion to re-organize and hold the first British line
14·10·15 12·20 am	The Battalion re-organized holding 1st British line

CASUALTIES

	Officers	Other Ranks
Killed	4	33
Wounded	5	163
Wounded & Missing	1	-
Missing	-	33
Total	10	229

R.G. Stewart
LIEUT. COLONEL
Commanding, 1st Bn. The Black Watch

20/10/15

16.E
6 sheets

S/S Kvaren

S/S Royne Heighno
Novr 1915
Vol. XVI

121/7779

Army Form C. 2118.

WAR DIARY
INTELLIGENCE SUMMARY

(Erase heading not required.)

Instructions regarding War Diaries and Intelligence Summaries are contained in F. S. Regs., Part II and the Staff Manual respectively. Title pages will be prepared in manuscript.

Hour, Date, Place	Summary of Events and Information	Remarks and References to Appendices
1915.		
November 1. LILLERS.	Corps reserve Training Strength of Batt. 25 officers, 626 other ranks. 2nd Lieut R.S. Gurtuve, promoted fr. Lce Cpl. 2/Serjeants Strigulenders, Jones, posted C. Coy.	
" 2. "	Corps reserve Training	
" 3. "	" " Capt & Adjt V.M. Fortune resumes duties as Adjt. from act.g bde major 1st Bde.	
" 4. "	Corps reserve Training. Capt J.N.O. Rycroft joins from a.d.c. G.O.C. 11th Corps. and takes command D. Coy.	
" 5. "	Corps reserve. Divisional Boxing tournament.	
" 6. "	Corps reserve. Training. 2nd Lieut R.J. Thomson to hospital - fever.	
" 7. "	Divine Service. Draft (Sgts 3, Cpls 3, prvts 74) arrives. Casualty O.R. 1 wounded (bomb accident)	
" 8. "	Corps reserve. Training.	
" 9. "	" " Battalion concert.	

… Army Form C. 2118.

WAR DIARY
INTELLIGENCE SUMMARY

(Erase heading not required.)

1915	Hour, Date, Place	Summary of Events and Information	Remarks and References to Appendices
November 10	LILLERS.	Corps Reserve. 1st Brigade inspected and addressed by Sir General Sir Henry Rawlinson Bt. KCB, CVO, Commd'g 4th Corps, with special reference to good work of 25th September.	
" 11	"	Corps Reserve. Training 2nd W.R. Unpleasant wounded by hand grenade when at practice. Casualty Officers 1 wounded.	
" 12	"	O.C. and Corps Reserve. Company Commanders visit Trenches A.1 - immediately N of LOOS.	
" 13	"	Corps Reserve. Baths.	
" 14. 7.30 a.m		Entrain for NOEUX-les-MINES	
9.30 a.m	MAZINGARBE.	Arrive by line of march at MAZINGARBE from NOEUX-les-MINES. Have dinner and teas. Parade 4.50 and march to trenches in A.1.	
8 p.m.	N. of LOOS.	N of LOOS. When relieve all 8th London Reg't. by 7.50 p.m. A,B,D in front line by night, C. in support. 77th Regiment (French) on our right, 8th R. Berkshire Reg't on left. Wind W. Weather fine. Sharp frost at night.	

Army Form C. 2118.

WAR DIARY
or
INTELLIGENCE SUMMARY.
(Erase heading not required.)

Instructions regarding War Diaries and Intelligence Summaries are contained in F. S. Regs., Part II and the Staff Manual respectively. Title pages will be prepared in manuscript.

Hour, Date, Place	Summary of Events and Information	Remarks and references to Appendices
1915 November, 15. N. LOOS	B. Coy withdraw to support, D to reserve line of trenches during daylight. Trenches very foul. Front trenches shelled with LHV and 4.9 howitzer occasionally throughout day. 4 officers 10th Glosters Regt attached A and D Companies for instruction. Working parties 1/Cameron Highlanders and 73rd pioneer Coy up in evening for batteries. Casualties O.R. 2 wounded. Wind W. Weather Sharp frost early, fine.	
" 16. " "	Maj Gen¹ Holland C.B, CVO, DSO visits Trenches. Some heavy shelling from 11 am to 2 p.m. Casualties OR 3 wounded Wind W. Weather foggy early, fair	
" 17. N. LOOS 11 am to 11·20am 8 p.m. PHILOSOPHE 9 p.m.	Bombardment of PUITS 14 by our guns. Slightly foed. Enemy reply but not strongly. 10th Glosters Regt relieve 35th who move back to brigade reserve in billets at PHILOSOPHE, 3 platoons C. Cy holding LENS Rd, 65 Metre p¹, NORTHERN SAP. Fredericks? Casualties O.R. 2 wounded. Wind W. Weather Heavy showers fell.	

Army Form C. 2118.

WAR DIARY
~~INTELLIGENCE SUMMARY.~~
(Erase heading not required.)

Instructions regarding War Diaries and Intelligence Summaries are contained in F. S. Regs., Part II. and the Staff Manual respectively. Title pages will be prepared in manuscript.

Hour, Date, Place	Summary of Events and Information	Remarks and references to Appendices
10/15		
November 18. PHILOSOPHE.	Brigade Reserve. 2nd Lieut Thompson back from temporal. on Wind W. Weather sharp frost early, then heavy rain	
" 19 PHILOSOPHE 1 p.m.	9th Bn Kings Liverpool Regt. relieve all 13" except recdoubt. "13"	
HOUCHIN 3.45 p.m.	to Divisional Reserve in billets at HOUCHIN. C. Coy's 3 Platoons	
11 p.m.	retired at night and rejoin 13".	
	2nd Lieut Kelly takes over duties of Transport Officer from 2nd Lt O.S. Brown.	
	General Sir H Rawlinson Comm. 4th Corps visits HOUCHIN. Wind E. Weather foggy.	
" 20 HOUCHIN	Divisional Reserve.	
" 21 "	" Divine Service	
" 22 "	" Draft 1 W.O., 1 Sergt, 57 O.R. arrives.	
" 23 "	" Field Marshal Sir John French G.C.B, O.M.V.C., in.spected 1st Brigade near MEUX-w-MINES and eulogy praised fine work of the Brigade at LOOS, and referring to the great record of the Battalion thought that the honour "LOOS" was a splendid one any home on our colours He referred	

Army Form C. 2118.

WAR DIARY
or
INTELLIGENCE SUMMARY.
(Erase heading not required.)

Instructions regarding War Diaries and Intelligence Summaries are contained in F.S. Regs., Part II. and the Staff Manual respectively. Title pages will be prepared in manuscript.

Hour, Date, Place	Summary of Events and Information	Remarks and references to Appendices
1915		
24. November HOUCHIN	also to the previous successes of the Brigade throughout this campaign. He also spoke to the Comm'g Officer on the good appearance of the Battalion. 2nd Lieut Adam and 19 other ranks rejoined from course of training. Draft 1 W.O, 1 Sergt, 2 Corpls & 5 other ranks from Cavalry all been who had been wounded.	
	Divisional Reserve. Training	
25 " "	Divisional Reserve. Billeting party on to PHILOSOPHE	
26. Nov. HOUCHIN 10am PHILOSOPHE 12 noon	March to PHILOSOPHE leaving A.D. Co'ys under Major Hamilton DSO at MAZINGARBE. Brigade Reserve.	
27. Nov. PHILOSOPHE	Brigade Reserve. D. Company up from MAZINGARBE.	
28 Nov. "	Brigade Reserve. A Company up from MAZINGARBE.	

(73989) W4141—463. 400,000. 9/14. H.&J.Ltd. Forms/C. 2118/10.

Army Form C. 2118.

WAR DIARY
or
INTELLIGENCE SUMMARY.
(Erase heading not required.)

Instructions regarding War Diaries and Intelligence Summaries are contained in F.S. Regs., Part II. and the Staff Manual respectively. Title pages will be prepared in manuscript.

Hour, Date, Place	Summary of Events and Information	Remarks and references to Appendices
1915		
November 29. N? HULLUCH.	In evening leave PHILOSOPHE and relieve 8th Royal Berkshires in Subsection B.1 opposite SE end of HULLUCH. A, B, C Coys in front line, D Coy in support. Wind E. Weather Thaw, rain.	
" 30. "	In Subsection B.1. 2nd Lts Bland and Mann, 20th Hussars attached for some shelling. Instruction to A and B Companies. Casualties O.R. 2 wounded. Wind S. Weather Fine, rain at night.	

E Stewart M Grant
Commdg 1/ The Black Watch.

6.J. 17.E
annex

1/Roy. Welshns.
Dec. 1915
Vol XVII

1st Bar
2

Army Form C. 2118.

WAR DIARY
or
INTELLIGENCE SUMMARY.
(Erase heading not required.)

Instructions regarding War Diaries and Intelligence Summaries are contained in F.S. Regs., Part II. and the Staff Manual respectively. Title pages will be prepared in manuscript.

1915.	Hour, Date, Place	Summary of Events and Information	Remarks and references to Appendices
December 1.	Near HULLUCH.	Subsection B1. Trenches very muddy. Wind S. Weather Showery.	
" 2.	" "	Bombardment: eng our guns on our front.	
	4.45pm near LONE TREE	Relieved by 8th Royal Berkshires and go to Support line – old German line – near LONE TREE. Casualty O.R. 1 wounded. Wind SSW. Weather Fair, rain in night.	
" 3.	" "	In Support B.1. Wind W. Weather Very wet.	
" 4.	" "	In Support B.1. Heavy fatigues. Casualty 0 R. 1 wounded. Wind WSW. Weather Wet.	
" 5.	Near HULLUCH.	Relieve 8th Royal Berkshires in B.1. Subsection. Wind W. Weather Fair, rain at night.	
" 6.	" "	In B.1. Firing many rifle grenades. Enemy attempt to reply but silenced by French mortars. Casualties O.R. 3 wounded. Wind W. Weather Heavy rain at intervals.	

Army Form C. 2118.

WAR DIARY
or
INTELLIGENCE SUMMARY.
(Erase heading not required.)

Instructions regarding War Diaries and Intelligence Summaries are contained in F.S. Regs., Part II. and the Staff Manual respectively. Title pages will be prepared in manuscript.

Hour, Date, Place	Summary of Events and Information	Remarks and references to Appendices
1915.		
December 7. Near HULLUCH.	More rifle grenades fired into enemy. Their reply stopped by trench mortar. Casualties O.R. 7 wounded	
" 8.	Wind W. Weather fair early, then rain	
	Some casualties in R.F.A. working party in our support line caused by heavy enemy shelling. Relieved by 6th Bn. Welch Regt. Owing to depth of mud on roads last company not in until 3 a.m. on 9th.	
11.30 pm MAZINGARBE	Move to Divisional Reserve in MAZINGARBE.	
" 9.	Casualties O.R. 6 wounded. Wind W. Weather fair.	
MAZINGARBE	Divisional Reserve. Baths.	
" 10.	Divisional Reserve. 2nd Lt J.A. INGLIS 3rd B- rejoined. Inspection by A.D.M.S. Fine day.	
" 11.	Divisional Reserve. Windy & some rain.	
" 12.	Divisional Reserve. Much colder.	
" 13.	Divisional Reserve. C.O. A.D.S. & Coy Commanders & and trenches. Dry cold day. Draft O.R. 105 arrive.	

Army Form C. 2118.

WAR DIARY
or
INTELLIGENCE SUMMARY.
(Erase heading not required.)

Instructions regarding War Diaries and Intelligence Summaries are contained in F.S. Regs., Part II. and the Staff Manual respectively. Title pages will be prepared in manuscript.

Place	Date	Hour	Summary of Events and Information	Remarks and references to Appendices
Near LOOS	Oct/14		Took over front line trenches in A.1. from Royal North Lancs. Quiet trenches. Very wet day.	
"	15		A.1. A good bit of shelling. Casualties O.R. 1 wounded. Sent O.R. 44 arrived. 1st Reinft.	1st Reinft. arrived
"	16		A.1. Lot of shelling in afternoon. Casualties O.R. 2 killed. 2nd Lt P.H.L.E. COBBURN rejoined from hospital. 2nd Lt CAMPBELL sent to hospital. 6th Bn CAMERONS joined.	
PHILOSOPHE	17		Relieved by Camerons in A.1. at 7 p.m. to go back to PHILOSOPHE in Brigade Reserve. Wet day, but not too bad. A lot of shelling. Casualties O.R. 1 wounded.	
"	18		Brigade Reserve. Wet + mild.	
"	19.		Brigade Reserve. Rain with burst of frost.	
Near LOOS	20.		Relieve CAMERONS in A.1 at 7.30 p.m. Cold dull day.	
"	21.		A.1. G.O.C. div. from round trenches 6.30 a.m. Wet day. Casualty Captain G.M. RICHMOND wounded. A lot of shelling. Colonel McCLINTOCH Inniskilling Fusiliers att d	
"	22		A.1. Lot of shelling all day. Very wet afternoon. Casualties 2nd Lt O.S. BROWN killed. O.R. 1 killed 7 wounded.	
"	23		A.1. relieved by Camerons 8 p.m. + go to GUN ALLEY in support. Very wet day. Colonel McCLINTOCH wounded at 6.30 a.m.	
"	24		In support. Very hot trenches especially New Reserve Trench. Wet morning. Hugh Quarter Arm. Shelled lot	

Army Form C. 2118.

WAR DIARY
or
INTELLIGENCE SUMMARY.
(Erase heading not required.)

Instructions regarding War Diaries and Intelligence Summaries are contained in F. S. Regs., Part II. and the Staff Manual respectively. Title pages will be prepared in manuscript.

Place	Date	Hour	Summary of Events and Information	Remarks and references to Appendices
LOOS	Sep 25		In Support. Head Quarters killed again. G.O.C. Corps visits New Horse Jacob in afternoon.	
"	26		Relieved at 7 p.m. by South Wales Borderers & go into Divisional Reserve at NOEUX LES MINES by bus from PHILOSOPHE near billets 10 p.m. Join day. Head Quarters & heavily shelled. Casualties O.R. killed 3 wounded 3. 7 others buried & still not yet not recovered. Deaths O.R. & 41 others	
NOEUX LES MINES	27.		Divisional Reserve. Inn etc.	
"	28.		Divisional Reserve. Baths. Inn etc.	
"	29		Divisional Reserve	
"	30		Divisional Reserve. Hon. Lau Nus. Sgn Stewart Left C.R. 24 men Enemy to [illegible]	
"	31.		Divisional Reserve. H. Col. L.?. Stewart with 5 regiment [illegible] 1st Royal	

John M Hamilton Major
Commanding 1st The Black Watch.

1ST DIVISION
1ST BRIGADE

1ST BATTALION
BLACK WATCH (R.HIGHLANDERS)
JAN - DEC 1916

1st Brigade.
1st Division.

1st BATTALION BLACK WATCH (R.Highlanders) JANUARY 1916.

1st Royal Star
Jan
Vol XVIII

18E
a sheet

Army Form C.2118

WAR DIARY
or
INTELLIGENCE SUMMARY.
(Erase heading not required.)

Instructions regarding War Diaries and Intelligence Summaries are contained in F.S. Regs., Part II. and the Staff Manual respectively. Title pages will be prepared in manuscript.

Place	Date	Hour	Summary of Events and Information	Remarks and references to Appendices
Haucourt	1st		Relieved R.R.R. & D.L.I. at 6 p.m. A.B.C Coys. whole line. D. Coy. in support in front line trenches	
"	2nd		B.I. Day & night, not much enemy activity. O.R. 1 killed, 3 wounded	
"	3rd		B.I. Day & night, not much activity	
Philosophe	4th		Relieved by 1st Cameron H'ldrs at 3 p.m. 1st Argyle Sussex Division H.Q. March Schwabe & Marne till 3 hour & told our Brigade in reserve. 152nd Brigade casualties O.R. 1 wounded	
"	5th		Brigade Reserve all day. Billets. Min-ly attack	
"	6th		Brigade Reserve. Fine day. Well.	
Mazingarbe	7th		Relieve CAMERON HIGHLANDERS B.I. starting at 3 p.m. Casualties O.R. 1	
"	8th		B.I. Casualties O.R. wounded 2.	
"	9th		B.I. Casualties O.R. wounded 4	
"	10th		Relieved by CAMERONS & go into Support in old GERMAN LINE & new Reserve Trench.	
"	11th		In Support. Draft 2nd Lt J.C. Monday from LONDON SCOTTISH & 27 O.R. arrive.	
"	12th			

Army Form C. 2118.

WAR DIARY
or
INTELLIGENCE SUMMARY.
(Erase heading not required.)

Instructions regarding War Diaries and Intelligence Summaries are contained in F. S. Regs., Part II. and the Staff Manual respectively. Title pages will be prepared in manuscript.

Place	Date 1916	Hour	Summary of Events and Information	Remarks and references to Appendices
NOEUX LES MINES	Jan 13th		Relieved by 15th Division & reach NOEUX at 9 p.m. when Bn. goes into billets in supt. Corps Reserve.	
ALLOUAGNE	14th		Entrain NOEUX for LILLERS & march to billets in ALLOUAGNE.	
"	15th		Coys recovn. refitting & cleaning up	
"	16th		Coys recovn. training	
"	17th		Coys recovn. training	
"	18th		Coys recovn. training	
"	19th		Coys recovn. training	
"	20th		Visit of Sir Joffre. Capt Lumsden + 100 men formed Guard of Honour at FERFAY. Remainder of Battn. lined Route of LILLERS. no Bn. Coys.	
"	21st		Coys recovn. training	
"	22nd		Coys recovn. training	
"	23rd		Coys recovn. training. Draft of 20 O.R. joined.	
"	24th		Coys recovn. training	
"	25th		Coys recovn. training. Inspection by Brigadier.	
"	26th		Coys recovn. training	
"	27th		Coys recovn. & ½ hour notice	
"	28th		Coys recovn. 4 hours notice. Training. 2nd Lieut W. URQUHART rejoined from Hospital.	
"	29th		Coys recovn. Training	
"	30th		Coys recovn. Training	
"	31st		Coys recovn. Training	

John McKenzie Major
Commanding 1st Bn The Black Watch

1st Brigade.
1st Division.

1st BATTALION ROYAL HIGHLANDERS (Black Watch) FEBRUARY 7/ 1916.

Army Form C. 2118.

WAR DIARY
or
INTELLIGENCE SUMMARY.
(Erase heading not required.)

Instructions regarding War Diaries and Intelligence Summaries are contained in F. S. Regs., Part II. and the Staff Manual respectively. Title pages will be prepared in manuscript.

Place	Date 1916 July	Hour	Summary of Events and Information	Remarks and references to Appendices.
ALLOUAGNE	1st		Divisional Reserve.	
"	2nd		"	
"	3rd		"	
"	4th		2nd Lt G.G. Moore to R.F.C. (Probation).	
"	5th		Draft 19 O.R. arrive.	
"	6th		Draft 45 O.R. arrive.	
"	7th		2nd Lt R.S. Guthrie A.A.I. T.M.B.	
"	8th		"	
"	9th		"	
"	10th		"	
"	11th		"	
"	12th		Divisional North Work.	
"	13th		2nd Lt Miller + 2 O.R. joined.	
"	14th		"	
"	15th		Casualties O.R. 2 killed	
MAZINGARBE	16th		Working party from Billets to N. Mines + 10 nt killed at Mazingarbe. Strong 12 File + 189 nct. thirty killed	
"	17th		Draft A. O.R. arrive.	
"	18th		"	
"	19th		"	
"	20th		Take on front line from North Hants Regiment. Left of Maroc Section. 2nd Lt J.A.S. Campbell to hospital	

2353 Wt. W2514/1454 700,000 5/15 D. D. & L.   A.D.S.S./Forms/C. 2118.

WAR DIARY or INTELLIGENCE SUMMARY.

(Erase heading not required.)

Army Form C. 2118.

Place	Hour, Date	Summary of Events and Information	Remarks and references to Appendices
MAROC (Section LEFT)	21st/22nd 1916	Fine day, cold with frost. Fairly quiet.	
"	22nd	Fairly quiet. Some shrapnel. Very little casualties. O.R. 1 killed 1 wounded.	
SOUTH MAROC	23rd	Snow. Very LAM. Relieved by CAMERONS 9 A.m. + 9 A.m. O.R. 2 Shrapnel. Casualties 2 O.R. wounded.	
"	24th	Hard frost. More snow. Very still.	
"	25th	Very LAM. More snow. Casualties 1 O.R. killed 5 wounded.	
MAROC (Half Section)	26th	Very cold but slept thro. Taken over from CAMERONS 7 L.m.	
"	27th	Thawing. Inundation very bad. Heavy shelling on left. Casualties 1 O.R. wounded.	
"	28th	Thaw + rain. Inundation very bad. Fairly quiet. Casualties 1 O.R. wounded.	
LES BREBIS	29th	Relieved by CAMERONS 3 p.m. + go into Brigade Reserve. Inundation very bad owing to thaws. Quiet day. Lieut. K. BUNN rejoined from 11 I.B.G. + posted to C Coy.	

John Millesonhton Lt Col
Commanding 1st Bn Black Watch

1st Brigade.
1st Division.

1st BATTALION ROYAL HIGHLANDERS (Black Watch)

MARCH 1916.

Army Form C. 2118.

WAR DIARY
or
INTELLIGENCE SUMMARY.
(Erase heading not required.)

Instructions regarding War Diaries and Intelligence Summaries are contained in F.S. Regs., Part II. and the Staff Manual respectively. Title pages will be prepared in manuscript.

20.E
3rd Bn

Hour, Date, Place	Summary of Events and Information	Remarks and references to Appendices
LES BREBIS Mon 1st 1916	Brigade Reserve. Training & Musketry.	
" 2nd	" Fine day but cold.	
" 3rd	Divisional Reserve. Training & musketry.	
" 4th	" " " Weather fine and mild. Cas. 2 O.R. wounded.	
" 5th	" Coy. drill. 2nd Lt. H. STG. FEILING to hospital.	
" 6th	" Stokes gun drill.	
" 7th	" Above exercises. 2nd Lt. D.M. MOFFATT R.A.M.C. joined rein Captain J.W.C. STUBBS to 1st Bn.	
" 8th	" Above "	
LOOS Sector " 9th	Took over from Royal Sussex Regiment left section of firing line, R.A. Coy. of Reserves in support.	
" 10th	Above. Issue Lt. E. Shelley + Brent moves. Casualties O.R. 1 K. 7 W.	
" 11th	Very cold. Shelling & trench mortars. Casualties 1 O.R. wounded.	
NORTH MAROC " 12th	Brigade Reserve. Relieved by CAMERONS. Casualties 2nd Lt D.A. MILLER & 9 O.R. wounded. O.R. 1 K. 3 W.	
" " 13th	Brigade Reserve. Training. Fine & warm.	
" " 14th	Brigade Reserve. Fine day & warm.	
" " 15th	Relieve CAMERONS 8 k a. relief.	
LOOS Sector " 16th	Fine day. 2nd Lt. J. Allan S. Casualties O.R. 7 W.	

Army Form C. 2118.

WAR DIARY
or
INTELLIGENCE SUMMARY.
(Erase heading not required.)

Instructions regarding War Diaries and Intelligence Summaries are contained in F. S. Regs., Part II. and the Staff Manual respectively. Title pages will be prepared in manuscript.

Place	Date 1916	Hour	Summary of Events and Information	Remarks and references to Appendices
LOOS. Sector	March 17th		Fine day. Lot of shelling. Casualties 2-2nd Lt shelling Lindsay wounded 1 O.R. wounded.	
N. LOOS.	18th		Relieved 5 CAMERONS + 2 Lt before H.Q. 1 O.R.I. Casualties O.R. 1 K. 2 wounded.	
"	19th		Fine day. Casualties O.R. 1 K. 15 wounded	
"	20th		Quiet day	
LES BREBIS	21st		Brigade Reserve	
"	22nd		" Wet day. Fine	
"	23rd		" Wet day. Fine	
"	24th		" Then snow. Showers in afternoon. Lieut. H.L.F. BOYD joined Bn.	
"	25th		" Fine day. Snow fell in hills. " Viscount O.F.D.K. DRUMGOON RIG joined Bn.	
"	26th		" Rain in morn. Clear later.	
MAROC section	27th		Relieve K.R.R. in right MAROC section at 9 p.m.	
"	28th		Quiet day. Fine weather. Casualty 1 O.R. wounded. Lieut. D. KIRK joined.	
"	29th		Quiet day + fine.	
SOUTH MAROC	30th		Relieved 5 CAMERONS + go into Support. Quiet day + fine	
"	31st		Quiet day. Fine + warm.	

John D Hamilton Lt Col.
Commanding 1/4th The Black Watch

1st Brigade.
1st Division.

1st BATTALION ROYAL HIGHLANDERS (BLACK WATCH)

APRIL 1916.

In line 1, M 29 b.o.s. should read M. 21 b.o.s, 1 Munik.

[signature]
21/2/38.

WAR DIARY or INTELLIGENCE SUMMARY

Army Form C. 2118

Place	Date	Hour	Summary of Events and Information	Remarks and references to Appendices
South MAROC	1/4/16		Fine & warm day. all quiet	
MAROC Sec.	2/4/16		Relieved Camerons	
MAROC Sec.	3/4/16		Quiet day, fine & warm. wounded 1 o.R. (whilst with 1/1 T.M. Battery)	
MAROC Sec	4/4/16		Another very warm. killed 2/Lt K. Gunn (Bde. Bomb Officer)	
South MAROC	5/4/16		Relieved by Camerons	
South MAROC	6/4/16		fine but cold	
South MAROC	7/4/16		fine & warm day	
PETIT SAINS R.Lef BARRACKS	8/4/16		Relieved by S.W.B. & took over billets from Gloucesters. fine & warm	
Petit SAINS	9/4/16		fine warm day. 2/Lt G.J. Moore transferred to R.F.C.	
PETIT SAINS	10/4/16		Beautiful day & warm	
PETIT SAINS	11/4/16		wet day	
PETIT SAINS	12/4/16		wet cold day & wet	
PETIT SAINS	13/4/16		cold day 1 killed 1 O.R. wounded 13 O.R. (accidentally owing to explosion of nose cap.) Maj. R.A. Bullock joined Bn.	
LOOS	14/4/16		Relieved 2/K.R.R.	
LOOS	15/4/16		wounded 1 Off. (2/Lt I. Dr. Brown)	
LOOS	16/4/16		wounded 10 o.R. rested. killed 1 o.R. wet day	
Loos & Bde. 17/4/16 Reserve			Killed 3 o.R. Maj. R.A. Bullock to 57th Bde as Bde. Major	
LOOS 10.C. & Reserve	18/4/16		v. wet day. killed 1 O.R. wounded 1 O.R. 2 Offs. joined Bn. 2/Lt w.P. Godfrey & 2/Lt A.B.Clarke	
LOOS 10.C &	19/4/16		wet & very wet. casualty 1 O.R. wounded	
LOOS	20/4/16		Relieved by CAMERONS - 1/lt McGeorge Quiet relief but the day casualty 1 o.R. wounded	

Army Form C. 2118.

WAR DIARY
or
INTELLIGENCE SUMMARY.
(Erase heading not required.)

Instructions regarding War Diaries and Intelligence Summaries are contained in F. S. Regs., Part II. and the Staff Manual respectively. Title pages will be prepared in manuscript.

Place	Date 1916	Hour	Summary of Events and Information	Remarks and references to Appendices
LOOS.	21.4.		Quiet day. Enemy trench mortar in afternoon. Casualties O.R. 2 killed 5 wounded.	
"	22.A		Very wet day.	
LOOS 7 O.G.1	23.A.		Relieved by Camerons & 2nd Lt support. Casualties O.R. wounded 3. 2nd Lt S. M'KENZIE & wounded.	
"	24.A.		Quiet day. 7 Scots Casualties 2 O.R. wounded.	
"	25.A.		Quiet day. Casualties O.R. 1 killed 3 wounded. 2/Lt J.C. MONDAY wounded.	
46 S. TREBIS.	26.A.		Relieved by 9th H.B. 3rd Brigade & so into Res. Reserve. Casualty O.R. 1 killed	
"	27.A.		Very fine & warm. Casualties 5 O.R. wounded by trench mortar at FERFAY.	
"	28.A		Very fine & warm. A good deal of shelling. 2/Lts D.A.F.K. DRUMLANRIG & hospital.	
"	29.A.		Very fine & warm. 2/Lt G.J. SINCLAIR & A 3 O.R. joined. 1 — Lt S.M. PRESTON to Cadet school joined.	
"	30.A		Very fine & warm. Casualties 2 O.R. killed 3 wounded.	

John M'Hamilton = Lt Col
Commdg. 1st Bn Black Watch

1.5.16.

1st Brigade.
1st Division.

1st BATTALION ROYAL HIGHLANDERS (BLACK WATCH)

M A Y 1916.

1 Royal Fus
Vol 22

WAR DIARY
or
INTELLIGENCE SUMMARY.
(Erase heading not required.)

Army Form C. 2118

22E
2 sheet

Place	Date	Hour	Summary of Events and Information	Remarks and references to Appendices
	May 1918			
LES BREBIS	1st		Div. Reserve. Very fine + hot. Transport moved back to PETIT SAINS.	
MAROC Section	2nd		Relieved ROYAL N. LANCS 3rd Brigade. Fine dry + quiet relief.	
"	3rd		Fine dry hot weather. Very quiet.	
"	4th		Fine. Very hot. Fairly quiet.	
"	5th		Very hot morning. Mist in afternoon. Casualties O.R. 1 W.	
"	6th		Fine dry weather.	
"	7th		Cooler + some showers. Draft of 25 O.R. arrive.	
S. MAROC	8th		Relieved by Cameron + 9th int. S. point. Cold + windy. Very quiet. 2nd Lt J ANDERSON	joined
				" H. McMILLAN joined
"	9th		Rain in afternoon. Casualties O.R. 1 W.	
"	10th		Fine morning. Very quiet.	
"	11th		Fine morning. Wet afternoon. Casualties O.R. 1 K.	
"	12th		Fine dry + warm.	
LES BREBIS	13th		Cold + wet. Relieved by S.W.B. + 9th int. Div. Reserve.	
"	14th		Divisional Reserve	
"	15th		" Capt W SANDERS & 9th Lancers joined. In attachment.	
"	16th		" Very fine day.	
"	17th		" Fine day. 2nd Lt W.R. BUCKNALL joined	
CALONNE	18th		Took over from KINGS 3rd Brigade. Casualties Captain P.H.L COLQUHOUN + 2nd Lt W.R. BUCKNALL wounded 2nd Lt T. WILSON + 2 O.R. Wounded	
"	19th		Very fine + fairly quiet. Casualty 1 O.R. W. Captain W.D. M. L. STEWART rejoined from HAVRE	
"	20th		Fine. A lot of shelling. Casualty 1 O.R. W.	

Army Form C. 2118

WAR DIARY
or
INTELLIGENCE SUMMARY

(Erase heading not required.)

Place	Date	Hour	Summary of Events and Information	Remarks and references to Appendices
CALONNE	2/1st		Very fine day. Lot of shelling. Casualties O.R. 2 K. 13 W. Trenches badly damaged.	
"	22nd		Very hot. Relieved by CAMERONS & went to Support. Casualties O.R. 1 K. 3 W.	
"	23rd		Fine day. Lot of shelling behind the lines.	
"	24th		Cooler & quieter.	
"	25th		Some heavy shelling. Casualties Cadet McSANDERS wounded. O.R. 3 K. 6 W.	
"	26th		Take over front line from CAMERONS. Fine & fairly quiet.	
"	27th		Fine day. Lot of shelling. Casualties Capt. H.L.F. BOYD wounded. O.R. 3 W.	
"	28th		Fine day. Rifle grenades & trench mortars active. Casualties O.R. 2 K. 4 W.	
"	29th		Fine day. Quiet except for Rifle grenades. Casualties O.R. 1 K. 7 W.	
BULLY GRENAY	30th		Relieved by CAMERONS & to in Brigade Reserve.	
"	31st		Fine day. No firm action.	

John McMamilton Lt Col.
Commanding 1st/7th R. Black Watch.

1. 6. 16.

1st Brigade.
1st Division.

1st BATTALION ROYAL HIGHLANDERS (BLACK WATCH)

JUNE 1916.

WAR DIARY
or
INTELLIGENCE SUMMARY

Army Form C.2118

1 Royal [Scots]

(Erase heading not required.)

Instructions regarding War Diaries and Intelligence Summaries are contained in F.S. Regs., Part II. and the Staff Manual respectively. Title pages will be prepared in manuscript.

Place	Date 1916	Hour	Summary of Events and Information	Remarks and references to Appendices
BULLY GRENAY	1st June		Brigade Reserve. Hamilton Infirmary Major T.N.O. Rycroft wounded. O.R. 1 K. 3 wounded.	
LES BREBIS	2nd		Divisional Reserve. Relieved 5 SUSSEX Staff of 5th Div. [illegible] Fine day.	
"	3rd		" do.	
"	4th		" do.	
"	5th		Arthur showery.	
"	6th		2 Lt. DENNISTON, STEWART, + TEMPLETON join.	
"	7th		Hon. T. LORD KITCHENER's Death.	
"	8th		Prime day. Battln. ordered	
"	9th		Fine day.	
MAROC Section	10th		Relieve SUSSEX 3rd Bde. in front line. Very heavy Trench Mortar Casualties 2 O.R. wounded.	
"	11th		Some very heavy Trench Mortars. Trenches quiet.	
"	12th		Fine day. Lt. J. ROBISON from 2nd Bn. attd. F.T.C. DIXON Lt. A.T. CAMERON MACFARLANE, Lt. J.R. WELLS 1st LOTHIAN + BORDER HORSE YEOMANRY join. Casualties 2 O.R. wounded	
"	13th		Cold + wet. Casualties 1 O.R. wounded	
NORTH MAROC	14th		Relieved by CAMERON HIGHLANDERS + go into Support. Casualties 1 O.R. wounded.	
"	15th		Some wet cold windy. Casualty 1 O.R. wounded.	
"	16th		Fine + warmer. Casualty 1 O.R. wounded	
"	17th		Fine day. Enemy T. Mortars [illegible]	
LES BREBIS	18th		Relieved by 4 N. LANCS. T.F. Lt. Dunn and Robertson A.W.B. McKenzie, Ian KISS + L. ZOCHSKEY from 19th Bn. Royal Fusiliers Join. Casualty 1 O.R. wounded.	
"	19th		Divisional Reserve.	

Army Form C.2?

WAR DIARY
or
INTELLIGENCE SUMMARY.
(Erase heading not required.)

Instructions regarding War Diaries and Intelligence
Summaries are contained in F. S. Regs., Part II.
and the Staff Manual respectively. Title pages
will be prepared in manuscript.

Place	Date 1916	Hour	Summary of Events and Information	Remarks and references to Appendices
LES BREBIS	20th June		DIVISIONAL RESERVE	
"	21st		Very fine day	
"	22nd		Relieve 1st GLOSTERS in front line. Very fine & warm + fairly quiet. 2nd Lt E.G.G FOREMAN to Hospital	
"	23rd		Fine & warm. Heavy bombardment in afternoon. Own shells [illegible]. 2nd Lt E.O. ARMYTAGE & 3 O.R. wounded	
"			R. MOFFAT & D.K. MUNRO join from Brigg. Casualty 1 O.R. wounded	
"	24th		A lot of rain. Own shelling + heavy trench mortars. Casualty 1 O.R. wounded	
"	25th		Relieved by CAMERONS + go into support. Batta. day. Lot of shelling	
"	26th		Some rain + cold. Lot of shelling	
"	27th		Very wet day + cold. Lot of shelling. Draft 43 O.R. arrive	
"	28th		Very wet day. Lot of shelling. Quiet night	
"	29th		Take over front line from CAMERONS. Both days + quiet night	
"	30th		Quiet day, Thunder shower. 2nd Lt J. KELLY to Hospital. Casualties 1 O.R. killed, 1 wounded	

John Williamson Lt Col
1st Bn. Black Watch.
1.7.16.

1st Bde.
1st Div.

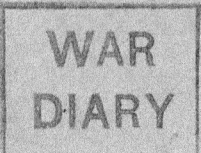

1st BATTALION

BLACK WATCH (R.Highlanders)

JULY 1916.

Army Form C. 2118

Royal Scots Vol 24

WAR DIARY
or
INTELLIGENCE SUMMARY.
(Erase heading not required.)

Instructions regarding War Diaries and Intelligence Summaries are contained in F. S. Regs., Part II. and the Staff Manual respectively. Title pages will be prepared in manuscript.

Place	Date	Hour	Summary of Events and Information	Remarks and references to Appendices
CALONNE Section	1st July		Holding front line. Very fine day. 2 Lt E.D. ARMYTAGE to hospital.	
"	2nd "		Carried out bomb attack at 8.30 P.M. Using Trench Mortars & Rifle Grenades. Canadian Lt J.A. INGLIS wounded. O.R. 2 wounded. "Bantams" 6 out.	
"	3rd "		Relieved by CAMERONS 9 P.M. Have minnies + tm at BULLYGRENAY + march to BARLIN	
BARLIN	"			
"	4th "		Wrote Orders. Fine morning. Wet afternoon	
"	5th "		Route march. Fine day	
"	6th "		March to BETHUNE + entrain at 12 noon for DOULLENS arriving at 4.15. March to NADRES arriving 9.15 P.M. 11 miles	
NADRES	7th "		March via convoy to MONDICOURT and BOIS. Very wet night. 7 miles	
MONDICOURT near BOIS	8th "		March 8 P.M. to BAIZIEUX about 12 miles	
BAIZIEUX				
ALBERT	9th "		March at 10.45 A.M. to ALBERT 9 miles	
BECOURT	10th "		March up to O.B. 17 + 2 near BECOURT 2 coys A + C at SCOTS REDOUBT	
"	11th "		Move up to front line at CONTALMAISON after dark. T.E.R.S. & M.I. PATERSON from 3rd Bn joined. Cam 15. 1 O.R. wounded.	
CONTALMAISON	12th "		Took CONTALMAISON Wood + established posts 700 yds. along Black Watch French Capt A. Cameron Cameron O.R. 20 wounded.	
"	13th "		Lot of shelling. Casualties O.R. killed 5 wounded 55	
ALBERT	14th "		Overnight CONTALMAISON Wood at 3 am. 2 Lt of shelling. Commandier 2nd Lt S.I. MURDOCH wounded O.R. 17 killed 4 gassed 36 wounded. Relieved by MUNSTERS + took to Divisional Reserve in ALBERT	

2353 Wt. W25H/1454 700,000 5/15 D. D. & L. A.D.S.S./Forms/C. 2118.

WAR DIARY or INTELLIGENCE SUMMARY

(Erase heading not required.)

Instructions regarding War Diaries and Intelligence Summaries are contained in F.S. Regs., Part II. and the Staff Manual respectively. Title pages will be prepared in manuscript.

Place	Date 1916	Hour	Summary of Events and Information	Remarks and references to Appendices
ALBERT	15th July		Divisional Reserve.	
"	16th	"	"	
BECOURT	17th	"	Move to E. BECOURT WOOD at 2 h.m. Rest of shelling	
"	18th	"	Wet morning. Rest of shelling	
O.G.2	19th	"	Move up in support of 3rd Brigade. Casualties 2nd Lt F.M. McDOUGALL wounded on duty. 2 O.R.	
			2nd Lt DENNISTON wounded & 6 wounded	
BAZENTIN Wood	20th	"	Relieve K.R.R. & front line 12 midnight Rest of shelling	
LOZENGE	21st	"	Relieved by CAMERONS + GLOSTERS 10 h.m. Casualties O.R. 3 wounded	
SHELTER WOOD	22nd	"	Move up to SHELTER WOOD at 9 h.m. Rest of shelling. Casualties O.R. killed 3 wounded 11	
BAZENTIN Wood	23rd	"	Relieve CAMERONS + GLOSTERS at 9 h.m. Rest of shelling. Casualties O.R. killed 1 wounded 10	
"	24th	"	In old Suit Let of shelling. Casualties O.R. killed 2 wounded 7. 2nd Lt J.E. DENNISTON joined	
			to W.7 Regt. 2nd Lt T. JOHNSON from 3rd Batt. + 2nd Lt. B.W. MACHIN joined.	
BAZIEUX	25th	"	Relieved by 7th Bde R.W.K. + 70 Brigade + took billets at 2.30 a.m. Very heavy shelling. Casualties 2nd Lt G.J. SINCLAIR wounded O.R. 1 killed 17 wounded 3 missing	
"	26th	"	Divisional Rest. Very fine.	
"	27th	"	"	
"	28th	"	"	
"	29th	"	"	
"	30th	"	"	
"	31st	"	"	

John McMillan Lt Col
Commdg 1st Bn Black Watch

COVER
FOR
BRANCH MEMORANDA.

Unregistered.

6ᵗʰ Armé

Notiziario * Interros
di Prigionieri

Referred to	Date	Referred to	Date

15ᵗʰ March to 30ᵗʰ August
1918

1st Brigade
1st Division.

1st BATTALION

THE BLACK WATCH

AUGUST 1 9 1 6

Operation Orders.
Brigade Report on Operations 18th August.

WAR DIARY
or
INTELLIGENCE SUMMARY.
(Erase heading not required.)

Army Form C. 2118.

Place	Date 1916	Hour	Summary of Events and Information	Remarks and references to Appendices
BAIZIEUX	1st August		Divisional rest & training day him & hot.	
"	2nd		"	
"	3rd		— Capt J.N.D. RYCROFT to hospital. Broke 2 blood vessels	
"	4th		— Major G.T. HUNTER-GRAY joined from 11.2.D.S. Capt W.D.M.L. STEWART to hosp.	
"	5th		"	
"	6th		— Capt H. RYCROFT to England.	
"	7th		"	
"	8th		"	
"	9th		" 1 N.Z.F.B. W. MACHIN to hospital. Draft 30 o.R. joined.	
"	10th		"	
"	11th		" Draft 47 o.R. joined.	
"	12th		"	
"	13th		"	
BÉCOURT	14th		Moved at 6.15 to bivouac near BÉCOURT wood.	
BAZENTIN	15th		In Brigade dugouts O&I near BAZENTIN le PETIT wood. Lt R.T. THOMSON to hospital	
"	16th		3 Platoons as brigade guard in INTERMEDIATE LINE at BAZ. Shell-holes. Casualties 2/Lt K.A. TEMPLETON 2/Lt W. PEPHERT killed	
"	17th		Casualties O.R. Killed 1, wounded 11, missing 2. Lt G. CAMERON to hospital — 2/Lt CAMERONS slightly wounded	
"	18th		by enemy shelling. Remained during relief	
"			M. Wood Ridge & at INTERMEDIATE LINE & AISNE. Casualties M.T.M. SCOTT Killed. Lt BREVCH. Lt MacDOUGALL wounded, 2/Lt D.A. MILLER, R.L.L. McPHERSON J.A. MUNRO wounded. L.J. STEPHENSON	See Append. I v D. & II
			O.R. 2/Lt T.R. SEALE 2/Lt 2/Lt F.R. DIXON wounded at duty O.R. Killed 12 wounded 75 missing 40.	
MAMETZ WOOD	19th		1 Brigade Reserve Casualties O.R. wounded 6.	
QUADRANGLE AREA	20th		Relieved by 3rd Brigade & to rest & support dugout.	

25

Army Form C.2118.

WAR DIARY
or
INTELLIGENCE SUMMARY.
(Erase heading not required.)

Instructions regarding War Diaries and Intelligence Summaries are contained in F. S. Regs., Part II. and the Staff Manual respectively. Title pages will be prepared in manuscript.

Place	Date 1916	Hour	Summary of Events and Information	Remarks and references to Appendices
QUADRANGLE AREA	21st August		Brigade Support. Fine day. Casualties O.R. 2 killed 7 wounded. Lt 1st Line	
"	22nd "		" Strength 9 157 O.R. men	
"	23rd "		"	
"	24th "		" Casualty O.R. 1 wounded. Draft of 4 N.C.O. joined from N.I.G.	
"	25th "		" Capt. R.D. McL STEWART injured from Hospital. Casualty 2nd Lt W. MacKAY. slightly wounded	
"	26th "		" 2nd Lt J.S. YOUNG R.O. DUFF 2 O.R. DICKIE joined from 11th BA	
HIGHWOOD	27th "		Relief 2nd WELSH to front line. Casualty 2nd Lt J.D. ROBSON wounded. Lt 9 Rations	
"	28th "		Front Line 9 Highwood. Casualties 2 O.R. wounded	
BAZENTIN LE GRAND	29th "		Relieved 5, 10 a Gloster at 4 a.m. + 5. to support Bazentin	
"	30th "		Very heavy rain. Casualties O.R. Lewis. wounded 14 Ration, 4.	
QUADRANGLE AREA	31st "		Relieved by 2nd Regiment + 90 front + support relief complete at 9 h. – front partly hit with mud	

John McMunn Lt Col.
Commanding 1st Bn Black Watch

6.9.16

Appendix No. 1

OPERATION ORDERS No. 1.
By
Major G.T. Hunter-Gray, Commanding 1st Bn The Black Watch

16th. August, 1916
----

1. The 1st Bn The Black Watch will seize the German Intermediate Line from S.2.d.7.5. to S.2.c.8.4. at ZERO (2am) 17:8:16.

2. The 3 Platoons of "D" Coy. will move out to their jumping places so as to arrive there at 1 am.

3. N.C.O's & Men of 13 & 15 Platoons will carry 2 Bombs each, and an extra Bandolier. Nothing else will be carried but Equipment & Entrenching Tool.
   30 Red Flares will be issued to each Platoon which will be lighted immediately the trench is taken, after which the Camerons will move forward and relieve them on the Left and Glosters will sideslip and relieve them on the Right.
   As the attack is taking place from the rear, all men should be warned to turn about after taking the trench.
   16 Platoon will carry 8 Bombs.

4. Scout Officer will report disposition to 16 Platoon Commander prior to movement at ZERO. 16 Platoon will move along trench as far as possible before ZERO but on no account is any Bombing to take place until Red Flares are shewn by the two attacking Platoons.

5. Guides will meet 13 & 16 Platoons at the Cemetery at 12 mn.

6. No. 13 Platoon will jump off at 1-30 am and get to their assaulting position and rush the trench at 2 am.

7. No. 15 Platoon will jump off at 1-45am and get to their position and rush the trench at 2 am.

8. all Officers & Platoon Commanders will be at Battalion Headquarters at 10-30 pm.

(sd) J.Millar, Captain for Adjt.,
1st Bn The Black Watch.

Appendix No. 2

OPERATION ORDERS No. 1.

By

Major G.T. Hunter-Gray, Commanding 1st Bn The Black Watch

17th. August, 1916

1. The Battalion will attack the Intermediate Line at ZERO to-morrow morning.

2. Instructions given verbally to Company Commanders with reference to Area :-

    ### 1st Line

    "B" Coy. Right   "A" Coy. Left.

    ### 2nd. Line

    "D" Coy. Right   "C" Coy. Left

    One Platoon "C" Coy. to go out from 70th. Avenue to work to road on left flank of Intermediate Line (Sgt. Docherty "D" Coy. will go with this Platoon).

3. One Platoon of "A" Coy. will occupy Lancashire Trench.

4. Intense Bombardment of Immediate Line at 4-13 am at which time the attacking force will move forward as far as possible. At 4-15 am the Artillery will lift 50 yards and fire 1 round per gun, after which they will lift another 50 yards and fire 1 round per gun, then lift another 50 yards and open a continuous barrage.

5. Each man will carry two bombs and each bomber 10 bombs. Every N.C.O. & man will also carry an extra bandolier.

6. 20 flares will be carried by each Platoon and lighted as soon as objective is gained.

7. "C" & "D" Coys. will each take forward 30 shovels & 30 picks.

8. Dump of ammunition, Bombs Picks, Shovels & Flares will be formed behind "A" & "B" Companies.

(sd) J. Millar, Captain for Adjt.,
1st Bn The Black Watch

Appendix III

1st INFANTRY BRIGADE.

NARRATIVE of OPERATIONS carried out on

18th AUGUST 1916,

against GERMAN INTERMEDIATE LINE.

References :-
Sketch Maps 1/10000
Map Ref S.2.

I. <u>Attack by 1st The Black Watch - 4:15 a.m. 18/8/16.</u>

1. The previous attempt made to take the Intermediate Line, by surprise, on night 16/17th August by 1st The Black Watch having failed, instructions were received from 1st Division to attack with one Battalion at dawn on August 18th.
       1st Brigade Order No 16 d/16-8-16.
       1st Div No. G 183 17/8/16.

2. The Black Watch were warned on the morning of the 17th that they would probably be required to attack.

3. Details of the attack were settled and communicated verbally to the O.C. The Black Watch by 1-30 p.m. Operation Orders were issued at 7 p.m.

4. The scheme of attack was for The Black Watch to assault in two lines, their objective being the Intermediate Line from S.2.d. to Track at S.2.c. with one Platoon working round each flank of the Intermediate Line and attacking from the North.
   Assault was at 4-15 a.m. on the 18th after a two minutes intense bombardment.
       1st Brigade Order No 17 d/17-8-16.

5. On the afternoon of the 17th August an endeavour was made to ascertain if the Intermediate Line was still held, as many Germans had been seen running back from it about midday.
   About 5-45 p.m. a Patrol of the 1st Cameron Highlanders entered the Intermediate Line at its corner at S.2.c.8.5. They found the trench badly knocked about and not held near this point although Germans were seen dug in about 100 yards behind it.
   At the same time the 10th Glosters had a bombing encounter with the enemy near the Block in Intermediate Line about S.2.d.8½.5.
   Immediately the Cameron Patrol entered the Trench Red and Green lights were sent up from behind it and a very heavy barrage commenced and lasted till nearly 8 p.m.
       Report by O.C. Camerons - Appdx I attached.

6. The Black Watch were ordered to relieve the Camerons in the front and support trenches West of the Track in S.2.d. and take over up to and including LANCS SAP from Right Battalion of the 46th Brigade at 6 p.m. on the 17th.
   The Relief, however, was delayed on account of the barrage brought on by the Reconnaissance of the afternoon and the Black Watch were not able to move forward of O.G.1 until 8 p.m.
       1st Bde No. BM 238 of 17/8/16.

7. While moving up to the front, The Black Watch came under heavy shelling which caused delay. The Battalion was only finally in its positions about 4-10 a.m. on the 18th - just before Zero.

2.

References :-

8. The Black Watch attacked in two Lines thus :-

'A' Coy	'B' Coy
'C' Coy	'D' Coy

9. The morning was very misty, a thick white fog restricted the view to a very few yards and conditions were probably far more difficult than during an ~~ordinary~~ ordinary night attack.

The Front Line advanced at 4-13 a.m. and at once came into the enemy's barrage which did not however become heavy till about 4-20.

They advanced to the edge of our intense bombardment and immediately it lifted advanced and came into contact with the enemy about 30 of whom were bayoneted by 'A' Company.

'A' Company could not discover any trench although they advanced another 70 yards to look for it. They came into a heavy fire of rifle grenades, bombs and artillery. The trench where crossed by this Company appears to have been shelled out of recognition.

In front of 'B' Company on the Right the trench existed in better condition and was defended by two lines of bombers one line in front of the trench and one behind. The front line was dealt with and the trench entered. As soon as our men entered the trench the second line of bombers threw bombs into it.

Report by O.C. 'B' Company.

The Right of the attack came under heavy machine gun fire.

Report by O.C. 'D' Company.

The Second Line followed the first at about 25 yards distance. Portions of this line appear to have lost direction and the line was broken up by heavy shell fire. The remainder reached the objective with the first line.

Report by O.C. 'C' Company.

10. When the assault had reached a point about 70 yards behind the Intermediate Line attempts were made to re-organize it. Parties had lost touch and sense of direction, it was not possible to see more than a few yards; there was no definite trench line for men to form on as they had expected. Eventually all withdrew to our front trenches in small parties.

Report by O.C. 'C' Company.

The casualties were 7 Officers and 140 other Ranks.

Report by O.C. 1/The Black Watch.

11. The causes of the failure of the attack appear to have been :-
(a) The thick mist which made what was planned a dawn attack more difficult than an night attack. The fog was exceptionally dense and quite unlike the ordinary morning mists sometimes met with.
(b)/

3.

References :-

11. (contd)

(b)   The heavy enemy barrage. The assault was fortunate in that the enemy took much longer than usual to put on his barrage, but when it did open it disorganised and broke up the second line of the attack.

(c)   The assaulting troops expected a definite trench line to capture and establish themselves in. The majority appear to have crossed the trench without recognising it as such amidst the maze of shell holes.

(d)   Our intense bombardment is reported to have been too light to seriously affect the enemy.

II. Attack by the 8th Royal Berks 2-45 p.m. 18/8/16.

1.   The attack by 1st The Black Watch on the morning of the 18th having failed the 8th Berks were warned that they would have to attack the INTERMEDIATE LINE at 2-45 p.m. as part of an extensive attack by several Divisions against the German positions.   1st Division Order No.171 of 16/8/16 and Addenda 1 & 2.

The 8th Berks had previously been warned to be in readiness to relieve The Black Watch any time after 5 a.m. on the 18th.   1st Bde Order No 17 of 17/8/16.

2.   The position was explained personally to the O.C. 8th Berks at about 8 a.m. and details of attack were then settled.
Orders for Relief of The Black Watch by the 8th Berks were issued at 8-23 a.m.   1st Bde No. BM 250 d-18/8/16.

3.   The scheme of attack was as follows :-   1st Bde Order No 18 dated 18/8/16.
8th Berks to attack INTERMEDIATE LINE, from Track in S.2.c. to point 100 yards east of Track in S.2.d., with three Companies. One Platoon to deliver a flank attack from Eastern end of 70th AVENUE (about S.2.c.6.6).
A Bombing Party of 10th Glosters to deliver a bomb attack Westwards along INTER-MEDIATE LINE and connect with the right of the 8th Berks attack.
Infantry to move forward at 2-45 p.m. under cover of a 2½ minutes intensive bombardment of the objective. Smoke was to be let off for 20 minutes commencing at Zero by the 15th Division on our Right.

4.   While the 8th Berks were relieving The Black Watch our Front Line was bombarded with heavies. The Officers of the 8th Berks are certain that it was our own heavy Artillery firing.

5.   This bombardment cut off inter-communication between Companies, so demolished LANCS TRENCH that the Platoon detailed to attack from 70th AVENUE was unable to reach its Starting Point, and prevented LANCS SAP being occupied.

6/

4.

References :-

6. Efforts to crawl across the demol--ished portion of Trench were stopped by Snipers and any effort to have moved considerable bodies of Men across the open prior to Zero would have given the enemy warning of the intended attack and precipitated his barrage

Addendum to 1st Divn Order No.171 dated 16/8/16.

7. It was decided that the Parties which should have assaulted from LANCS SAP and 70th AVENUE should join in the Frontal Attack.

8. The Trench at S.2.d.3.2½. was also flattened, one Platoon and a Machine Gun Section were buried, and inter-communication cut off.

9. At 2-45 p.m. the assault was delivered in two Lines.

10. The smoke discharged by the 15th Division blew across our front in a dense cloud and caused the left company of the assault to lose direction. The majority of this Company bore too much to the Right and eventually joined with the other two Companies who came under heavy machine gun fire about 100 yards from our Front Line which prevented further progress.
 A small party on the right of the Assault reached the INTERMEDIATE LINE but failed to enter it.

11. The assaulting Troops endeavoured to consolidate a shallow trench about 100 yds in front of our Front Line and held on to it for a considerable time under very heavy shell fire but were eventually forced to retire back to our own line again.
 The casualties were 8 Officers and 150 Men.

12. The Bombing Party of the 10th Glosters waited in position ready to bomb down the INTERMEDIATE Line as soon as the 8th Berks assaulting lines approached it. They never saw the 8th Berks and therefore never commenced their attack, but they saw the Germans in some strength lining their parapet and firing at the advancing Berks. One of our Vickers Guns came into action at the block and apparently inflicted serious losses on the enemy who got down into their trench and continued to fire their rifles in the air.

13. The following causes prevented the objective being reached :-
 (a) Intensity of enemy's machine gun fire which stopped the right of the attack.
 (b) The Undue number of casualties amongst the Officers - all the Officers with the left Company became casualties at an early stage of the operations - and this, combined with the smoke caused disorganisation in the left of the attack.
 (c)

p.5

13. (cont²)

(c) Lack of time for carrying out relief and carefully organising the attack.
Tools, Bombs etc carried up for The Black Watch attack in the morning could not be properly collected for the Berks use in the afternoon. Supplies of these articles are and cannot be sufficiently numerous to admit of successive attacks, at short intervals, being fully provided with new ones.

(d) I consider that the Eastern portion of the INTERMEDIATE Line in German occupation was never properly bombarded. In conversation with the G.S. Officer of the III Corps to-day, I found he thought that our Block in the Inter-mediate Line was almost on the Track in S.2.d. whereas in fact it is some 250 yards to the East of it.

III. The following points in connection with the three attacks delivered against the Intermediate Line by this Brigade appear to require special attention.

(a) In bombarding a Trench such as the Inter-mediate Line which is partly held by us, partly by the enemy the Artillery observation should to some extent be carried out from the Trench its-self to ensure effective bombardment up to the Block. Map references of trench blocks cannot be accurate.

(b) I suggest that when the location of any important point such as a trench block is required it should be obtained by aeroplane, a flare being lighted at a prearranged hour at the doubtful point. Where this is done there should be no general lighting of flares.

(c) Two daylight attacks became to some extent disorganised owing to the difficulty of seeing; in the first instance this was owing to fog and in the second owing to smoke.
The precautions as regards compass bearings etc usual for a night attack should also be taken for a day attack.

(d) Ample time to prepare an assault must be given. During times of heavy and constant hostile shelling, as the present, even 10 hours may be insufficient to effect a Battalion relief and prepare for an assault from Trenches.

(e) The enemy now put on a barrage of great intensity in a very short time. The normal interval between their flares going up and the barrage open--ing is 40 seconds.
It is possible that more counter-battery work during an assault might be an assistance to the Infantry.

(f)/

III. (contd).

(f) Except in very favourable circumstances it is not possible to get reports back _quickly_ or to clear up the situation rapidly.

If the ground can be observed from some point outside the barrage some information may be obtained early notwithstanding the smoke of bursting shells.

Observers and Liasion Officers posted in the barrage zone are useless.

Commanding Officers and Company Commanders do all that is possible to inform Brigade Head Quarters of the situation.

(g) Hostile trenches can be bombarded out of recognition and when this occurs the assaulting Infantry maybe left without a definite objective except a red line on the map.

(h) It would be a great assistance if any photographs, of their objectives, which are taken could be sent to Brigade Head Quarters without delay. At present this is not done.

John W. Hamilton Lieut.Colonel,

19th August 1916. Commanding 1st Infantry Brigade.

1st Brigade.

1st Division.

1st BATTALION ROYAL HIGHLANDERS (BLACK WATCH)

SEPTEMBER 1916.

WAR DIARY
INTELLIGENCE SUMMARY
(Erase heading not required.)

Army Form C. 2118.

Vol 26. 1st Hastisatch

Place	Date 1916	Hour	Summary of Events and Information	Remarks and references to Appendices
QUADRANGLE AREA	1st Sept		Brigade in support. Casualties O.R. killed 2, wounded 8. Strength 29 O.R. missing.	
HIGHWOOD	2nd		Relieve Northants & K.R.R. 2nd Brigade in front line. Casualties 2nd Lt J.ANDERSON wdd. 1 T.M.B. wounded. O.R. 5 wounded.	
"	3rd		Attack Germ line at 12 noon & carried from on enemy to our front line. N.D. of men (D.I.M. 62/4/6) 2nd Lt MCH S.PRESTON & J.R.WELSH 2nd Lt R.T.CROSSLEY wounded, O.R. killed 37 wounded 123. 36 thought O.R. 70 missing	
BAZENTIN LE GRAND	4th		Relieve 5 Glos Regiment & took supporting at 9 am. A.K.A.H.Stokley & Co reconnoitring 2nd Lt T.JOHNSON killed. O.R. killed 2 wounded 5, missing 5.	
BLACKWOOD	5th		Relieved by 1st Gloucesters & moved at 8.30 p.m. to cont of Bazentin. Casualties O.R. killed 3 wounded 4	
"	6th		Reorganising O.R. 1 wounded. Strength O.R. 30 + min.	
"	7th		" " " Strength O.R. 3 [illegible]	
"	7th		2.1/M R took 6 MACFARLANE-GRIEVE, M.E.ROSE, DNM MCGREGOR join from 3rd A + 2nd Lt D.O.MICALL, M.G. JOHNSTONE, J.S. HAMILTON P.R. HUGHES join 2 R.J. MASTERSON from 11th Bn.	
"	8th		Resting 2nd Lt A.C.TARBUTT – SR + S.R. (?) from 11th D.	
MILLENCOURT	10th		Moved at 1.30 p.m. by 2nd & 4th & butt line & from 3rd Y mile – ALBERT	
WARLENCOURT	11th		Arrived at 2.30 a.m. & GARDEGRAVE 4 s/c to billet at 4/25 about 2 mile.	
"	12th		Army School [illegible]	
"	13th		"	
"	14th		"	

WAR DIARY or INTELLIGENCE SUMMARY

Army Form C. 2118.

(Erase heading not required.)

Place	Date 1916	Hour	Summary of Events and Information	Remarks and references to Appendices
LA HOUSSOYE	15th Sept		Army Reserve - Training. Afternoon Wet.	
BRESLE	16th		March at 5.10 a.m. gallery — at 7.30. fine day	
"	17		Lieut J.G. Hambro DSO from service of 15th Bde. Command 1 Bn Intermer by Major V.M. Fortune A.S.D. Reports Ammo & March to ALBERT on 18th	
"	18th		Marched to ALBERT. Very wet day	
ALBERT	19th		Marched to relieve 47th Bn in Gough Drop (narrow street) 2nd Lts E.W.D. Wilson, J.C. DENG, A.W. MATHER, P.W. MACKAY, P. URQUHART joined from 3rd Bn 2nd Lt T.C. JACOBS from 11th Bn	
GOUGH DROP	20th		Completed relief of 47th Bn. 2nd Doctor 5 am attacked DROP ALLEY in conjunction with NEW ZEALANDERS. 2nd Lt J.E. DENNISTON (m) and 17 wounds OR (K3)(W12) casualties	See operations I II III
GOUGH DROP	21st		Consolidation of DROP ALLEY. Casualties OR (K2)(DOW 2)(W20)(M1) Relieved by 3rd Royal Welsh & moved to MAMETZ	
MAMETZ WOOD	22nd		In Support. 2nd Lts L.J. SERGEANT from 3rd Bn, 2nd Lt R.K. ARBUTHNOTT from 3rd Bn Casualties OR (K7)(W35)(M3)	
"	23		In Support	
"	24		Relieved 2nd RMF Fusiliers with two Coys in FLERS LINE (C & D) A&B remains at MAMETZ WOOD	

Army Form C.2118.

WAR DIARY
INTELLIGENCE SUMMARY.
(Erase heading not required.)

Instructions regarding War Diaries and Intelligence Summaries are contained in F.S. Regs., Part II. and the Staff Manual respectively. Title pages will be prepared in manuscript.

Place	Date	Hour	Summary of Events and Information	Remarks and references to Appendices
FLERS LINE	25th	6 AM	Enemy made determined bombing attack (Ref. append. I)	I II III
		7.15	Enemy driven back having 7 dead in our trench (Ref. append. II)	
W.N. 2 cap. at MATNETZ WOOD		12.35 pm	Attacked enemy two gun Machine Gun append. I. II. III	
		11.45	Two cap FLERS LINE relieved by 2nd K.R.R. (Casualties 2nd Lt P.R. Husband (K Capt W.D. MacL. Shewake - OR who (K.35.) (W.74) (MM 7) GRIEVE)	(W) 2nd Lt W.E. ROSS (W.2Lt. G.M. MacFARLAND
MATNETZ WOOD	26th		Support	
"	27th	6pm	Relieved by 20th London Regiment & marched to BRESLE	
BRESLE	28th		Capt J.N.O. Rycroft Rejoined and assumed duties of adjt. a. & TARBUTT to hospital. Draft of 60 OR joined	
"	29		Cleaning up	
"	30		Training. Draft of 42 OR joined. Lt. Col V.M Fortune proceeded on leave. Maj G.T Hunter-GRAY assumed Command	

C. Fuller Capt. for H Col.
Comdg 1/4th The Black Watch

OPERATION ORDERS NO. 1

War Diary
Appendix 4.

By

Lieut-Col. J.G.H.Hamilton D.S.O., Commanding 1st Bn The Black Watch

2nd. September, 1916.

Reference Maps - Sheets 62d.N.E. 62c.N.W.
1/20,000.   57d.S.E. 57c.S.W.

1. As part of a combined attack by the British and French the 1st. Bde. will on 3rd. inst. attack WOOD Lane and the German Trench in High Wood. The Divisions on our flanks are not attacking. Zero will be notified later.

2. (a) 1st Cameron Highlanders will attack on our right from S.10.b.9½.8. to where German front line enters the wood at S.4.d.2.7. inclusive.
   (b) 1st Bn The Black Watch will assault on left objective from S.4.d.2.7. including Mine Crater to S.3.d.9.8. also the following Communication Trenches :- (a) About S.4.c.4.9. (b) Along Western face of wood. both of which will be blocked 40 yards North of Captured line.

3. Each Company will detail mopping up parties who will be given special bombs for dealing with dug-outs. The attack within the Wood will be assisted by :-
   (1) Various appliances operated by Special Brigade R.E.
   (2) A Mine being exploded under the Eastern corner of High Wood.

4. The Black Watch will attack with 3 Companies in front line from right to left "C""A""D"., "B" Coy. moving into our present front line at ZERO and holding it with help of 5 Lewis Guns & 2 Vickers.

5. Each assaulting Coy. will have 3 Platoons in first line closely followed by one Platoon carrying Tools and Bombs in Buckets for consolidating captured position.

6. "C" Coy. will detail one Platoon to capture and hold mine crater, one Section of this Platoon carrying tools. They will be assisted by one section R.E.(20 men) and will take two Lewis Guns with them.
   The far lip of the crater will be held and a trench dug 30 or 40 yards to the North.
   "D" Coy. will tell off special parties to block communication trenches mentioned in para 2.

7. The line when captured will be immediately consolidated and parties sent out from each Coy. to occupy shell holes about 50 yards in front. After consolidating "A" Coy. will withdraw to our Original line and "C" & "D" Coys. will close inwards and hold the captured line and posts in front.

8. The Lewis Gun Officer will detail two Lewis guns to occupy the crater and will arrange to send forward two guns to each Coy. as soon as the German line is captured. One gun will be established in the forward line and one in the German main line. The Machine Gun Coy. will detail one Gun for the crater as soon as it is captured.

9. Each man will carry each two Mills Bombs and Bombers their full compliment. Coy. Sergt. Majors will remain at their dumps and arrange to send forward supplies of ammunition and bombs.

10. Coy. Signallers will remain at their present Signal Stations till after line is captured.

(sd) J.Millar, Capt for Adjt.,
1st Bn The Black Watch.

Issued to :-
4 Companies	4
Signallers	1
Lewis Gunners	1
File	1
War Diary	2
Total	9 issued

Operation Report dated 3/9/16.

1. The attack started at ZERO - 12 noon - in accordance with attached orders

2. Before ZERO our crater Company was shelled badly by our own Stokes Guns and had many casualties, all the oil cans except 3 in this section were also put alight.

3. The Jack pipes also blew back into our own trench.

4. The Flammenwerfer were put off at night time but seemed to go too high and did not traverse.

5. The right Company succeeded in reaching the crater and trench to left and took about 40 prisoners.

6. The Companies on left failed to reach their objectives being taken on by Machine Gun and rifle fire immediately they topped the parapet.

7. All went well at crater at first and work of consolidating was well on hand and trench started to connect with with our old front line.

8. A Bombing Platoon started to bomb to our left and advanced about 50 yards, capturing a machine gun and 4 prisoners.

9. One Vickers Gun and 3 Lewis Guns were knocked out in crater about 3-45pm by Rifle Grenades or bombs.

10. At about 3-50pm the Cameron Highrs. on our left withdrew to their own line.

11. At 3-52pm I heard that the crater had been lost, it had been steadily shelled by our own guns from the time it was occupied by us.

12. We are now holding our original line with 4 Companies 1st Black Watch on right, two Companies of 10th. Glosters on left with 1 Coy. 10th. Glosters in support.

13. I estimate my casualties at about 5 Officers and about 300 Other Ranks.

(sd) J.G.H.Hamilto , Lieut-Colonel.,
Commanding 1st Bn The Black Watch.

5-20pm
3/9/16.

Brigade Operation Orders No. ~~22~~ 32.
By
A.J.Reddie, D.S.O. Brig-Gen. Comdg. 1st Infy Bde.

Reference) Sheet 57.c.S.W. 1/20,000.
Map   )

An attack will be carried out to-night by the 2nd. Canterbury Bn. 2nd. Brigade, 1st. New Zealand Division.
OBJECTIVES:- GOOSE ALLEY from M.30.c.15.80 to FLERS SUPPORT M.29.d.66. to FLERS TRENCH M.29.d.45 to junction with DROP ALLEY thence along DROP ALLEY to M.29.d.20.

The attack will be delivered at ZERO, from the Roads in M.30.c. and M.35.b.

An Artillery Barrage will be placed on the objectives at ZERO, this barrage will be lifted to allow attacking troops to enter their objectives and will then be placed on FLERS LINE N.W. of objective.

ZERO will be at 8-30pm.

The 1st Bn The Black Watch will deliver a Bombing Attack at 8-30pm (in conjunction with the above attack) from COUGH DROP up DROP ALLEY to M.29.d.20 and there gain touch with the 2nd. Canterbury Battalion.

On completion of the attack, the Officer Commanding 1st Bn The Black Watch, will be prepared to take over the whole of DROP ALLEY from the 2nd. CAnterbury Battalion, who will establish strong points at M.30.c.15.80 - M.29.d.66 - and M.29.d.45.

Acknowledge.

Headquarters of 2nd. Canterbury Battalion are at M.36.a.86.

Advance Copy to O.C. 1st. Black Watch issued at 3-10pm. by runner Pte. Johnson.

20:9:16
(sd) xxx Yates, Capt. for.,
Bde. Major, 1st Infy. Bde.

Later Messages

(1) A party of 100 men should reach your Headquarters at 7pm. with extra bombs.

20th. Sept. 1916.   (sd) xxx Yates Capt. for.,
Bde. Major, 1st Infy. Bde.

(2) Two STOKES MORTARS are being sent up at once and ammunition carriers will follow.

20th. Sept. 1916.   (sd) xxx Yates Capt. for.,
3pm.   Bde. Major, 1st Infy. Bde.

OPERATION ORDERS Append II NO.1 - Copy No.11.
By
 Major V.M.Fortune, D.S.O.Commanding 1st Bn The Black Watch

Reference Map - Sheet 57.c.S.W. 1/20,000

The Battalion will, in conjunction with the NEW ZEALANDERS attack DROP ALLEY to-night at ZERO, which will be at 8-30pm. "B" Coy. will attack DROP ALLEY at 8-30pm. under arrangements already made. "A" Coy. will place two Platoons and one Lewis Gun at the disposal of "B" Coy. "B" Coy. will endeavour to join up with New Zealanders at M.29.d.2.0.

After capture, DROP ALLEY, up to junction with New Zealanders, will be be consolidated and will be conected to COUGH DROP.

One Vickers Gun will be placed at the disposal of O.C."B" Coy. if required, who will notify Battalion Headquarters.

After the capture of DROP ALLEY, the Black Watch will be prepared to take over the whole of DROP ALLEY.

It is the intention of the Commanding Officer to relieve that part of DROP ALLEY captured by "B" Coy., by the two Platoons of "A" Coy. at the disposal of "B" Coy. and to relieve that part captured by the New Zealanders by the two remaining Platoons of "A" Coy.

Lieut. Doig No. 1. Machine Gun Company will remain near Battalion Headquarters and be ready to move Machine Guns into DROP ALLEY as required.

Two STOKES MORTARS are put at the disposal of "B" Coy. for defensive purposes only.

Later in the evening COUGH DROP will be converted into a strong post by the R.E.

(sd) J.Millar, Captain for Adjt.,
20th. Sept. 1916.   1st Bn The Black Watch.

Issued to:-   No. of Copy.
    4 Companies   1-4
    L.M.G.O.   5
    Intelligence Officer   6
    Signal Officer   7
    Battalion File   8
    Canterbury Rifles (2nd.Bn)   9
    Artillery Laison Officer   10
    War Diary   11
                              Total   11 Copies issued.

append III

Operation Report :- dated 21:9:16. for War Diary.

One Company plus one Platoon holds DROP ALLEY from junction with FLERS LINE M.29.d. central to junction with COUGH DROP M.35.a.6.4.
   This Coy. has two Vickers.
   One Company less one Platoon from M.35.a.6.4. to about M.35.b.5.4.
   One Company from M.35.a.8.3. to 6.4. to 4.3. to 1.3. This Coy. has one Vickers Gun.
   One Coy. from M.35.b.6.4. to M.35.b.7.3. This Coy. has one Vickers.
   8th. Berks Coy. from M.35.b.7.3. to about M.35.d.3.5. This Coy. has one Vickers.
   Two STOKES MORTARS in COUGH DROP and two at Bn. H.Qrs. not yet in position.

4-10p.m.
21:9:16

(sd) J.Millar, Captain for Adjt.,
    1st Bn The Black Watch.

Operation Report:-dated 21:9:16. for War Diary.

In conjunction with New Zealanders "B" Coy. attacked DROP ALLEY at 8-30pm last night. Having made good the junction of DROP ALLEY and COUGH DROP during the afternoon they succeeded in gaining touch with the New Zealanders. Consolidation was proceeded with.
   Between 12 m.n. and 1 am during our internal relief the New Zealanders appeared to be counter-attacked and a few individual New Zealanders passed through our line and touch was lost.
   A Barricade has been erected about M.29.d.2.0. Consolidation is being proceeded with and the situation is being cleared up in front of our barricade.

----

5 am. 21:9:16

(sd) J.Millar, Captain for Adjt.,
    1st Bn The Black Watch.

No. 1.

OPERATION ORDER

War Diary
Appendix No. 1.

By
Major V.M. Fortune, D.S.O., Commanding 1st Bn The Black Watch

24th. September, 1916.

1. The Battalion Headquarters, "C" & "D" Coys. will move in the following order at 9 pm. "C"., "D"., Bn.H.Q., and will be established in FLAG LINE by 12m.n. with Bn. H.Q. about M.35.d.4.6.
   "C" Coy. will occupy FLAG LINE immediately to the WEST of the NEW ZEALANDERS with "D" Coy. immediately to the WEST of them.

2. The 2nd. R.M.F. will to-day attack the FLERS LINE up to and including the X Trench at M.29.d.3.2,- 4½,9½. After the capture of the objective:-
   (a) A new trench will be dug from M.29.d.3.9. to M.29.c.9.4. The 2nd R.M.F. beginning from the former point and the 2nd. Welsh Regt. from the latter point.

   (b) Both trenches of the FLERS LINE will be filled in, in front of the objective for 50 yards, or as far as may be possible.
   ZERO will be at 8-30pm. to-night.

3. "C" & "D" Coys. will be required to do one of the following :-
   (a) If the R.M.F. attack is unsuccessful they will take over the line as it is held at present by the 2nd. R.M.F. and will be prepared to repeat the operation to-morrow, at a time to be given out later. In this case "C" Coy. will take over the FLERS SUPPORT LINE including the BLOCK down GOOSE ALLEY.
   "D" Coy. will take over the FLERS FRONT LINE including BOYAU connecting DROP ALLEY with GOOSE ALLEY.

4. Two Companies 2nd. R.M.F. and one Company S.W.B. are being left at the disposal of O.C. 1st Bn The Black Watch, and will be behind the two Coys. of the Black Watch.
   Further Operation Orders will be issued to-morrow.

(sd) J.Millar, Capt. for Adjt.,
1st Bn The Black Watch

Issued to:-

"C" Coy.	1
"D" :	1
Signal Officer	1
File	1
War Diary	2
Total	5 Issued.

No. 2. OPERATION ORDER No. 2. War Diary
L Coy.   By   Appendix 1.
Colonel V.M.Fortune D.S.O., Commanding 1st Bn The Black Watch
----
                    25th. September, 1916.

1. "C" & "D" Coys. The Black Watch at ZERO will seize enemys' trenches in FLERS FRONT and SUPPORT LINES up to C.T. in M.29.d.4.9. inclusive - "C" Coy. will be responsible for C.T.

2. After Objective is gained at least 50 yards of FLERS FRONT and SUPPORT LINE will be filled in and position wired as soon as possible.

3. As soon as possible after position is captured a fire trench will be dug from M.29.c.9.4. to M.29.d.3½.9. for this purpose O.C.S.W.B. Coy. will hold his Coy. in readiness and provide them with tools.

4. 6 Stokes and 1-2" Mortars will carry out short bombardments up to ZERO. 2 Stokes are at disposal of each Coy. Commander and the Officer & N.C.O. i/c. of each pair must keep in close touch with Company Commanders. Gas Bombs will be fired but in no area to be occupied by our troops.

5. "B" Coy. 2nd. R.M.F. will place two Platoons at disposal of O.C. "C" Coy. for carrying if required.
   "D" Coy. 2nd. R.M.F. will place two Platoons at disposal of O.C. "D" Coy. for carrying if required.

6. O.C. "C" Coy. will place a flag on barricade in GOOSE ALLEY 20 minutes after ZERO.

7. RED Flares will be called for 30 minutes after ZERO and will be shewn by Platoons and advanced posts, and again 2 hours after ZERO.

8. The two Coys. of the 2nd. R.M.F. behind the two Coys. of the Black Watch will keep in close touch with them as the Black Watch move forward.

                              (sd) J.Millar, Capt for Adjt.,
                                   1st Bn The Black Watch

Issued to:-
    "C" Coy. Black Watch   1
    "D" :   --:--   1
    "B" :   2nd. R.M.F.   1
    "D" :   --:--   1
    "B" :   2nd. S.W.B.   1
    1st. T.M.B.   1
    New Zealanders   1
    File   1
    War Diary   2
                     Total   10 Copies issued.

Appendix 2.

Narrative of Operations on 25th. September, 1916.

(1) During the night 24th/25th. September, 1916., 1st Bn The Black Watch, (less two companies), relieved the 2nd. Royal Munster Fusiliers, and two Companies South Wales Borderers, in the FLERS FRONT & SUPPORT LINE, in M.39.d.

The Two Companies 2nd. Royal Munster Fusiliers and one Company South Wales Borderers, were left at disposal of O.C. Black Watch,. After relief the Companies were disposed as follows:- Holding Sap & FLERS FRONT LINE - one Company Black Watch. Behind them one Company 2nd. R.M.F. and behind them one Company S. W. B. Holding Sap in FLERS /SUPPORT LINE and GOOSE ALLEY Sap - one Company Black Watch. Behind them in FLERS SUPPORT - one Company 2/R.M.F.

(2) At 6 am on 25th. September, 1916., the enemy made a determined Bombing attack against the FLERS SUPPORT - FLERS FRONT & GOOSE ALLEY SAPS. They succeeded the Trench Junction at M. 39.d.4.8. and the FLERS SUPPORT & GOOSE ALLEY SAPS. By 7-30am they had been driven out, the original barricades were re-occupied and all was quiet. They left 7. dead in our Trench.

In the Counter-Attack our Bombers followed the enemy into their Trench, which was full of dead, but, had to return from Sniping on the flanks.

(3) At ZERO hour on the 25th. September, the two Companies Black Watch, supported by two Companies 2/R.M.F. & one Company S.W.B. assaulted the FLERS SUPPORT & FRONT LINE and established barricades at about M. 39. d.4½.9½. & 3.9½. There was not much resistance in the FLERS FRONT LINE, but, the FLERS SUPPORT LINE was strongly held, and the enemy made repeated Bombing Attacks to retake barricade at M.39.d.4½.9½. Owing to the resistance in SUPPORT LINE, it was found impossible to push further up the front line, although there was not much resistance actually in the front line.

About 10 Wounded & Unwounded Prisoners were taken, and about 40 Germans Killed in addition to several who were Bombed in Dug-outs.

The Lewis Gunners also accounted for several Germans who retired over the open.

Our Casualties were :- 4 Officers & 118 Other Ranks.

(4) The Consolidation of the Captured Position was carried out with the assistance of the two Companies 2/R.M.F. & one Company S.W.B.

(5) At 6 pm the New Zealand Division took over FLERS SUPPORT LINE and GOOSE ALLEY. During the night 25th/26th. the 2/K.R.R. C. took over the FLERS FRONT LINE.

Major.,

27:9:16. Commanding 1st Bn The Black Watch. (R. Hrs.)

1st Brigade.
1st Division.

1st BATTALION ROYAL HIGHLANDERS (BLACK WATCH)

OCTOBER 1916.

Army Form C. 2118.

1st Bn. The Black Watch
OCTOBER 1916

Vol 27

WAR DIARY
INTELLIGENCE SUMMARY.
(Erase heading not required.)

Instructions regarding War Diaries and Intelligence Summaries are contained in F.S. Regs., Part II. and the Staff Manual, respectively. Title pages will be prepared in manuscript.

Place	Date 1916	Hour	Summary of Events and Information	Remarks and references to Appendices
BRESLE	1st / 2nd		Training carried out	
MIANNAY	3rd		1st Brigade moved to MIANNAY by bus.	
"	4th / 5th / 12th		Training continued.	
	13th		Lieuts J.W.H. Robertson & A.K. Hamilton - 2/Lt J.L. Stephen & A. Fernakin joined.	
	14th / 30th		Training continued.	
	31st		1st Brigade moved by Bus to HENNANCOURT.	

V M Fortune
LIEUT. COLONEL
Commanding 1st Bn. The Black Watch

Nov. 3rd 1916

1st Brigade.
1st Division.

1st BATTALION ROYAL HIGHLANDERS (BLACK WATCH)

NOVEMBER 1916.

Army Form C. 2118.

WAR DIARY
or
INTELLIGENCE SUMMARY.

(Erase heading not required.)

1st Bn. The Black Watch
November 1916

Vol 28

Instructions regarding War Diaries and Intelligence Summaries are contained in F. S. Regs., Part II. and the Staff Manual respectively. Title pages will be prepared in manuscript.

Place	Date November	Hour	Summary of Events and Information	Remarks and references to Appendices
HENENCOURT WOOD	1st to 4th		At HENENCOURT where training was continued — very muddy.	
	5th		Marched to BECOURT CAMP.	
BECOURT CAMP	6th to 15th		At BECOURT Camp where training was continued.	
HIGH Wd	16th & 17th		Marched to camp S. of HIGH WOOD on 17th	
	18th 19th		Moved into STARFISH PRUE TRENCHES.	
	20th 21st		Moved into front line with 2 Coys in SNAG TRENCHES — 9.2 Coys in FLERS SWITCH — HQ in HEXHAM Rd. Relieved 1st Cameron H/rs	
MAMETZ Wd	22nd to 26th		Relieved by 1st Northhants & moved to NE Corner MAMETZ Wd.	
HIGH WOOD	27th to 1st Dec		Moved to camp S of HIGH Wd & moved to camp nr BAZENTIN LE PETIT Dec 1st. St Andrews Night (30th) was celebrated here.	

Casualties in November
Officers — 2 Killed (2nd Lt H.St L. Serling & 2nd Lt T.B. Anderson)
3 Wounded.
O.R. 3 Killed 10 wounded.
In addition 2nd Lt M Macmillan was killed & 1 O.R. wounded by a bomb accident at 1st Div. Bomb School.

Following officers joined
Major A.D. Murray 2/Lt. M A Barlow Jackson 3/4/16 — 2/Lt D Ramsay — 2/Lt G.S.M. Burton 2/Lt J.R. Stewart
2/Lt M. Tool 13/11/16 Asst. G.W. Armfield (Cavalry) 24/11/16 — 2/Lt J.D.M.M. Crichton 28/11/16

D.D.&L. J. A.D.S.S./Forms/C. 2118.

1st Brigqde
1st Division.

1st BATTALION ROYAL HIGHLANDERS (BLACK WATCH()

DECEMBER 1916.

Army Form C. 2118.

1st Bn. 42 Black Watch
December 1916

WAR DIARY
INTELLIGENCE SUMMARY
(Erase heading not required.)

Vol 29

Place	Date	Hour	Summary of Events and Information	Remarks and references to Appendices
Bazentin le Petit Camp	Decr 5th		At Bazentin Le Petit Camp.	
"	Dec 5th "8"		Moved up to Front Line and relieved 1st 1st Camerons with coys in Matadoes in Pioneer & Inch Support Trench & 2 platoons in Hexham Trench. HQ at Hexham Rd. 2 Coys in Bacourt L'Abbe.	
Bazentin le Petit & No 4	9th–13th		Relieved by 8th Berks. 2 Moved into Bazentin Le Petit (2 coys) to No.4	
" No 4	13th–14th		2 coys Moved into 7th A's Support and 2 coys moved into Camp No 4 at Bazentin Le Petit.	
Mametz Wood	17th–21st		Moved into camp NE corner of MAMETZ WOOD	
	21st–25th		Moved up to Front Line and relieved 1st Camerons with 2 coys in Pioneer & Inch Support Trench. 1 coy in BACOURT L'ABBE & 1 coy in FLERS SUPPORT.	
BAZENTIN LE PETIT	25th 29th		Relieved by 1st 8th Berks and Moved in BAZENTIN LE PETIT Nth. Officers Christmas Dinner was celebrated here on Dec 27th	
FRICOURT FARM	29th–1st Jan		Moved from huts Fricourt FARM camp. Officers New Year Dinner was celebrated here on Dec 31st.	

Casualties in December
Officers 1 wounded
OR 6 killed 22 wounded

2353 Wt. W2514/1454 700,000 5/15 D. D. & L. A.D.S.S./Forms/C. 2118.

Army Form C. 2118.

WAR DIARY
1st Bn the Black Watch
INTELLIGENCE SUMMARY

December 1915

(Erase heading not required.)

Instructions regarding War Diaries and Intelligence Summaries are contained in F. S. Regs., Part II. and the Staff Manual respectively. Title pages will be prepared in manuscript.

Place	Date December	Hour	Summary of Events and Information	Remarks and references to Appendices
			The following officers joined during the month.	
			Lt. J. R. Livingstone Learmonth 6-12-16	
			2/Lt. O. Grieve 30-12-16	
			2/Lt. J. C. Stephens from Hosp. 30-12-16	
			The following drafts arrived during the month.	
			14th Dec O.R. 20	
			20th " " 69	
			25th " " 14	
			30th " " 62	

C. J. Hunter Gray Major for.
Commanding 1st Bn The Black Watch

4/1/17.

1ST DIVISION
1ST INFY BDE

1ST BATTALION
THE BLACK WATCH.
JAN - DEC 1917

WAR DIARY.

1st. Bn. THE BLACK WATCH.

1st. INFANTRY BRIGADE.

1st. DIVISION.

JANUARY 1917.

WAR DIARY or **INTELLIGENCE SUMMARY.** 1st Bn The Black Watch

Army Form C. 2118.

Vol 30

Place	Date	Hour	Summary of Events and Information	Remarks and references to Appendices
ALBERT	1917 January			
FRICOURT Camp	1st to 9th		Battalion employed on Road Fatigues	
ALBERT	10th 11th to 22nd		Moved to Gillets in Rue D'Aubigny ALBERT. Battalion carried out Elementary Training & Staff Rides. Every third day 50 men were taken for fatigue. On the 18th 100 men under Lieut P.K. Campbell moved down to the New Area South of the Somme.	
WARLOY	23rd		A few shells into ALBERT between 5 a.m & 7 a.m – 1 O.R. killed. Moved to WARLOY via HENINCOURT	
WARLOY	23rd to 31st		Company & Battalion Training carried out. Also Staff Ride for Officers	

Officers

The following Drafts joined the Battn. January 6. 31 O.R.
Lieut C.W. Kimber 10th 2/Lieut R. Lang 10th " 13th 23 O.R.
2/Lieut W.S. Taylor 10th Lieut P.K. Campbell 13th 28 19 O.R. W. Fr Com. 1st Black Watch
" E. Brown 10th 2/Lieut G.J. Sinclair 13th 1st Bn Command 1st Black Watch
" E.B. Valentine 10th " V.C. Lane 28th 2nd February 1917
" J.A. Smith 10th

30 E 1 sheet

WAR DIARY.

1st.Bn.THE BLACK WATCH.

1st.INFANTRY BRIGADE.

1st.DIVISION.

FEBRUARY 1917.

Army Form C. 2118.

WAR DIARY
or
INTELLIGENCE SUMMARY.
(Erase heading not required.)

Instructions regarding War Diaries and Intelligence Summaries are contained in F. S. Regs., Part II. and the Staff Manual respectively. Title pages will be prepared in manuscript.

Vol 31 1st Bn The Black Watch

Place	Date	Hour	Summary of Events and Information	Remarks and references to Appendices
	January			
WARLOY	1st to 3rd		Battalion and Brigade training.	
HAMEL	4th to 6th		4th Brigade moved to billets in HAMEL.	
	5th to 6th		Battalion training carried out.	
MARLEY	7th		Battalion moved to Dugouts at MARLEY. Route march to Corps Commander (French) near MORCOURT.	
CHUIGNES	8th to 13th		Battalion moved to huts at CHUIGNES.	
	9th to 13th		Training carried out.	
Trenches	14th to 17th	4th	Battn: moved into the line taking over from the 2nd KRRC Line held by 2 Coys in front line, 1 Coy in Support, 1 Coy in Reserve. Battn: Front. Ry. Met. Barlew 62c. S.W. 2 / 10.10.0. N.29.c.3.4. to N.22.D.5.6½.	
	15-16-17"		Front Line	
	18 to 21"		Battn: relieved in front line by Cameron Highlrs Battn: moved to Battn: in Support.	
	22nd to 27		Battn: moved to Front Line. Battn: front same as above.	
	27		moved to Battn: in Reserve.	
	28		Battn: in Reserve.	

Cover:

WAR DIARY
or
INTELLIGENCE SUMMARY: 1st Bn: The Black Watch

The following Officers joined the Bn: during the month of Feb:

Lieut. Stewart Smith   9-2-17
 "   Fraser J.W.   "
 "   Allan J.G.   "
 "   Hart R.N.   17-2-17
Lieut. Colquhoun H.C.   22.2.17

The following drafts arrived.

30. O.R.   22-2-17
53 "   28-2-17

Casualties during the month.

O.R. 4 Killed. 13 Wounded.

M Wauchope Lt Col
March 2

WAR DIARY.

1st. Bn. THE BLACK WATCH.

1st. INFANTRY BRIGADE.

1st. DIVISION.

MARCH. 1917.

Army Form C. 2118.

WAR DIARY
or
INTELLIGENCE SUMMARY.
(Erase heading not required.)

1st Bn. The Black Watch. March 1917

Vol 32

Place	Date	Hour	Summary of Events and Information	Remarks and references to Appendices
	March			
ASEVILLERS	1-2		Batt. in Reserve. Batt. employed doing fatigues.	
"	3	—	Batt. moved to huts and bivouacs at Chuignolles.	
CHUIGNOLLES	4-10		Batt. training & carried out.	
"	11	—	Batt. moved into trenches (taking over front line from 2nd Royal Sussex. (3rd Brigade)	
TRENCHES	12-14		Front line. The one point of importance is not for these 3 days is: — The immense labour & grim shown by the enemy of his intended retirement.	
"	15	—	Front line. Batt. relieved by the 1st Cameron Highlders. Batt; moved to Reserve dug-outs at BECQUINCOURT.	
"	16	—	Batt; in Reserve. News received of the enemy's retirement from his positions on our front.	
"	17	—	Reserve. Advanced Batt: Head. 2rs moved to Boulogne Reserve. C and A Coys. attached to 10th Gloucester Regt.	

Page 2

Army Form C. 2118.
March 1917
1st Bn. The Black Watch

WAR DIARY
or
INTELLIGENCE SUMMARY.
(Erase heading not required.)

Instructions regarding War Diaries and Intelligence Summaries are contained in F.S. Regs., Part II. and the Staff Manual respectively. Title pages will be prepared in manuscript.

Place	Date	Hour	Summary of Events and Information	Remarks and references to Appendices
	March			
TRENCHES	18	—	Batt: relieved 10th Gloucesters (front batt:). Held line overlooking the Somme.	
TRENCHES	19-20.	—	Batt: Head Qrs moved to O.G.3. Batt: dispositions same as on 18th March. Two peaceful days.	
"	21	—	Batt: moved to emp: ends at BECQUINCOURT.	
BECQUINCOURT	22-28.	—	Batt: employed constructing roads and railway at FAY.	
"	29.	—	Moved to billets at ROSIÈRES. Two Coys moved to PUSEAUX. Employed constructing Railway. Two Coys at ROSIÈRES employed on Salvage work.	
ROSIÈRES	29-31.			

Army Form C. 2118.

March 1917.

1st Bn. The Black Watch

WAR DIARY
or
INTELLIGENCE SUMMARY.
(Erase heading not required.)

March.

The following casualties occurred during the month.

1. Officer.   Wounded.
17. O.R.   — do —
2. — do —   Died of wounds.
3. — do —   Killed.

The following drafts arrived during the month.

18 O.R.   5th March. 1917.
10 — do — 11th "   "
32 — do — 25th "   "
1 Officer 25th "   "

M. Johun
LIEUT. COLONEL
Commanding, 1st. Bn. The Black Watch.

WAR DIARY.

1st.Bn. THE BLACK WATCH.

1st.INFANTRY BRIGADE.

1st.DIVISION.

APRIL.1917.

Army Form C. 2118.

WAR DIARY
or
INTELLIGENCE SUMMARY.
(Erase heading not required.)

1st Bn. The Black Watch

1917

Vol 33

Place	Date	Hour	Summary of Events and Information	Remarks and references to Appendices
ROSIÈRES	April 1st	—	Batt: Head Qrs: and A+B Coys at ROSIÈRES. Employed doing Sewage work. C + D Coys at PUZEAUX employed making Redoubt.	
do	2nd	—	Do	
do	3rd	—	H.Q and A+B Coys moved to CURCHY.	
CURCHY	4th	—	A+B Coys moved to MORLEMONT.	
do	5th	—	C+D Coys joined Batt. H.Q from PUZEAUX.	
do	6th–15th	—	Batt: employed working on Roads in and about NESLE.	
do	16th	—	Moved to CHUIGNES	
CHUIGNES	17th–30th	—	From 17th – 20th Training 21 – 30th do	
			The following Drafts arrived during the month O.R. 67. Platoon Training, Company Training.	
			Casualties during the month O.R. 4 Accidm. Injury Wounded.	

T2134. Wt. W708—776. 500000. 4/15. Sir J. C. & S.

WAR DIARY.

1st.Bn. THE BLACK WATCH.

1st.INFANTRY BRIGADE.

1st. DIVISION.

MAY, 1917.

Army Form C. 2118

WAR DIARY
INTELLIGENCE SUMMARY.
(Erase heading not required.)

1st Batt: The Black Watch

1917

Vol 34

Place	Date	Hour	Summary of Events and Information	Remarks and references to Appendices
CHUIGNES	May 1st–19th 1917		Batt: training.	
— do —	19th		Batt: moved to billets at MARCELCAVE	
MARCELCAVE	19th–26th		Batt: training.	
— do —	26th		Batt: entrained for FLÊTRE	
FLÊTRE	27th–31st		Arrived at FLÊTRE 27th. Batt: training. The following reinforcements arrived during the month 12. 77 O.R. Casualties. NIL.	

Hugh Edgar
Capt: & adjt
Commdg 1st Batt The Black Watch

3HE
1 sheet

WAR DIARY.

(With Appendix).

1st. Bn. THE BLACK WATCH.

1st. INFANTRY BRIGADE.

1st. DIVISION.

JUNE, 1917.

WAR DIARY

INTELLIGENCE SUMMARY

1st Batt: The Black Watch

June 1917

Army Form C. 2118.

Place	Date	Hour	Summary of Events and Information	Remarks and references to Appendices
FLETRE	1st - 10th		Batt: training.	
-do-	11th		Moved to billets at BAVINCHOVE.	
BAVINCHOVE	12th - 18th		Batt: training.	
-do-	19th		Batt: training.	
WORMHOUDT	20th		Batt: marched to WORMHOUDT.	
ZUYDCOOTE	21st		Batt: marched to ZUYDCOOTE.	
OUST DUNKERQUE	22nd		Batt: moved by train to COXYDE, from COXYDE station by road to RINCK CAMP at OUST DUNKERQUE.	
-do-	23rd		Batt: relieved the 15th Hants. Regt. on the line on the night of the 23/24th. Sector held. Rt. Map. LOMBARTZYDE. 1/20,000. From the Sea to M.15.B.3.42. Line held by 3 Companies in the front line and 1 Company in Reserve. Front Line held by 2 Coys., 18 posts supported by a second and third line. Enemy artillery very active during the night. Our front slightly weaker	Appdx I
TRENCHES	24th	29 E		35E

Army Form C. 2118.

WAR DIARY
or
INTELLIGENCE SUMMARY.

(Erase heading not required.)

1st Batt: The Black Watch

1917

Instructions regarding War Diaries and Intelligence Summaries are contained in F. S. Regs., Part II. and the Staff Manual respectively. Title pages will be prepared in manuscript.

Place	Date	Hour	Summary of Events and Information	Remarks and references to Appendices
TRENCHES	June 24th-29th		in fine. No happenings of importance to report.	
-do-	29th		Batt. moved to Batt: in Support area in NIEPORT BAINS. on the night of the 29/30. Batt relieved by 1st Cameron Highlanders.	
NIEUPORT-BAINS	30th		The following reinforcements arrived during the month. 10 OR. 1 Officer. Capt B.C.A. Short. Casualties during the month. Officer Wounded - 2/Lt P.W. MACKAY & 2/Lt W.S. Taylor. OR - Ranks Killed 3. Died of wounds 2. Wounded 22.	

Commanding 1st Bat The Black Watch
4th July 1917

SECRET. *Appendix I*

Copy No. 18

1st Battalion The Black Watch Order No. 1.

23rd June 1917.

1. The Battalion, less 'A' Company, will relieve the 15th Bn Lancashire Fusiliers tonight 23/24th June 1917 as follows :-

Coy of B.W.	Relieves Coy of L.F.	Section
'C'	'A'	Right Front
'D'	'B'	Centre Front
'E'	'C'	Left Front.

Companies will move up in the following order :- 'C', 'D', 'B', Hd Qrs by Platoons at 3 minutes interval. The leading Platoon of 'C' Company to pass Cross Roads at OOST-DUN -KERQUE - LES BAINS at 10-30 pm.
    Platoon Guides and a Guide for Head Quarters will be provided by the 15th Lancs Fusiliers and will be at LAITERIE (300 yds West of NIEUPORT BAINS on Road running along the sea front) at 11 pm.
 (a) Dress - Battle Order, great coats to be left in packs.
 (b) Wiring Gloves - These will be drawn from the Quarter Master forthwith by Companies.
 (c) Tools - 10 shovels to be drawn from Q.M.Stores by each Company & Hd Qrs forthwith.
 (d) Water - Petrol tins will be drawn as above; water bottles are to be filled before moving off.
 (e) R.G. Carriers - Only 2 per Section will be taken into the Line: the remainder to be handed in to the Q.M's Store forthwith.
 (f) Training Squad. - The Party under training will report to Lieut Kimber when the Battalion moves, and will remain at 1st Line.
 (g) L.G. Ammunition - To be taken up by Companies.
 (h) Sign Boards - The Pioneer Sgt will hand boards detailed to O.C. Head Quarters immediately these are completed.

2. ADVANCE PARTIES. The following Advance Parties will be at the Cross Roads at Western entrance of NIEUPORT BAINS at 8 pm to-day and will be met by a Lancs Fusilier Guides
 (a)   Each Company will detail a Party to take over Trench Stores, representative for each Post in the Front Line and Company Signallers.
 (b)   Head Quarters - 1 Officer, H.Q.Signallers, 1 Runner per Coy, 1 Stretcher Bearer, and 1 Cook to take over kitchen.
    The above parties to move at 3 minute intervals, 'C' Company leading, followed by 'D', 'E' and Hd Qrs.
    'C' Coy Party to pass Cross Roads at OOST DUNKER LES BAINS at 7-30 pm.

 (c) The Intelligence Officer with all Scouts, Observers and Snipers will be at the Lancs Fusiliers Bn H.Q. at 7 pm. The Bombing Officer and N.C.O. will move with this party.
    The N.C.O. detailed for the extreme left post will accompany the above party, reporting to 2/Lieut Tarbutt forthwith for instructions.

3. TRANSPORT. (a) Lewis Gun Limbers will accompany the 1st Platoon of each Company and on the guns being drawn will return to the Transport Lines.
 (b)   One Limber will follow Head Quarters with Company Messes etc.
    All Officers' Servants will accompany this Limber.
 4 Scouts will meet the Limber at WEST end of PONT SIRDEY to guide messes to the different Head Quarters.

4. MAPS. Big Scale Maps and Defence Scheme will be taken over by Company Commanders from those they relieve immediately on going into the Line.
    "Dug-Outs" maps will be sent to Battn Hd Qrs at the earliest possible opportunity showing accomodation etc.

5. VERMORAL SPRAYERS. On arrival in the Line, if it is found necessary, instruction, in the use of the sprayers, will be given to details sent to the Medical Officer.

6/

6. PACKS. Packs will be handed into the Q.M. Stores to-day as under :-

"B" Company - 3-30 pm
"C"   "   - 3-45 pm
"D"   "   - 4 pm.

7. VALISES. To be handed in any time before moving off.

8. RATIONS. Ration Parties will draw rations while in the Line at 11 pm at Rationing Point each night. Commencing from night of 24th/25th and will continue to do so until futher orders.

9. YUKON PACKS. These will be taken up to-night in L.G. Limbers, and Companies are responsible for using the same in the Line and for their return on the Battalion being relieved.

10. SHELLING. Whilst in the Line, any Unit that reports shelling must also report directly the shelling stops or slackens off.

11. GAS. Companies will report immediately on completion of relief the number and nature of all gas appliances taken over in their sector.

12. ARMS. L.Guns and Rifles must be very sparingly oiled while in this Area. They must be dry cleaned after oiling. Ammunition must be kept dry and cleaned.

13. STRETCHER BEARERS. Will move under the orders of the M.O.

14. REPORT. Company Commanders will report relief complete, immediately after completion, to Battalion Head Quarters.

15. RETURNS. The following will be rendered daily whilst in the Line :-

Daily Fighting Strength   - 2-30 pm
Daily Casualties (to12 Noon) - 2-30 pm
Burial Return (Allied & German) - 2-30 pm (NIL not required)
R.E. Stores required   - 7 pm (previous day)
Bombs required   - 8 am.

16. TRENCH STORES. Lists of Stores taken over will be sent to Battn Hd Qrs as soon as the relief has been completed.

A. Basil Clark, Capt & A/Adjt
1st Battalion The Black Watch.

Issued to :-	Copy Nos		Copy Nos
'A' Company	1	Major Hon A.D.Murray	16
'B' Company	2 & 3	Adjutant	17
'C' Company	4 & 5	War Diary	18 & 19
'D' Company	6 & 7	Office	20
Head Quarters	8 & 9	Transport Officer	21
C. O.	10		
15th Lancashire Fusiliers	11		
L.G.O.	12		
Intelligence Officer	13		
Medical Officer	14		
Quarter Master	15		

WAR DIARY.

1st. Bn. THE BLACK WATCH.

1st. INFANTRY BRIGADE.

1st. DIVISION.

JULY. 1917.

Army Form C. 2118.

WAR DIARY
INTELLIGENCE SUMMARY.
(Erase heading not required.)

Instructions regarding War Diaries and Intelligence Summaries are contained in F.S. Regs., Part II. and the Staff Manual respectively. Title pages will be prepared in manuscript.

July 1917. 1st Batt: The Black Watch

Place	Date	Hour	Summary of Events and Information	Remarks and references to Appendices
NIEUPORT BAINS	July 1-2		Batt: in Support.	
— do —			On the night of 2/3, we raided enemy's trenches at M.9.C.5.22. The Objective being first on the extreme right of the line by the sea. Object raid was to procure prisoners or some identification of enemy holding the land. Raiding party consisted of 2 N.C.O's + 14 O.R. under Lieut. G. Fergusson. The raid which was known to take place at 1-30 a.m. on the morning of the 3rd was preceded by a short intense Artillery Bombardment. Party entered enemy trenches with little opposition, showing that the attack was a complete surprise to the enemy. Four khaki little took place within the trenches, glances which dispelled were knocked, any of the enemy killed and two prisoners taken one of which was killed on the Evening of the trench and not was taken.	

WAR DIARY

INTELLIGENCE SUMMARY. 1st Batt: The Black Watch

July 1917

Place	Date	Hour	Summary of Events and Information	Remarks and references to Appendices
	July			
	1st		Apart to the enemy's parapet. The other men brought back to our lines severely wounded and died on trip to Dressing station. to the 5th Company 2nd Regt: Battn: Cyclists. Brigade and were trained in the 2nd Essaults Battn: 8th Jaeger Regt. Rest Company.	
	2nd		Our own party returned to own trenches safely.	
NIEUPORT BAINS	3rd		Battn: in Support. In the night of the 3rd Battn: moved to Camp at St Idesbald to the right of the 2nd KRRC.	
ST IDESBALD	4th–16th		Battn: training.	
do.	17th		Battn: moved to Camp at Bray Dunes.	
BRAY DUNES	18th		" " " " LE CLIPON	
LE CLIPON	19th–31st		Battn: onto Brigade training.	

WAR DIARY
INTELLIGENCE SUMMARY
1st Battn. The Black Watch

July 1917

Army Form C. 2118

Place	Date	Hour	Summary of Events and Information	Remarks and references to Appendices
	July		The following Casualties took place during the month.	
			5 O.R. Wounded	
			1 do Died of wounds	
			10 do Missing	
			The following reinforcements arrived during the month.	
			36 O.R.	

V.M. Fortune
LIEUT. COLONEL
Commanding 1st Bn. The Black Watch

Aug. 7th 1917

WAR DIARY.

1st.Bn. THE BLACK WATCH.

1st.Infantry Brigade.

1st.DIVISION.

AUGUST 1917.

WAR DIARY

INTELLIGENCE SUMMARY. 1st Batt. The Black Watch.

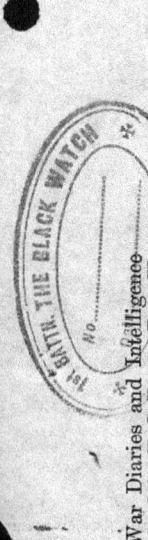

Place	Date	Hour	Summary of Events and Information	Remarks and references to Appendices
	August 1917			
ECLIPON CAMP	1st - 31st		Company Batt: and Brigade training.	
	25th		Batt: passed with 1st Division for inspection by G.O.C. 4th Army.	
			The following reinforcements joined during the month.	
			36. O.R.	
			2 Lt. W.D. Thompson	
			2 Lt. P.D. Mackay	
			Lt. B.C. Johnson	
			Capt. H.L.T. Boyd	

31st August 1917

[signature]
LIEUT. COLONEL
Commanding, 1st Bn, The Black Watch.

WAR DIARY.

1st. Bn. THE BLACK WATCH.

1st. INFANTRY BRIGADE.

1st. DIVISION.

SEPTEMBER 1917.

Army Form C. 2118

WAR DIARY
or
INTELLIGENCE SUMMARY.
(Erase heading not required.)

1st Batt. The Black Watch

1917

Place	Date	Hour	Summary of Events and Information	Remarks and references to Appendices
Le Clipon Camp	Sept.			
	1st-30th		Batt: Brigade and Divisional Training.	WMF
			The following reinforcements arrived during the month.	WMF
			50. O.R.	

(signature)
LIEUT. COLONEL
Commanding 1st Bn. The Black Watch.

WAR DIARY.

1st. Bn. THE BLACK WATCH.

1st. INFANTRY BRIGADE.

1st. DIVISION.

OCTOBER 1917.

WAR DIARY
INTELLIGENCE SUMMARY

Army Form C. 2118.

1st Bn. The Black Watch

1917

Place	Date	Hour	Summary of Events and Information	Remarks and references to Appendices
LE CLIPON CAMP	October 12-20		Batt. and Brigade training.	
	21st		Batt. moved to billets in ZEGGERS CAPPEL.	
	22nd		Batt. moved to billets in LEDRINGHEM.	
LEDRINGHEM	23rd-25th		Batt. training.	
	26th		Batt. moved to billets at HERZEELE	
HERZEELE	27th-31st		Batt. training.	
			The following reinforcements arrived during the month. Officers - 3. O.R. - 30. Casualties - Nil.	

J. M. Clark
Capt. & Adjt.

Lieut. Colonel
Commanding 1st Bn. The Black Watch

WAR DIARY.

(With Appendix).

1st. Bn. THE BLACK WATCH.

1st. INFANTRY BRIGADE.

1st. DIVISION.

NOVEMBER. 1917.

Army Form C. 2118.

WAR DIARY
INTELLIGENCE SUMMARY.
(Erase heading not required.)

1st Batt. The Black Watch

November 1917

Vol 40

Place	Date	Hour	Summary of Events and Information	Remarks and references to Appendices
HERZEELE	1st - 5th		Batt: training.	WMF
			Batt: moved to Schools Camp on the Watou – Poperinghe road.	WMF
SCHOOLS CAMP	5 - 6th			WMF
DAMBRE CAMP	7th - 12th		Batt: moved to Dambre Camp at (Ref: Map 28 NW 1/20,000) B.27.c.9.9.	WMF
			Batt: employed in training and improving camp.	WMF
CANAL BANK	13th - 14		Batt: moved to Dugouts on the banks of the Canal de L'YSER.	WMF
IRISH FARM	15th - 16th		Batt: moved to Camp at IRISH FARM (Ref: Map 28 NW 1/20,000) C.27.a.2.6.	WMF
	17th - 18th		Batt: relieved the 1st Camerons High'rs into the line. Batt: taking over line to the N.W. of PASSCHENDAELE on the night of the 17th/18th.	WMF
	19th		Batt: relieved by the 6th Batt. Loyal North Lancs. During this period the line the following Minor Operations were carried out; vide appendix I.	WMF WMF WMF
			Moved to dugouts on the banks of the Canal de L'YSER.	WMF
CANAL BANK	20th - 21st			
	22nd - 26th		Moved to ROAD CAMP on the WATOU – POPERINGHE road. Battalion training.	WMF
	27th		Moved to PIGEON CAMP near PROVEN. Battalion training.	WMF

[signature] Lieut. Colonel
Commanding 1st Bn.

APPENDIX I.

The Battalion relieved the 1st Cameron Highlanders on the night 17/18th November 1917 in the Sector VANITY FARM to VIRTUE FARM. On the same night the 10th Glosters relieved the 8th Royal Berks on the Left, and the 2nd Rifle Brigade (8th Division) relieved the 42nd Battalion Royal Highlanders of Canada on the Right.

Owing to the bad going and heavy shelling, the relief was not carried out until 8 am 18th November.

'C' Company took over the salient formed by VOCATION FARM - 'A' Company were in Support to 'C' Company from VINE COTTAGE to VALOUR FARM - 'B' & 'D' Companies in Reserve, the former near MEETCHEELE, the latter near BELLEVUE.

On the 18th November VIRILE FARM was occupied and posts put out in front; but touch with 10th Glosters was only got by patrol as a very marshy re-entrant separated the two Battalions.

Captain H.L.F. Boyd Commanding 'C' Company was killed by a sniper on the morning of the 18th.

An attempt to seize VOX FARM at midnight 18/19th failed, the enemy being encountered in strength.

On the night 19/20th the Battalion was relieved by the 1st Loyal North Lancs without a casualty, and went into billets in the CANAL BANK.

Casualties :- Officers. Killed 2   Wounded 2
               Other Ranks. Killed 18   Died of Wounds 4
                           Wounded 58   Missing 6

Lieut Colonel,
30th November 1917. Commanding 1st Battn The Black Watch.

WAR DIARY.

1st. Bn. THE BLACK WATCH.

1st. INFANTRY BRIGADE.

1st. DIVISION.

DECEMBER.1917.

SECRET

Army Form C. 2118.

WAR DIARY
or
INTELLIGENCE SUMMARY.
(Erase heading not required.)

Instructions regarding War Diaries and Intelligence Summaries are contained in F. S. Regs., Part II. and the Staff Manual respectively. Title pages will be prepared in manuscript.

Dec. 1917   1st Battalion The Black Watch.

Place	Date	Hour	Summary of Events and Information	Remarks and references to Appendices
	December 1917			
PIDGEON CAMP	1st - 2nd		Battalion training.	
	3rd		Battalion moved by train to billets at DEKORT FARM.	
	4th		Battalion moved into the line. Battalion in Support. Relieved 1st Batt Camerons High'rs	
			Reference map BIXSCHOOTE 20. S.W.H.	
			Head Quarters at U.20 a 5. 9½.	
	5th – 8th		A Coy CHAMPAUBERT FARM. U.14.15	
			B " U.19.13.3.9½.	
			C " COLONEL'S FARM. U.20.c.	
			D " STAJUETTE FARM. T.24 d.	
			Battalion moved into front line on the night 8/9th	
FRONT LINE	9th – 12th		Front Line.	
			Sector held U.H.13.9.0 – U.5.13.8.8	
			Front line a series of posts held by 2 Coucheries.	
			Main line of resistance MANGELARE – VELDHOEK – HILL 20 – FAIDHERBE POSTS	
			" " " held by 2 Coucheries.	
			Battalion relieved by 1st Battn. S.W.B.s on the night 12/13 and	
			moved to DEKORT FARM.	
	13th		Battalion moved to rest billets at EIKHOEK CAMP.	

SECRET

Army Form C. 2118.

WAR DIARY
of
INTELLIGENCE SUMMARY.
(Erase heading not required.)

1st Battalion The Black Watch

Nov 1917

Instructions regarding War Diaries and Intelligence Summaries are contained in F. S. Regs., Part II. and the Staff Manual respectively. Title pages will be prepared in manuscript.

Place	Date	Hour	Summary of Events and Information	Remarks and references to Appendices
EIKHOEK CAMP	December 1917 14th 20th		Battalion training.	
	21st	—	Battalion moved to DEKORT FARM	
	22nd 28th		Battalion moved into the line. Battalion in Support	
	29th 31st		Battalion in Support	
			The following reinforcements arrived during the month.	
			Officers. 2	
			O.R. 6	
			Casualties. O.R Killed 2, Wounded 5, Died of wounds 1	

L. Garboth Major
Commanding 1st Bn The Black Watch

1st January 1918

1ST DIVISION
1ST BRIGADE

1ST BATTALION
THE BLACK WATCH
~~JAN - DEC 1918~~
1918 JAN - 1919 MAR

Page 1

1st Batt: The Black Watch

WAR DIARY
or
INTELLIGENCE SUMMARY
(Erase heading not required.)

Army Form C. 21

1918

Place	Date	Hour	Summary of Events and Information	Remarks and references to Appendices
Line.	January 1st	—	Batt: in Support.	96 42
			Dispositions	
			Reg. Map. BIXSCHOOTE 20 S.W. 4 1/10000	
			Batt HQ at U.20.A.5.9½.	
			A. Coy. „ CHAMPAUBERT Fm. U.14.B.	
			B. „ „ CHAUMÉ Fm. U.19.A.	
			C. „ „ COLONELS Fm. U.20.C.	
			D. „ „ STAVELE Fm. T.24.D.	
			Batt: moved into the front line on the evening of the 1st relieving the 1st Batt: Cameron Highlanders.	
			Dispositions.	
			Batt: Front. U.4.13.9.0 — U.5.13.3.3.	
			Front line a series of posts held by 2 Companies.	
			Main line of resistance. MANGELAARE — VELDHOEK — HILL 20 — FAIDHERBE fms.	
			Held by 2 Companies.	
Line.	2nd — 5th		Batt: in the line. This line was exceptionally quiet. Very little firing was	42 E = 42 E

Page 2

Army Form C. 2118

WAR DIARY
or
INTELLIGENCE SUMMARY.
(Erase heading not required.)

Instructions regarding War Diaries and Intelligence Summaries are contained in F. S. Regs., Part II. and the Staff Manual respectively. Title pages will be prepared in manuscript.

Place	Date	Hour	Summary of Events and Information	Remarks and references to Appendices
	5th	—	The Battn. was shortly engaged in wiring the outpost line and Main line and in work on its defences generally.	A/2
	—	—	The Battn. was relieved on the night of the 5/6th by the 1st South African Bushmen and moved to Brigade in support area at DEKORT F.M.	A/2
	6th	—	Moved to EIKHOEK CAMP.	A/2
	7th–12th	—	Battn. training.	A/3
	13.	—	Battn: moved to Brigade in Support area at DEKORT F.M.	A/2
	14–20th	—	Battn. training. also engaged in work on the Corps line of defence.	A/2
	21st	—	Battn: moved to Battn. in Support Area.	A/2
			Dispositions:	
			Battn. HQ. at U.20.A.5.9½.	
			A.Coy. CHAMPAUBERT F.M. U.14.B.	
			B. CHAUNE. F.M. U.19.A.	
			C. COLONELS. U.20.C.	
			D. GOURBI F.M. U.S.A.	
	22nd–24th		Battn. moved into the line on the night of the 24th relieving the 1st Battn. Cameron Highlanders	A/2

WAR DIARY
INTELLIGENCE SUMMARY

Place	Date	Hour	Summary of Events and Information	Remarks and references to Appendices
	25th – 27th		Front Line. Dispositions. Front. U.4.D.5.6. – U.5.B.9.3. Front line a series of posts held by 3 Companies. Left Coy. U.4.C.5½.7 – U.4.D.6.9. 1 Platoon in front line posts, remainder of Coy in Main line. CENTRE COY. U.4.D.6.9. – U.5.A.8.3. 1½ Platoons in front line posts, remainder of Coy in Main line. Right Coy. U.5.A.8.3. – U.5.B.9.3. 1½ Platoons in front line posts, remainder of Coy in Main line. Reserve Company in V.9.B. + V.9.C. On the night of the 25th in conjunction with the Bath. on our right we withdrew our line slightly, on the Right Company front. Right Company front now runs U.5.A.8.3 – U.5.A.9½.5½ – U.5.B.9.4½.	

WAR DIARY or INTELLIGENCE SUMMARY

Army Form C. 2118.

Place	Date	Hour	Summary of Events and Information	Remarks and references to Appendices
	27th	—	On the night of the 27th/28th Battn was relieved by the 16th Highland Light Infy 32nd Division and moved to Biercito no RENINGHOT Camp.	
	28th		Moved to EIKHOEK CAMP.	
	29th-31st		Battn training.	
			The following reinforcements joined the Battn during the month.	
			4 Officers and 114 O. Ranks.	
			2/Lt Col. L.P. Evans V.C. D.S.O. joined from 17th and assumed vice Lt Col CW Van Fortune D.S.O. to attend an reconnaissance 4th Army Musketry School.	
			Casualties.	
			2 O. Ranks wounded.	

L Moran Lt Col
L/C The Black Watch
Cmdg 14th Bn The Black Watch

June 31st 1917

Feb 1 Royal A?? Vol 43

WAR DIARY
INTELLIGENCE SUMMARY.
(Erase heading not required.)

Army Form C. 2118.

Place	Date	Hour	Summary of Events and Information	Remarks and references to Appendices
EIKHOEK CAMP	1st-8th		The battn. carried out company training.	1/2
	4th		Battn. paraded for regimental football match with the 18th Belgian Regt. at OOSTVLETEREN. The result was a draw 1-1.	2/2
	9th		The battn. moved 15th Support Bde Area in the POELCAPELLE SECTOR; billeted in NISSEN HUT CAMP at HILLTOP FARM	3/2
HILLTOP FM.	11th-14th		Four companies unemployed in improving the defences of the Army Battle Zone. Coy. training, All N.C.Os. carried out reconnaissance of assembly positions in rear of the Corps line.	4/2
	15th		Battn. at the baths at RIEGERSBERG.	4/2
	16th		Three companies employed on Army Battle Zone. One company employed carrying R.E. material to POELCAPELLE.	5/2
	17th-18th			5/2
	19th		Work in camp	7/2
	20th		The battn. relieved the 2/K.R.R.C. in the Support Bn Area with Bn HQ at HUBNER HALLES C 11 b 7.3. (SHEET 28); A and B. Coys. at MARINE VIEW D 7 a. (SHEET 28) and C and D Coys in PHEASANT TRENCH. U 30 b. and d. (SHEET 20)	7/2
	22nd to		The battn. relieved the 1/A.N.H. in the Right Bn Sector, extending from V38 a. 90.30. 20 to V30 d. 50.95, with B. Coy on the Right sub-sector, C. Coy. in the Centre, and D Coy. on the left; A. Coy. in support at WINCHESTER FM D 2 a. (SHEET 28).	
	26th		The battn. was relieved in the line by the 1/Cameron Highlanders, and returned to the Support Bn. Area.	2/2
	26th			
	28th		The battn. relieved the 1/Cameron Highlanders in the line, with the same dispositions as above, except that A Coy occupied the Centre Sector and C. Coy. was accommodated in a pillbox near ST JULIEN, and the MOUSETRAP TRACK	4/2

WAR DIARY
INTELLIGENCE SUMMARY.
(Erase heading not required.)

Army Form C. 2118.

Page 2.

Place	Date	Hour	Summary of Events and Information	Remarks and references to Appendices
			OFFICERS — The f/m provided 6th U.K. from six months tour of eg/M duty	
			1.2.18 LIEUT (A/CAPT) R COOK.	
			15.2.18 LIEUT A.C. TARBUTT	
			The following were struck off the strength of the batt. during the month	
			4.2.18 LIEUT J.G ALLAN ——— to R.E. coys in U.K	
			8.2.18 LIEUT D.N. M°GREGOR — MEDICAL BOARD in U.K.	
			4.2.18 FIRST LIEUT J.G KRAMER M.O.R.C — to H.Q 86TH DIVN. A.E.F	
			The following joined the batt.	
			3.2.18 MAJOR. S.H. RAYNES BRITISH COLUMBIA REGT. (7th attchd)	
			4.2.18 LIEUT G.E. BIRKETT R.A.M.C.	
			5.2.18 LIEUT M.S. JAMESON A.S.C. (H.T)	
			T/LIEUT. G I KIRKCALDY A.S.C. was granted permanent commission in the Black Watch, and taken on the strength. 19.2.18	
			CASUALTIES during the month —	
			KILLED 2. O.R	
			DIED OF WOUNDS 1. OR	
			WOUNDED 16 OR	
			61. OR	
			REINFORCEMENTS received during the month	

L. Musurus LIEUT-COL.
CMDG 1ST THE BLACK WATCH

SECRET

1 Royal Highlanders
1st Bn. Black Watch

WAR DIARY
or
INTELLIGENCE SUMMARY
(Erase heading not required.)

Army Form C. 2118.

Place	Date	Hour	Summary of Events and Information	Remarks and references to Appendices
	1916			
	1ST/12TH	Night	Battn in the line on a frontage extending from V38.a.90.20 to V30.d.50.93 with B Coy on the Right; A Coy on the centre; D Coy on the left; C Coy in a pillbox near SAINT JULIEN beside the MOUSETRAP TRACK. Battn HQ at HUBNER Fm D.I.C. 50.70	NR
	3RD	9PM	C. Coy carried out a raid on enemy posts in the MORAY Ho enclosure (V31.d) under command of 2/LIEUT ARTILLERY, M.G.S, and T.M.S. The posts were definitely located by a patrol under 2/LIEUT R RAMSAY on the night of the 2ND/3RD. The strength of the assaulting party amounted to two officers (2/LIEUT R K ARBUTHNOT and 2/LIEUT R RAMSAY) and 63 other ranks. This raiding party crept close up to the barrage and at ZERO the raiders the position. The operation was entirely successful, but it was found that the garrison had fled. Our German only was found in the position, and he was so badly hit by shell fire that no identification could be obtained. The raiding party returned to our lines without sustaining any casualties.	NR
			On the same night 2/LIEUT D SMITH DCM with 2 O/R carried out a daring patrol on an enemy post on the road EAST of TRACUS Fm. The party crept close up to the post. Three bombs were hurled into the position. The garrison fled and a rifle was found to be the field.	
			Very active patrolling marked the whole tour of the front line.	

J Wilson
LIEUT. COLONEL
Commanding, 1st. Bn. The Black Watch

Army Form C. 2118.

WAR DIARY
or
INTELLIGENCE SUMMARY.
(Erase heading not required.)

Instructions regarding War Diaries and Intelligence Summaries are contained in F. S. Regs., Part II. and the Staff Manual respectively. Title pages will be prepared in manuscript.

Place	Date	Hour	Summary of Events and Information	Remarks and references to Appendices
	4th/5th		The battn. was relieved in the line by the 2/Welch Regt. and returned to Hospital Farm.	KR
Hospital Fm	5th/9th		(B.19.d.3.1) by Bus from Wieltje to Elverdinghe	KR
			Training and recreation	KR
	10th		The battn moved to Huddleston Camp (C.7.d.)	KR
Huddleston Camp	11th/12th		Company Training	KR
	13th		The battn moved into Support Bn. Area with Bn HQ A. Coy. and D. Coy. at Kempton	KR
			Park (C.15.B.); B. Coy at Gournier Fm (C.9.d.15.70.); C. Coy at Langemarck.	KR
	14th		A Coy moved to Langemarck	KR
Support. Bn Area	15th/16th		Range practice and working parties	KR
	17th/18th		The battn relieved 1/Cameron Highlanders in the line with the following dispositions	KR
			C. Coy in the Right sub-sector with coy hq at Millers Ho (V.13.a. 45.65); A Coy	KR
			in the Left sub-sector with coy hq at Taube Ho (V.7.a.70); D. Coy in support	KR
			with coy hq at Imbros Ho (V.18.d.65.00); B Coy in reserve with coy hq	
			in Eagle Trench (V.24.d.); Bn HQ at Souvenir Ho (V.18 a 33.64).	
	18th	4.15am	An enemy raiding Party (estimated strength 70) attempted a raid	KR
			V.8.c.0.2. and C.2.a. after shelling our T.M. & M.G positions. Enemy attacked in	

A6945 Wt. W14422/M1160 350,000 12/16 D. D. & L. Forms/C./2118/14.

M. Wilson Lieut. Colonel
Commanding. 1st. Bn. The [illegible] Highd Bn.

WAR DIARY
or
INTELLIGENCE SUMMARY.
(Erase heading not required.)

Army Form C. 2118.

Place	Date	Hour	Summary of Events and Information	Remarks and references to Appendices
			and the party which approached 1/8 C.2.2 was repelled by L.G. fire. The other party succeeded in reaching 1/8 C.O.2. Two of our sentries were captured, a fourth who had also been captured made his escape by felling the escort with a blow from his steel helmet.	AR
	17th/21st		The battn. in the line	AR
	21st/22nd		The battn. returned by the 1/4 N. LANCS., and returned to HUDDLESTON CAMP 3	AR
	22nd		The battn. moved to billets in the CANAL BANK aloud C.13.a	AR
	22nd/25th		The battn. in the CANAL BANK — Specialist training	AR
	25th/26th		The battn. relieved 1/Cameron Highlanders in the support battn. area with battn. HQ, A. Coy, and C. Coy in CANE TRENCH (C9 b 00.05 to C9 d 43), B. Coy at the PIG and WHISTLE (U.28 b 45.25.), D. Coy in the STATION HOTEL, LANGEMARCK	AR
	26th/28th		The battn. in the support battn. area — working parties	AR
	29th/30th		The battn. relieved the 1/Cameron Highlanders in the line, with B. Coy in the RIGHT sub-sector; D. Coy in the LEFT sub-sector; C. Coy in support, and A. Coy in reserve with Coy. HQ at DOUBLE COTT; Battn. HQ at SOUVENIR H.Q.	AR
	30th/31st		The battn. in the line	AR

M. Moore
LIEUT. COLONEL
Commanding 1st Bn. The East Lancs.

WAR DIARY
or
INTELLIGENCE SUMMARY.

(Erase heading not required.)

Army Form C. 2118.

Place	Date	Hour	Summary of Events and Information	Remarks and references to Appendices
	4TH		REINFORCEMENTS — 35 O/R.	
	10TH		20 O/R	
	18TH		10 O/R	
	19TH		10 O/R TOTAL 75 O/R	
			CASUALTIES — KILLED — 7 O/R WOUNDED 11 O/R	
			DIED OF WOUNDS - 2 O/R MISSING 3 O/R	
			LIEUT A KILGOUR — WOUNDED 19.3.18	
			LIEUT A KILGOUR — REJOINED BN 27.3.18	
			STRUCK OFF STRENGTH	
	1ST		2/LIEUT A LEISHMAN — To Home Establishment	
	8TH		2/LIEUT G A BURNETT DCM } on 6 months loss of duty	
	13TH		LIEUT (A/CAPT) P.H.H.C COCKBURN M.C	
			To II Army Central School as Asst/Instructor	
			HONOURS AND AWARDS	
	20TH		MILITARY CROSS LIEUT (A/CAPT) R K ARBUTHNOT.	
			2/LIEUT. R. RAMSAY	
			MILITARY MEDAL	
			2238 SGT J THOMPSON 3133 PTE P T DOUGLAS	
			14TH A/0244 A/LCPL J D SIM	
			PTE. W E ANDERSON No 40164	
	28TH		MERITORIOUS SERVICE MEDAL No 43081 L/CPL W COCKBURN 30TH PTE J INGLIS No 18016	

J. M. ??? LIEUT. COLONEL
Commanding, 1st Bn, The Black Watch.

1st Brigade.

1st Division.

1st BATTALION

ROYAL HIGHLANDERS (Black Watch)

APRIL 1918.

WAR DIARY
INTELLIGENCE SUMMARY

for the month of April, 1918

Army Form C. 2118.

(Erase heading not required.)

Instructions regarding War Diaries and Intelligence Summaries are contained in F. S. Regs. Part II. and the Staff Manual respectively. Title pages will be prepared in manuscript.

Place	Date	Hour	Summary of Events and Information	Remarks and references to Appendices
	April			
YPRES-STADEN RLY.	1ST/2ND		The battn. in the line with Bn HQ at SOUVENIR HQ; B Coy in the right sub-sector; D Coy in the left sub-sector.	A/2
	2ND/3RD		C Coy in support, and A Coy in reserve with Coy HQ at DOUBLE COTT.	
			The battn. relieved in the line by 1/4 NORTH LANCS returned to billets in the CANAL BANK (C.13.c.B.2)	A/2
CANAL BANK	3RD/7TH		Company Training	A/3
	7TH		The battn. marched to ELVERDINGHE, with Bn HQ near the OLD MILL	A/3
	8TH		The battn. marched to PESELHOEK; entrained and proceeded to CHOQUES via BORRE arriving at CHOQUES at 10 p.m.; detrained and marched to billets in LAPUGNOY	A/2
	8TH/11TH		The battn. in LAPUGNOY	A/2
	11TH	1:30 p.m.	The battn. entrained at LAPUGNOY and proceeded to billets in VAUDRICOURT.	A/2
	11/12TH		The battn. in VAUDRICOURT.	A/2
	12TH		The battn. marched to billets in BEUVRY.	A/2
	12/13TH		The battn. in BEUVRY	A/2
	13/16TH		The battn. in BEUVRY	A/6
	16/17TH		The battn. relieved the 4TH b NORTH LANCS REGT in the left battn. sub-sector of HI GIVENCHY SECTOR with Bn HQ in SOUTHMOOR HQ at A.6.d.9.5; D Coy on the left with H.Q. at CALLAO, A Coy in the centre in GRENADIER RD.; C Coy on the two islands holding NEW CUT, WARE ROAD and OB from 12 2ND LIEUT. COLONEL BERKELEY STREET. Commanding 1st Bn The Black Watch.	

Two platoons in the BANTIN SOUTH and Two platoons in the BANTIN NORTH sub-sectors.

(2)

Army Form C. 2118.

WAR DIARY
~~INTELLIGENCE~~ SUMMARY
(Erase heading not required.)

Place	Date	Hour	Summary of Events and Information	Remarks and references to Appendices
			C Coy in the centre, holding New Cut, Ware Road, and O.B. from to sap K; A Coy on the right	A.2
			to Berkeley Street A.9.d.65 (Ref Map sheet. Gorre 1/20,000); a counter attack platoon under	
			2/Lieut P.H. Mackay, together with the local reserve of A and C Coys was accommodated in the	
			tunnel system in Givenchy, with a battle end at about A.9.c.3.6 and other into Piccadilly	
			and Caledonian Road.; B Coy garrisoned the system of Keeps, with one platoon in Herts	
			Keep A.9.d.7.4, one platoon in Moat Fm A.9.c.2.7, and two platoons in Givenchy Keep	
			and Givenchy Tunnel.	
	16/21st		The battn. in the line	N/a
	17th	10am	The enemy opened a slow bombardment of the Keep system with shells of very large calibre	N.2
	18th	1am	The bombardment became intense with shells of all calibres up to 12 inch, and at	N.2
		9am	an infantry attack developed	
			The enemy had previously attacked in this sector on 9th April, when he overran the	
			defences of the Corps on the left, and the brigade holding the Givenchy sector was	
			unable to deliver a successful counter-attack with the troops in the tunnel system.	
			On this date a frontal attack was not delivered, and moreover the enemy's	
			knowledge of the ground was at fault, and a great emphasis of the sector	

A.O. 945 Wt. W11422/M1160 350,000 12/16 D. D. & L. Forms/C./2118/14.

A.P. Stein LIEUT. COLONEL
Commanding 1 Bn. The Black Watch

WAR DIARY
INTELLIGENCE SUMMARY.
(Erase heading not required.)

(3)

Army Form C. 2118.

Place	Date	Hour	Summary of Events and Information	Remarks and references to Appendices
	18TH		On the 18th, the situation had materially changed. The left flank of the battⁿ was exposed on the LE PLANTIN plain, while C Coy held a narrow salient along WARE RD and SCOTTISH TRENCH. Moreover the enemy had profited by the experience on the 9TH, and had successfully marked down the battle route of the tunnel system	A/12
		8 AM	At 8am the hostile infantry advanced to the assault and soon the front system where the battage had been most intense. Almost immediately they secured the entrance to the tunnel, thereby cutting off the local reserve of A and C Coys, with the special counter-attack platoon. At the same time, D Coy and the garrisons of MOAT Fm and GIVENCHY KEEP were engaged from the NORTH and from the EAST. The most desperate fighting raged in front of GIVENCHY KEEP, where CAPT D. COOKE and LIEUT A. KILGOUR were killed in the first assault, and finally the garrison was reduced from 2 Officers and 40 other ranks to 1 W.O and 8 O.R yet they continued still to withstand all the efforts of the enemy. Lt LIEUT ADDISON D.C.M and 6 O.R. was sent up to support the garrison, and our position in the KEEP was again firmly established. Moreover, at MOAT FARM the enemy had secured close behind a creeping barrage and had	A/12

J. Horne LIEUT. COLONEL
Commanding, 1st Bn The Black Watch

WAR DIARY
INTELLIGENCE SUMMARY
(Erase heading not required.)

(4)

Army Form C. 2118.

Place	Date	Hour	Summary of Events and Information	Remarks and references to Appendices
			reached a point within 40 yards of our defences. The garrison of the MOAT was also much reduced in strength but, gallantly led by Lieut BURTON, it held the enemy at bay throughout the attack. On the left D.Coy was similarly attacked from the NORTH, and 2/Lieut BALMAIN was killed. Heavy losses had been sustained up till now by Capt ROBERTSON, whose rifle and Lewis Gun fire was thought to bear on the hostile troops as they advanced, and were after some time brought to the end, the Line was in the left half of the enemy trenches in possession of WARE RD, SCOTTISH TRENCH, PICCADILLY, the CRATERS, and AVENUE TRENCH later a company of CAMERON HIGHLANDERS reinforced the battn and was directed to employ it in a counter attack aided by our artillery barrage. The arrangements were of necessity hastily planned and the barrage was not effective but Lieut J.A. SMITH with No 8 platoon of The Black Watch reached the 1st Objective after killing and capturing a party of the enemy. The counterattack was unsuccessful.	
	30th	4AM	Two companies 1/NORTHAMPTONSHIRE REGT counterattacked and recovered the PICCADILLY Line, under a heavy artillery and M.G. barrage.	
	31/22ND		The Battn relieved in the line by 1/CAMERON HIGHLANDERS returned to the RES	

A.P.Moran Lieut. Colonel
Commanding 1st B'ttn Black Watch

WAR DIARY
INTELLIGENCE SUMMARY

(5)

Army Form C. 2118.

Place	Date	Hour	Summary of Events and Information	Remarks and references to Appendices
BATTN. AREA			with Bn HQ at the Pred. Bridge. D Coy at Vauxhall and Westminster Bridges; B Coy in billets near the Pred. by the canal bank.	1/12
	23rd	10 p.m	The battn. relieved by a battn. of the 165th Bde, returned to billets in Houchin	1/12 1/12
	24th	1.30 a.m	The battn. marched to Noeux-les-Mines	1/12
	24/30th		The battn. in camp near the Rue de Mazingarbe, in Noeux-les-Mines — bathing, musketry, company training	1/12
				1/12 1/12
			CASUALTIES.	
			Killed — Capt D Cooke	
	18th		Lieut (A/Capt) G J Sinclair	
			Lieut A Kilgour	
			2/Lieut R M Hume	
			2/Lieut W Balmain MM	
			Wounded & Missing —	
			Lieut (A/Capt) R K Arbuthnott M.C.	
			Missing — Lieut D C Stewart Smith	
			Lieut G I Kirkaldy	
			Lieut J C Stephen	
			2/Lieut P H Mackay	
			2/Lieut A Glencross MM	
			2/Lieut R Ramsay M.C	
			Wounded —	
			Lieut J W Kimber	1/12

W Murray
Commanding 1st ... LIEUT COLONEL

WAR DIARY
INTELLIGENCE SUMMARY.
(Erase heading not required.)

Army Form C.2118

Place	Date	Hour	Summary of Events and Information	Remarks and references to Appendices
	18TH		LIEUT M.S. JAMESON (A.S.C. H.T.) attchd — MISSING	IM
			MAJOR S.H. RAYNES (BRITISH COLUMBIA REGT attchd)	
			— WOUNDED 18.4.18; DIED of WOUNDS 20.4.18	IB
			STRUCK OFF STRENGTH.	
	2ND		CAPTAIN J.TH MABILL R.A.M.C. 6TH 2/LIEUT H.J. FOXCROFT	
	6TH		CAPTAIN I.D BROWN 2ND CAPT. D MACINTYRE R.A.M.C.	
	22ND		CAPTAIN N.D MACLEOD M.C. 27TH CAPT. I.D BROWN	
			CASUALTIES — Officers —	
	18TH		KILLED — 35 WOUNDED — 66	
			MISSING — 258	
			DIED of WOUNDS — 7	
			REINFORCEMENTS — 68 other ranks	
			HONOURS AND AWARDS	
			DISTINGUISHED CONDUCT MEDAL — { No 8843 CPL J. YARKEY.	
			No 2604 SGT H. SHARP	
			MILITARY MEDAL — No 1380 CPL J. MIDDLETON; No 40164 PTE H.I ANDERSON	IM
			No 12018 PTE A. INGLIS ; No 40653 L/CPL T. ARRAN	
			No 2041 PTE J. NORTON	

X.P. Mearns LIEUT. COLONEL
Commanding 1st B. The Black Watch

WAR DIARY
or
INTELLIGENCE SUMMARY.
(Erase heading not required.)

SECRET — Army Form C. 2118.

1st B. Watch

Place	Date	Hour	Summary of Events and Information	Remarks and references to Appendices
NOEUX-LES-MINES	May 1918			
	1st & 2nd		COMPANY TRAINING	
	2nd		Bn. HQ moved to the RED CHATEAU in the CAMBRIN locality with one attached garrison in .... of Corps	W2
			B Coy, less two platoons, garrisoned the PONT FIXE .... and was attached for tactical purposes to 1/CAMERON HIGHLANDERS; two platoons of B Coy garrisoned MAISON ROUGE and KEYES KEEP, and were attached for tactical .... to 1/6 A.N. HANTS.	
			D Coy garrisoned portion of VILLAGE LINE, with Coy HQ about H.90.b.9.4. and were attached for tactical purposes to 1/CAMERON HIGHLANDERS.	W3
	2nd/30th		The batt. in the line, disposed as above.	W2
	30th		The battn was relieved in the line by 1/S.W. BORDERERS and 2/WELCH and returned to camp in NOEUX-LES-MINES 1. by the RUE DE MAZINGARBE.	W2
NOEUX-LES-MINES	30th/28th		Platoon Tactical training, range practices and specialist training	W2
	27th		Battn sports	W2
	28th		About 2 P.M. when A and C Coys had paraded ready to march off to C Coy. FIFTYNINE casualties from a solitary shell burst immediately in rear of whom 6 were killed and 4 died of wounds	W2

LIEUT ....
Commanding ....

Army Form C. 2118.

WAR DIARY
or
INTELLIGENCE SUMMARY.
(Erase heading not required.)

Instructions regarding War-Diaries and Intelligence Summaries are contained in F.S. Regs., Part II. and the Staff Manual respectively. Title pages will be prepared in manuscript.

Place	Date	Hour	Summary of Events and Information	Remarks and references to Appendices
	28th		The battn relieved 2/K.R.R. Corps in the Right Battn Subsector of the Hohenzollern Sector, the frontage extended from G.5.c.0.1. to G.4.a.7.9 and following was the disposition — A Coy in the right company sub-sector with coy HQ about G.10.c.8.8 ; C. Coy in the left sub-sector with coy hq about G.4.c.1.9 ; B Coy in support with coy hq about G.9.b.8.8 ; D Coy in reserve with coy HQ about G.2.d.6.3 ; Bn HQ about G.1.a.5.8. (Ref. Map Sheet, Gorre 1/20,000)	A/2
	29/31st		The battn in the line.	A/2

HONOURS AND AWARDS

BAR TO DISTINGUISHED SERVICE ORDER — LIEUT-COL. H.P. EVANS V.C. D.S.O

MILITARY CROSS — LIEUT (A/CAPT) I.H. H.ROBERTSON
— LIEUT (A/CAPT) G.S.M. BURTON
— LIEUT (A/CAPT) B.G. VALENTINE
— LIEUT. T.A. SMITH
— LIEUT. W. ADDISON D.C.M

JHEvans
LIEUT. COLONEL
Commanding 1st. Bn. The Black Watch.

Army Form C. 2118.

WAR DIARY
or
INTELLIGENCE SUMMARY.
(Erase heading not required.)

Instructions regarding War Diaries and Intelligence Summaries are contained in F. S. Regs., Part II. and the Staff Manual respectively. Title pages will be prepared in manuscript.

Place	Date	Hour	Summary of Events and Information	Remarks and references to Appendices
			DISTINGUISHED CONDUCT MEDAL. No 8508 C.S.M. H. BENNETT	
			No 3188 SGT A FRASER	
			BAR TO MILITARY MEDAL. No 10108 PTE J SKEA	
			MILITARY MEDAL	
			No 4383 C.S.M J. McHARDY D.C.M ; No 3197 SGT J ROBERTSON ; No 11142 PTE J LINDSAY	
			No 40644 SGT W. ROBERTSON : No 285011 CPL D. BRATCHIE ; No 43344 PTE A. REID	
			No 11948 PTE D KIDD : No 9865 PTE T. WHEATLEY ; No 17819 PTE R. CRAWFORD	
			No 8064 PTE J SAMSON ; No 40047 PTE W CUSHNIE ; No 2512 SGT J COUGHAN	
			No 18146 PTE A WILLIAMS ; No 3109 PTE J GIBSON ; No 40191 PTE A HARLEY	
			No 43332 PTE J PIRNIE ; No 8301 SGT L. SIMMONS ; No 20937 N.CPL J. McDONALD	
			No 14411 PTE R. CLARK ; No 43112 PTE D BRICKNAL ; No 43651 PTE R LEGGATT	
			No 3355 PTE A INNES ; No 1178 PTE J CURRIE ; No 9354 PTE A COWAN	
			No 15196 CPL W HUTCHISON ; No 2354 PTE R. McCULLOCH ; No 11013 PTE J REAY	
			No 10020 CPL T SMITH ; No 9364 PTE J McMAHON attchd 1st BDE Signals.	

M. [signature]
LIEUT. COLONEL
Commanding, 1st. Bn. The Black...

Army Form C. 2118.

WAR DIARY
or
INTELLIGENCE SUMMARY.

(Erase heading not required.)

Place	Date	Hour	Summary of Events and Information	Remarks and references to Appendices
			REINFORCEMENTS	
	8.5.18		OFFICERS — 2/Lieut R.K. Fyall ; 2/Lieut H.H. Smith ; Lieut D.C. Daly	2/2
	15.5.18		2/Lieut C.A. Smith.	1/2
	17.5.18		2/Lieut J. Buchanan (A.& S.H.) ; 2/Lieut H.R.T. Taggart (A.& S.H)	
			2/Lieut J.P.C. Houston (A.& S.H.) ; 2/Lieut H.B. Webster (A.& S.H)	
	20.5.18		2/Lieut L. Clarke (Labour Corps)	
	24.5.18		2/Lieut C.I. Sutherland (A.& S.H) ; 2/Lieut J.N. Hood (A.& S.H.)	1/2
			2/Lieut D. Baxter	
			OTHER RANKS —	
			3/5/18 — 11 O.R. ; 15/5/18 — 65 O.R. ; 16/5/18 — 6 O.R	
			20/5/18 — 20 O.R. ; 28/5/18 — 8 O.R. ; 26/5/18 — 65 O.R	
			31/5/18 — 66 O.R.	
			STRUCK OFF STRENGTH —	
	2.4.18		2/Lieut I.K. Higginbotham — Hospital in U.K	1/2
	31.5.18		Major A. Gartside H.A.I. (attached) — Command

Major [signature]
2/R Sussex Regt. Lieut. Colonel.
Commanding 1st Bn. The Black ....

Army Form C. 2118.

WAR DIARY
or
INTELLIGENCE SUMMARY.
(Erase heading not required.)

Instructions regarding War Diaries and Intelligence Summaries are contained in F. S. Regs., Part II. and the Staff Manual respectively. Title pages will be prepared in manuscript.

Place	Date	Hour	Summary of Events and Information	Remarks and references to Appendices
			CASUALTIES	
			OFFICERS — NIL	
			OTHER RANKS —	
	4.5.18		KILLED — ONE	
	26.5.18		— SIX	
	28.5.18		DIED OF WOUNDS — FOUR	
	6.5.18		WOUNDED — ONE	
	16.5.18		— ONE	
	18.5.18		— ONE	
	19.5.18		— ONE	
	28.5.18		— FIFTYONE	

LIEUT. COLONEL
Commanding, 1st. Bn. The Black Watch.

1 Rty Highrs
Army Form C. 2118.
Ref Map Sheet Gorre 1/20000

SECRET

WAR DIARY
or
INTELLIGENCE SUMMARY
(Erase heading not required.)   June

Instructions regarding War Diaries and Intelligence Summaries are contained in F.S. Regs., Part II. and the Staff Manual respectively. Title pages will be prepared in manuscript.

Place	Date	Hour	Summary of Events and Information	Remarks and references to Appendices
Hohenzollern Sector	1st /5th		The battn. in the line — Right Battn Subsector of the Hohenzollern Sector. Frontage extended from G.5.c.0.1 to G.4.a.7.9 and following was the dispositions — A Coy in the Right Coy subsector with coy headquarters about G.10.a.88 ; C Coy in the Left Coy subsector with coy headquarters about G.4.c.1.9 ; B Coy in Support with coy headquarters about G.9.3.88 ; D Coy in Reserve with Coy Headquarters about G.3.d.6.3 ; Bn Headquarters about G.1.d.5.8. (Ref Map Sheet Gorre 1/20,000)	J.A.
	5th		The battn. was relieved in the line by the 1/4 North Hants Regt and returned to billets in Annequin, less B Coy, D Coy and one platoon of A Coy. B Coy relieved one company of 1/4 North Hants Regt attached Cameron Highlanders in Left batta sub-sector and became company in reserve Left Battn with coy headquarters about A.26.d.1.5. D Coy with one platoon A Coy attached, remained as Reserve Coy Right Battn with the same dispositions as before ; C Coy occupied Annequin Keep with Coy Headquarters at F.29.d.1.3. ; A Coy occupied Annequin Right with Coy HQ at F.29.d.8.2. ; Bn HQ established at F.29.c.80.05.	27E 5-mins J.A.

O. Anderson LIEUT. COLONEL
Commanding 1st. Bn. The Black Watch

WAR DIARY
or
INTELLIGENCE SUMMARY.
(Erase heading not required.)

Army Form C. 2118.

Place	Date	Hour	Summary of Events and Information	Remarks and references to Appendices
ANNEQUIN	5TH	6PM	The battn. less B Coy, D Coy and one platoon A Coy in ANNEQUIN — working parties daily	1A
	9TH		The battn. relieved 1/Bn. CAMERON HIGHLANDERS in the LEFT BATTN sub-sects following was the disposition	
			D Coy occupied the RIGHT COMPANY sub-sect with coy headquarters at G386?	
			B Coy occupied the LEFT COMPANY sub-sect with coy headquarters at A3?C9?	
			A Coy garrisoned RAILWAY and GLOSTER KEEPS, with coy headquarters at G3a??	
			C Coy manned SUSSEX TRENCH and HUMANITY TRENCH with coy hq at G3?a??	
			Bn HQ was established in a island under the RAILWAY EMBANKMENT at A3?a?a	2A
	10TH		The battn. in the line	2A
	11TH			2A
	13TH		The battn. was relieved in the line by 4/SEAFORTH BORDERERS and moved to billets in NŒUX - LES - MINES, with Bn HQ in H. MARIE	
NŒUX - LES - MINES	13TH		The battn. carried out tactical training in BOIS D'OHAIN and in the training area adjacent to NŒUX. During the period	
	21ST		the battn. published the orders of "Q" BATTN and was responsible for manning the defences of NŒUX in the event of attack	2A

J. Roberts ──── LIEUT. COLONEL

Commanding 1st Bn The Black Watch

Army Form C. 2118.

WAR DIARY
or
INTELLIGENCE SUMMARY.
(Erase heading not required.)

Place	Date	Hour	Summary of Events and Information	Remarks and references to Appendices
CAMBRIN SECTOR	21ST		The battn. relieved 1/Bn. The NORTHAMPTONSHIRE Regt. in the RIGHT BATTN. SUB-SECTOR of the CAMBRIN SECTOR. — FRONTAGE extended from TWIN SAP (A 27 b 55.45) inclusive to MILL SAP (A 31 b 8.0) inclusive — Following with dispositions — A Coy occupied RIGHT Coy SUB-SECTOR with Coy Hq at A 27.32.6 ; C Coy occupied LEFT FRONT COMPANY SUB-SECTOR with Coy Hq at A 21 c 85.60 ; D Coy occupied RIGHT SUPPORT Coy sector with enemy Hq at A 27 a 3.3 ; B Coy occupied LEFT Coy SUPPORT SECTOR with enemy Hq at A 26 b 5.5 (by day) and A 20 d 90.35 (by night) ; Bn HQ. was established at A 20 d 55.40. Two platoons from SUPPORT Bn in CAMBRIN were attached to garrison LEWIS KEEP and MAISON ROUGE.	
	28TH		D Coy relieved C Coy in LEFT FRONT Coy SUBSECTOR ; C Coy returned to RIGHT SUPPORT SECTOR.	J.8.
	29TH		B Coy relieved A Coy in RIGHT FRONT Coy SUBSECTOR ; A Coy returned to LEFT SUPPORT SECTOR.	J.8.
	30TH AUG		C Coy relieved D Coy ; D Coy again returned to RIGHT SUPPORT SECTOR.	J.8.
	30TH		The battn. in the line — very active patrolling carried out. LEFT (OR FRONT. LIEUT. COLONEL J. Anderson Commanding 1st Bn. The Black Watch.	J.8.

WAR DIARY
or
INTELLIGENCE SUMMARY.
(Erase heading not required.)

Army Form C. 2118.

Place	Date	Hour	Summary of Events and Information	Remarks and references to Appendices
			CASUALTIES — OFFICERS — 2/Lieut. C.A. Smith Wounded 24.6.18	
			Other ranks — KILLED — 1.O.R. — 3.6.18 ; 1.O.R. — 4.6.18 Total — 2.O.R	
			DIED OF WOUNDS — 1.O.R. — 31.5.18 ; 1.O.R. — 11.6.18 Total — 2.O.R.	
			WOUNDED — 1.O.R. — 2.6.18 ; 2.O.R. — 3.6.18 ;	
			1.O.R. — 4.6.18 ; 3.O.R. — 5.6.18 (2.gas) ;	
			1.O.R — 6.6.18 ; 1.O.R. — 7.6.18 (gas) ; 1.O.R — 8.6.18 ; 1.O.R — 24.6.18	
			Total — 11.O.R	2.off.
	10th		STRUCK OFF STRENGTH — Major (A/Lt-Col.) L.P. Evans V.C. DSO — to command 14th S.R. Regt.	p.p.
	3rd		Lieut. J.W. Fraser to Base Depot for duty	p.p.
	10th		JOINED BATTN — Capt. (A/Lt-Col.) F. Anderson DSO. M.C. — to command battalion	p.p.
	12th		Major T.H. Cunningham DSO — Major on Headquarters	
			REINFORCEMENTS — JOINED — 2.6.18 — 1.O.R ; 3.6.18 — 18.O.R ;	
			6.6.18 — 7.O.R ; 7.6.18 — 12.O.R ; 9.6.18 — 8.O.R	
			14.6.18 — 60.O.R. ; 17.6.18 — 24.O.R ; 19.6.18 — 14.O.R	
			21.6.18 — 30.O.R ; 23.6.18 — 5.O.R. ; 27.6.18 — 2.O.R	
			30.6.18 — 1.O.R Total — 182. O.R	p.p.

J. Anderson LIEUT. COLONEL
Commanding 1st. Bn. The Black Watch

Army Form C. 2118.

WAR DIARY
or
INTELLIGENCE SUMMARY.

(Erase heading not required.)

Instructions regarding War Diaries and Intelligence Summaries are contained in F. S. Regs., v are II. and the Staff Manual respectively. Title pages will be prepared in manuscript.

Place	Date	Hour	Summary of Events and Information	Remarks and references to Appendices
	29TH		REJOINED BATTALION 2/LIEUT. C.A. SMITH.	J.A.
	12TH		SICK IN COUNTRY 2/LIEUT. G.N. FERGUSON. M.C. M.M.	2.A.
	19TH		LIEUT. D.C. DALY	6.A.

J. Matson LIEUT. COLONEL
Commanding, 1st. Bn. The Black Watch.

1 Royal Hrs

Army Form C. 2118.

CONFIDENTIAL

WAR DIARY
or
INTELLIGENCE SUMMARY.

(Erase heading not required.)

REF. MAP SHEET. GORRE 1/20,000

Place	Date	Hour	Summary of Events and Information	Remarks and references to Appendices
CAMBRIN SECTOR	1ST/11TH		The battn in the line in CAMBRIN RIGHT SUB-SECTOR — FRONTAGE intended from TUNY SAP (A.27.b.55.45) inclusive to MINE SAP (A.24.b.8.0) inclusive — Following was the dispositions — Right front company — B Coy with Coy HQ at A.24.b.2.6; LEFT FRONT COMPANY — C Coy with Coy HQ at A.24.c.85.60; RIGHT SUPPORT COMPANY — D Coy with Coy HQ at A.26.b.5.5. (by day) and A.20.d.90.35 (by night); Bn HQRS was established at A.20.d.55.40. Two platoons from SUPPORT BATTN CAMBRIN was attached to garrison LEWIS KEEP and MAISON ROUGE.	8AM
	7TH	9.45PM	D Company, consisting of FOUR OFFICERS, Capt J.W.H. ROBERTSON O.C., 2/Lieut D SMYTH D.C.M., 2/Lieut J BUCHANAN (A&SH attached The BLACK WATCH) 2/Lieut H CLARKE, together with 120 other ranks raided the enemy's trenches in A.21.d and A.22.c (REF MAP SHEET AUCHY (S) 1/10,000). A copy of the OPERATION ORDER is attached. Farthy with a report on the raid. The raid was entirely successful and six prisoners of the 369TH REGIMENT was captured.	8PM
	11TH		The battn was relieved in the line by the 1st Battn The Gloucestershire R[egt]	A/E 15 March

F[?] Mick Major F/ LIEUT. COLONEL
Commanding, 1st Bn. The Black Watch.

A0945 Wt. W14422/M160 350,000 12/16 D.D. & L. Forms/C/2118/14.

Army Form C. 2118.

WAR DIARY
or
INTELLIGENCE SUMMARY.
(Erase heading not required.)

Place	Date	Hour	Summary of Events and Information	Remarks and references to Appendices
	12th/13th		Rest and attend to billets in NOEUX-LES-MINES	R.M.
	13th		A composite company consisting of six officers — CAPT. J.W.H. ROBERTSON O.C. Company: CAPT. G.S.N. BURTON O.C., LIEUT. J. BROWN, LIEUT. J.S. YOUNG, LIEUT. J.B. STEWART, 2/LIEUT. D. SMITH D.C.M. — and 220 other ranks was detailed to proceed to ROMESCAMP to form a composite battalion, representative of the BRITISH ARMY in FRANCE. The batt. composed one company detailed by the 4TH GUARDS BRIGADE, one company 1st Batt. The BLACK WATCH, one company 1st Batt. The ROYAL WEST SURREY REGT. (The QUEEN'S), and one company detached by the Overseas Forces, including one platoon CANADIANS, one platoon AUSTRALIANS, one platoon NEW ZEALANDERS, and one platoon SOUTH AFRICANS. The batt. was accompanied by the band of the 3rd Batt. The IRISH GUARDS. The company entrained at PERNES, and arrived at ROMESCAMP on the morning of the 14th.	R.M.
	13th		The composite battalion entrained at ABANCOURT the evening of the 13th	

R.M.E. NAPIER, LIEUT. COLONEL
Commanding 1st. Bn. The Black Watch

Army Form C. 2118.

CONFIDENTIAL WAR DIARY
or INTELLIGENCE SUMMARY.
(Erase heading not required.)

Place	Date	Hour	Summary of Events and Information	Remarks and references to Appendices
	13TH		different at the Gare du Champs de Mars in Paris only on the 13th not reported to billets in the French-American Hospital in the Grand Palais.	
	14TH	6.45 AM	The battn. paraded in the courtyard of the Grand Palais and marched to rendezvous in the Bois de Boulogne where the Allied Troops were inspected by M.M. le Président Poincaré and le Général Joffre. At 9 AM the battn. marched off, in rear of the Belgian contingent, had the saluting base in the Avenue du Bois de Boulogne, and proceeded along the now Honour[?]fare, through the Porte de la Concorde, to the Champs d'Elysées. The march occupied over a period of two and a half hours, and throughout the march the streets were thronged with citizens. Everyone of the company of Highlanders was loudly acclaimed with shouts of "Vive l'Ecosse", "Les Braves Ecossais" and its path was littered with roses. Towards the end of the march the pipers began to play and the international bystander[?] became intense. The line of advance was a triu-	

R.M.L.[?] N[?] LIEUT. COLONEL
Commanding 1st Bn. The Black [Watch]

Army Form C. 2118.

WAR DIARY
or
INTELLIGENCE SUMMARY.
(Erase heading not required.)

CONFIDENTIAL

Instructions regarding War Diaries and Intelligence Summaries are contained in F. S. Regs., Part II. and the Staff Manual respectively. Title pages will be prepared in manuscript.

Place	Date	Hour	Summary of Events and Information	Remarks and references to Appendices
			the company was almost entirely cut off from the leading company of H. Guards	KM.
	15TH		There was no parade.	KM
	16TH		The company entrained at the Gare de Champs de Mars, and proceeded via Etaples to Calonne Ricourt, reaching the battalion at Noeux-les-Mines on the evening of the 18TH.	
Noeux-Les-Mines.	17TH/28TH		The batt. in Noeux-Les-Mines — re-organisation, baths and company training.	KM
	9TH		The batt. relieved the 2ND Battn. The King's Royal Rifle Corps in the Hohenzollern Right Subsector — frontage scheduled from G.5.0.0. to G.4.a.8.8. and following was the Disposition — Right Front Coy — A Coy with Coy HQ about G.1.D.a.8.8; Left Front Company — C Coy with Coy HQ about G.4.c.1.9.; Support Coy — B Coy with Coy HQ in Central Keep — G.3.a.5.0.; Reserve Coy — D Coy with Coy HQ at G.2.d.6.3. Batt. Headquarters was established at G.2.d.0.0.	KM
	21ST/26TH		The battalion in the line.	KM
	26TH		The batt. was relieved in the line by the 1ST Battn. Loyal North Lancs Regt and assumed the role of Support Battn. — Hohenzollern.	KM

Roy Leitch, Lieut. Colonel
Commanding 1st Bn. The Black Watch

CONFIDENTIAL

Army Form C. 2118.

WAR DIARY
or
INTELLIGENCE SUMMARY.
(Erase heading not required.)

Instructions regarding War Diaries and Intelligence Summaries are contained in F. S. Regs., Part II. and the Staff Manual respectively. Title pages will be prepared in manuscript.

Place	Date	Hour	Summary of Events and Information	Remarks and references to Appendices
			with Headquarters in ANNEQUIN FOSSE. A, B, and C, COMPANIES were disposed in billets in ANNEQUIN and were responsible for manning the defences of ANNEQUIN LOCALITY, while D COMPANY, was attached to 1ST CAMERON HIGHLANDERS as RESERVE COMPANY in the HOHENZOLLERN WEST SUBSECTOR with Coy HQ about A 26 d 3.3	
	30TH/31ST		The batt. in ANNEQUIN — boarding watching parties, and carrying out simple Tactical Schemes, and reconnaissance of the locality	RM
	31ST		The batt. relieved the 1ST Batt. Cameron Highlanders in the HOHENZOLLERN LEFT SUB-SECTOR. — FRONTAGE as shown from G.4. a.3.8. to A.37.b.6.3., and following was the disposition — RIGHT FRONT COMPANY — D COY with Coy HQ about G.3.b.9.8.10.; LEFT FRONT COMPANY — B. COY with Coy HQ about A.37.c.90.65.; KEEPS COMPANY (RAILWAY and GLOSTER) — A COMPANY with Coy HQ about G.3.a.7.3.; SUPPORT COMPANY — C COY with Coy HQ about G.3.a.35.40.; together with D COY CAMERON HIGHLANDERS attached as RESERVE COMPANY in VILLAGE LINE with Coy HQ about A.36 d.3.5. Battn. HQ was established in a	RM

F. L. LIEUT. COLONEL
Commanding, 1st Bn. The Black Watch.

CONFIDENTIAL

Army Form C. 2118.

WAR DIARY
or
INTELLIGENCE SUMMARY.
(Erase heading not required.)

Place	Date	Hour	Summary of Events and Information	Remarks and references to Appendices
			HONOURS AND AWARDS	
			MILITARY CROSS — 2/Lieut. D. Smith D.C.M.	RJM
			2/Lieut. L. Clark	
			DISTINGUISHED CONDUCT MEDAL — No 270 Sgt P. McNulty	
			No 201194 Sgt G. Sievewright M.M.	
			MILITARY MEDAL — No 2411 Pte A. Thomson	RJM
			No 1711 Pte A. Harvey	
			No 656 Pte G. Thomson	
			No 7339 L/Sgt G. Hunter	
			No 18466 Pte L. Dixon	
			No 43107 Pte R. Cairnie	
			No 43350 Pte F. Seaton	
			MEDAILLE MILITAIRE — No 656 Pte G. Thomson M.M.	

Rtilika Major
— LIEUT. COLONEL
Commanding, 1st. Bn. The Black Watch.

CONFIDENTIAL

WAR DIARY
or
INTELLIGENCE SUMMARY.

Army Form C. 2118.

Summary of Events and Information

REINFORCEMENTS JOINED   OFFICERS.

LIEUT (A/CAPT.) R. COOK 13.7.18 ; CAPT (A/MAJOR) H.G. MILES D.S.O. 15.7.18 ;
LIEUT W. WHYTE and 2/LIEUT J PENNINGTON 22.7.18 ; LIEUT R.J MATERION 23.7.18 -- KIA

OTHER RANKS. - 8.7.18 - 2 O.R. ; 9.7.18 - 7 O.R. ; 14.7.18 - 7 O.R. ; 19.7.18 - 7 O.R.
21.7.18 - 6 O.R. ; 22.7.18 - 6 O.R. ; 24.7.18 - 6 O.R. ; 26.7.18 - 7 O.R. ; 27.7.18 - 10 O.R. ; 28.7.18 - 1 O.R.

OFFICERS STRUCK OFF - 3.7.18 LIEUT. J.W. FRASER to BASE ; 17.7.18 MAJOR T.H.
CUNNINGHAM D.S.O. (Seaforths) to 8/SEAFORTHS. 18.7.18 LIEUT W. MACKENZIE -- KIA
evacuated sick to U.K. ; 2/LIEUT G.H. FERGUSON A & S.H. - sick to U.K.

DEATHS - OFFICERS. - 2/LIEUT H.R. TAGGART. (A&S.H. attached.) died of wounds 24.7.18 -- KIA

OTHER RANKS - 1 - 7.7.18 ; 1 - 7.7.18 died ; 1 - 11.7.18 (died of wounds)
1 - 9.7.18 (died of wounds) ; 1 - 26.7.18 (in action)

WOUNDED - OFFICERS. - 2/LIEUT. J BUCHANAN (A&S.H. attached).
OTHER RANKS - 6.7.18 - 4 O.R. ; 17.7.18 - 1 O.R. ; 7.7.18 (Raid) - 33 O.R. -- KIA
24.7.18 - 5.O.R. ; 24.7.18 - 1.O.R. (at duty)
29.7.18 - 1.O.R. (at duty)

Emile Major
LIEUT. COLONEL
Commanding 1st Bn. The Black Watch

S E C R E T.

Copy No. 15

War Diary.

Herewith orders for raid to be carried out by 'D' Company, 1st Battalion The Black Watch, on night 7th/8th July 1918.

ACKNOWLEDGE.

J S Young Lieut & Adjt.
for. Lieut Colonel,
6th July 1918   Commanding 1st Battalion The Black Watch,

SECRET.   Copy No. ...15......

1st BATTALION THE BLACK WATCH.

OPERATION ORDER NO.1.

Reference Map LA BASSEE CANAL (4) 1/10,000 15/6/18 and attached Maps.

1. On the 7th July, 'D' Company and four Lewis Gun Sections of 'C' Company, will raid the enemy's trenches in the area - A.21.d.85.15. - A.22.c.22.05. - A.22.c.33.75. - A.21.d.85.70.

2. Object of attack is to secure identifications, inflict casualties on the enemy, and destroy enemy defences and dug-outs.

3. ASSEMBLY.

   (a) No. 16 Platoon, No. 1 Section No. 13 Platoon, and two Lewis Gun Sections of 'C' Company, will assemble in accordance with instructions N. and S. of the Southern exit of ROBERTSON'S TUNNEL.

   (b) No. 14 Platoon, Nos 3 and 4 Sections No.13 Platoon, will assemble in accordance with instructions N. of the Northern exit of ROBERTSON'S TUNNEL.

   (c) No. 15 Platoon, No.2 Section No.13 Platoon, and two Lewis Gun Sections of 'C' Company, will assemble in the old front line and at the exit of HILL TUNNEL in accordance with instructions.

4. APPROACH MARCH & ASSEMBLY.

   (a) At 6-0 p.m. 7/7/18, 'D' Company will move from CAMBRIN, sections at 200 yards distance. Nos 14 and 16 Platoons will assemble in ROBERTSON'S TUNNEL - No.15 Platoon will assemble in HILL TUNNEL.
   Teas will be arranged in Tunnels at 7-30 p.m.
   Lewis Gun Sections of 'C' Company and Sections of No.13 Platoon will report to their respective Platoon Group Commanders at 7-30 p.m.

   (b) Platoon Groups will commence assembly at 8-30 p.m.; assembly to be completed at 9-15 p.m.
   Rum will be issued to troops in their assembly positions at 9-15 p.m.
   Great care will be exercised to avoid detection while moving into assembly positions and when in assembly positions.

   (c) O.C. 'C' Company will remove necessary barricades and wire from assembly position on the night 6th/7th July.

5. METHOD OF CARRYING OUT ATTACK.

   No. 13 Platoon are responsible for capturing, clearing and holding enemy's front line from A.21.d.85.15. to A.21.d.85.70. and forming blocks in the enemy's front line on the flanks.

   No. 16 Platoon will enter the enemy's front line about A.21.d.85.15. and will advance across the open and along the C.T. to enemy's Reserve line about A.22.c.20.20. The Lewis Gun Section will form a block at A.22.c.15.06. The section carrying Mobile Charges will advance on the Left, and on reaching the enemy's Reserve line, will work Southwards, the remaining two sections will work Northwards along the enemy's Reserve line and will join with No.14 Platoon.

/2

<u>No.14 Platoon</u> will enter enemy's front line about A.21.d.9.4. and will advance across the open to the enemy's Reserve line about A.22.c.23.40.; on reaching the enemy's Reserve line, the Lewis Gun Section will form a block in DOCK ALLEY.
The section carrying Mobile Charges will advance on the Right of Platoon, and will work Northwards along the enemy's Reserve Line. One section will work Northwards joining hands with No.15 Platoon, one section will work Southwards joining hands with No.16 Platoon.

<u>No.15 Platoon</u> will enter enemy's front line about A.21.d.65.70., and will advance across the open and along the C.T. to the enemy's Reserve line about A.22.c.28.63.
One section will form a block in the enemy's Reserve line at A.22.c.25.70. The section carrying Mobile Charges will advance on the Right, and will work Northwards along the enemy's Reserve line.
Two sections will work Southwards, joining hands with the Lewis Gun Section of No.14 Platoon in DOCK ALLEY.

<u>Lewis Gun Sections of 'C' Company.</u>

Two sections will take up a position on the craters near the enemy's front line on the Right flank – two sections will take up a position on the craters near the enemy's front line on the Left flank.
These sections will engage any suitable targets, assist in covering the advance, and will block No Man's Land in the event of any attempt of counter attack from the flanks.

6. <u>ARTILLERY.</u>
Artillery will cut wire on a wide front.
Artillery will put down a creeping barrage on the German Front line at Zero.

ZERO to ZERO plus 5	On German Front line.
ZERO plus 5 to ZERO plus 7	100 Yards beyond German Front line.
ZERO plus 7 to ZERO plus 11	On German Reserve line.
At ZERO plus 11	Infantry enter German Reserve line.
ZERO plus 11 to ZERO plus 35	Protective barrage.
ZERO plus 35 to ZERO plus 40	Barrage returns to German Reserve line.
At ZERO plus 40	"Cease fire".

(a) Hows and 6" Newtons will deal with special targets during the raid.
(b) Counter Battery work will be carried out.
(c) A faint barrage will be carried out further South.
(d) The creeping barrage will consist of 18 Pr H.E.
(e) On reaching protective barrage, a few rounds of smoke will be fired.

7. 3" STOKES.

1st T.M.B. will employ 6 guns in conjunction with raid.
3 Guns will thicken the Artillery Barrage.

	Targets.	Rate of fire.
ZERO to ZERO plus 2	A.21.c.9.2. A.21.d.91.45. A.21.d.89.65	Rapid
ZERO plus 2 to ZERO plus 8	A.22.c.25.15. A.22.c.30.47 A.22.c.32.66.	Rapid
ZERO plus 8 to ZERO plus 25	CHATEAU ALLEY DOCK ALLEY 200 Yards E. of junctions with Reserve Line	Slow

3 Guns will fire from ZERO to ZERO plus 40 on the German Front line at

A.27.b.5.2.
A.22.a.05.05.
A.21.d.96.76.

8. MACHINE GUNS.

20 Vickers Machine Guns will co-operate firing on selected targets.
(For details see App.I not attached.)

9. DRESS.

(a) All ranks will wear shorts.
(b) Raid disc will be worn.
(c) All ranks will carry rifle and bayonet, 50 rounds S.A.A. and two Mills Bombs (except Nos 1 and 2 Lewis-Gun.)
(d) Platoon Commanders will carry a French Horn.
(e) Sections carrying Mobile Charges (1 per section), will wear YELLOW arm bands, and in addition carry one 'P' Bomb per man.
(f) Nos.14, 15 and 16 Platoons will carry 1 pair long handled wire cutters per section.
(g) Nos.14, 15 and 16 Platoons will carry one electric torch per section.
(h) Rifle Bombing sections will not be employed as such.

10. WITHDRAWAL.

(a) At ZERO plus 21, Nos. 14, 15 and 16 Platoons will withdraw by same lines as those of advance - signal to do so will be given by Platoon Commanders on French Horn.
Lewis Gun sections will cover the withdrawal.

(b) No. 13 Platoon and L.G. Sections of 'C' Company will withdraw after Nos. 14, 15 and 16 Platoons have passed through, or at ZERO plus 35.

(c) Bugles will sound Gs at the exits of tunnels to guide people returning

(d) A vertical searchlight beam will be shown from near Brigade Hd Qrs as a guide for direction.

4

(e) All ranks will collect as soon as possible after the raid in the same tunnel from which assembly was carried out and will hand in their raid discs. An issue of rum will be given on return.

(f) Platoons will remain in the Tunnels till dawn before returning to CAMBRIN.

11. MEDICAL ARRANGEMENTS.

A Regimental Aid Post will be found in ROBERTSON'S TUNNEL to which all stretcher cases will be taken, and to which all walking wounded will report.
An Advanced Dressing Station will be formed in WALPOLE STREET.

12. REPORTS ETC.

O.C. 'D' Company will make special arrangements for collect-
-ing reports, regarding casualties and prisoners, and for ascertaining if all have returned.

13. SIGNAL COMMUNICATION and Hd Qrs.

Battalion Hd Qrs will not move.
Hd Qrs 'D' Company will be established at the O.P. in the Northern Arm of ROBERTSON'S TUNNEL, to which a line will be laid from Battalion Hd Qrs.

14. ZERO hour will be at 9-45 p.m.

15. SYNCHRONIZATION OF WATCHES.

Brigade time will be given to all concerned.
Attacking troops will however take their time for advance from the opening of the Artillery Barrage.

16. GENERAL REMARKS.

(1) It is essential to keep close to the barrage and keep correct direction.

(2) Nos. 14, 15 and 16 Platoons will be prepared to assist No. 13 Platoon in capturing and clearing Front line.

(3) No. 15 Platoon will be responsible for sending back all prisoners, who will be collected at Company Hd Qrs in ROBERTSON'S TUNNEL. O.C. 'A' Company will arrange escort for taking any back to Brigade Hd Qrs as soon as possible.

Lieut Colonel,
6th July 1916. Commanding 1st Battalion The Black Watch.

Issued to :-
Brigade H.Q. 1, 2,
Cmdg Off. 3
'D' Coy 4 to 8
M.O. 9
Q.M. 10
1/Can.Eng 11
Left Bn Right /
Brigade / 12
Office 13
War Diary 14, 15.

1/TMB 16

Report on Raid carried out by 'D' Company,
1st Battalion The Black Watch at 9-45 pm 7th July 1918.
200 Yards S. of the CAMBRIN - LA BASSEE Road.

At 9-15 p.m. all troops were in their assembly positions.

The area to be raided necessitated crossing old carters, which had been carefully reconnoitred and marked with number boards.

The attack was carried out on a front of 250 Yards, and the enemy's lines were penetrated to a depth of 200 Yards.

The enemy showed no activity while the troops were in their assembly positions.

At 9-45 p.m., our Artillery and T.M. Barrage opened punctually and with great accuracy. The Infantry left their assembly positions and were able to pass through our wire and get within 40 Yards of our barrage. A slight westerly breeze greatly assisted our Infantry in seeing the exact position of our barrage. The light was good when our troops left their assembly positions, and the smoke of our bursting shells completely concealed our attacking troops from the enemy's view.

At ZERO plus three minutes the barrage lifted, and our troops rushed the enemy's front line. No. 13 Platoon were responsible for the capture of this objective, and were assisted by the Platoons who were going through to the enemy reserve line. A light machine gun was found about A.21.d.8.5.; this gun was destroyed.

The enemy's front line had been much damaged, and in places difficult to recognise. There were no enemy discovered here on the right; in the centre, three prisoners were taken after a short fight, during which a few of the enemy were killed; on the left, a post of about six men were seen to enter a dug-out. Efforts were made here to extract the Bosche, who fired up the stairs of the dug-out, and threw bombs. A prisoner was employed to tell the occupants to come out, which they commenced to do, but on seeing our troops, rushed back into their dug-out. The dug-out was then freely bombed, but no mobile charge or K.J. Bombs were available.

The party proceeding down the Southern communication trench succeeded in capturing two prisoners, who came out of a dug-out. Two dug-outs were discovered in this trench.

On reaching the enemy's support line, no enemy could be discovered. The trench was much knocked about. Several dug-outs were discovered about A.22.c.2.6.; the entrances of these were destroyed with mobile charges.

One prisoner was captured by the party on the left.

Our casualties were :-

	Officers	O.R.
Missing	-	3
Wounded	1	23 (1 at duty)

Many of the wounded were very slight, and 2 Other Ranks reported missing are believed killed.

Result of Raid.

Number of prisoners	6
Estimated number killed	25

Many dug-outs were blown in and may have inflicted heavy casualties on the enemy.

Identification.

The prisoners belonged to the 369 Infantry Regiment, 10th Ersatz Division.

2.

The following points were noticed during the attack :-

(i) No hostile Machine Guns opened fire during the whole of the operation, two guns however fired along our front and on the craters at about 11-15 p.m. during which time search parties were out looking for five men who were originally reported missing.

(ii) At 9-57 p.m. the enemy fired several lights, which went up in a corkscrew and burst into 2 pink lights. This appeared to be the S.O.S. signal. A few green and white lights were fired by the enemy about 5 minutes after ZERO.

(iii) About 9-47 p.m. the enemy fired a few T.Ms about the Northern exit of ROBERTSON'S TUNNEL, and on the craters; this soon slackened in intensity.

The enemy in reply to S.O.S. signal, opened at 10 p.m. all along our reserve line, on O.Ps and points in rear. The enemy's bombardment extended far to the S. of the point attacked which no doubt was partly due to the feint barrage about G.1.

(iv) Direction was very well kept in spite of smoke and dust which prevented anyone seeing more than about 40 Yards while close to the barrage. Owing to the direction of the wind, the smoke soon cleared away.

The good keeping of direction under difficult conditions is attributed to the training which had been carried out.

(v) It appears that gas was met by the attackers between the enemy's front and support line, and it is suggested that our bombardment may have burst cylinders containing gas. No projectors or T.Ms were located in the enemy's lines.

(vi) The wonderful accuracy of our barrage at ZERO was undoubtedly responsible for the attackers getting too close to the barrage in subsequent lifts (especially on the right) and was responsible for a few casualties.

On the right of the attack one battery appeared to be firing shrapnel which was bursting high and rather short.

(vii) In spite of the intensity of our barrage, the enemy in certain places put up determined fights, making free use of bombs and rifle grenades, and then attacked with the bayonet, but were in this respect inferior to our troops. No wounds are reported to have been inflicted by the bayonet.

J. Anderson

8th July 1918

Lieut Colonel,
Commanding 1st Battalion The Black Watch.

Head Quarters,
    1st Infantry Brigade.

    Attached herewith report on raid carried out by 'D' Company of my Battalion.
    I consider that all ranks showed great dash and spirit during the operation.
    I intend forwarding as soon as possible, the names of a few Other Ranks who distinguished themselves during the raid.

                                        J. Anderson
                                                    Lieut Colonel,
8th July 1918   Commanding 1st Battalion The Black Watch.

C.R.A.
B.G.C., 1st Inf. Bde.
========================

1st Division No. G.327/45
8th July 1918.

    The Div. Comdr. wishes to express his keen appreciation of the raid carried out by the 1st Black Watch last night.

    The artillery work appears to have been excellent, and every advantage was taken of it by the Infantry.

    The results point to most careful and efficient preparation and organisation, also to very skilful handling of the troops and gallantry and determination on their part.

General Staff.   Lieut-Colonel.
                1st Division.

Dear Anderson.

I forward Lt Uwena. You know I
heartily agree. I was very sorry indeed
to hear the casualties had been so high
I had hoped we had got off lighter.

Yrs sincerely

L S Thornton

8/7/18.

BATTALION ORDERS BY LIEUT. COLONEL W.H.L.P.L.G. ALEXANDER, D.S.O., M.C.

COMMANDING BRITISH COMPOSITE BATTALION

PARIS.   MONDAY, 1/7/19.

1. **DETAIL.**
   Reveille   6.0.a.m.
   C.O.C. under detachment arrangements.
   Breakfasts   7.a.m.
   Sick Parade   8.a.m.

2. **GENERAL ORDER.**
   The following is the translation of a General Order from the President of the French Republic to the President of the Council, Minister of War.——— PARIS, July, 14th. 1919.

   "My dear President,
   "amidst enthusiastic acclamations Paris saw this morning a thing
   "which no other city in the world had seen hitherto: the living
   "personification of the armed nations, united in brotherhood for
   "the defence of their liberties.
   "The splendid march past of the Allied Troops bodied forth to our
   "eyes all the aspirations of the people, victory and the future
   "seemed already to be passing gloriously before us.
   "Amongst all those brave soldiers who arrived here yesterday from
   "the battlefront and who will return thither, their souls rendered
   "bright by the sight, our French Battalion showed themselves, as
   "always, admirable in bearing and well worthy of the fine Allied
   "Units.
   "I shall be grateful to you if you will transmit my congratulations
   "and my emotion to the Military Governor of Paris, to the Officers
   "and to the men.
                (signed)   RAYMOND POINCARÉ,
                                        THE PRESIDENT.

   "From/ President of the Council,
              Minister of War,
   "To/   The Military Governor of Paris,
              Commanding the Group of Armies in Paris.

   "My dear Governor,
   "I receive from the President of the French Republic the attached
   "letter, which I beg you to communicate to the fine troops,
   "whose magnificent march past made such a great impression on the
   "population of Paris.
   "Please be good enough to add the congratulations of the Minister
   "of War, to those of the Head of the State.
                (signed)   G.CLEMENCEAU.

   "The Military Governor, commanding the group of Armies in Paris is
   "happy and proud to bring to the knowledge of the troops of the Allied
   "Nations and of the French troops, all of whom were so brilliantly
   "represented at our National Fete, the congratulations of the
   "President of the Republic and of the President of the Council,
   "Minister of War.
   "He adds his own personal congratulations for the impression and of
   "strong resolution which the troops imparted to all.

                (signed)   GUILLAUMAT,
                        COMMANDING GROUP OF ARMIES OF PARIS.

                                        W.Faulkner
                    ADJUTANT, BRITISH COMPOSITE BATTALION.

WAR DIARY or INTELLIGENCE SUMMARY

Army Form C. 2118.

1 Bn. History Aug 1918 Vol 49

Place	Date	Hour	Summary of Events and Information	Remarks and references to Appendices
HOHENZOLLERN LEFT SUB-SECTOR	31/8TH 5TH		The Battn. in the line — FRONTAGE — following was the disposition — Right Front Company — D Coy with Coy HQ about G.3.b.95.40; Left Front Company — B Coy with Coy HDQRS about A.27.90.65; Keeps Company (Railway and Gloster Keeps) — A Coy with Coy HDQRS about G.3.a.75.3; Support Company — C Coy with Coy HDQRS about G.3.a.25.40; together with D Coy 1st The Cameron Highlanders attached as Reserve Company in Village line with Coy HDQRS about A.26.d.23. Battn. HDQRS was established in a cellar beneath the Railway at A.25.U.85.30	RW RW RW
	5TH		The Battn. was relieved in the line by 1st Battn Cameron Highlanders and returned to billets in ANNEQUIN, to assume the rôle of SUPPORT BATTn. HOHENZOLLERN SECTOR	
ANNEQUIN	5TH/10TH		The battn. in ANNEQUIN — B Coy C Coy and D Coy was disposed in billets in the village proper manning the defences of ANNEQUIN locality, while A Coy was attached to 1st Cameron Highlanders in the line, as Reserve Coy. HOHENZOLLERN LEFT SUB-SECTOR; with Coy HDQRS about A.26.d.23 — Battn. HDQRS in ANNEQUIN FOSSE.	RW RW

R.W. White
LIEUT. COLONEL
Commanding 1st. Bn. The Black Watch.

WAR DIARY
or
INTELLIGENCE SUMMARY.
(Erase heading not required.)

Army Form C. 2118.

Place	Date	Hour	Summary of Events and Information	Remarks and references to Appendices
	10th		The battn. was relieved in ANNEQUIN LOCALITY by the 1st. GLOSTER REGT and returned to billets in NOEUX-LES-MINES, with headquarters in the RUE d'ARRAS.	K.M.
	11th		Owing to some hostile artillery activity, the battn. was withdrawn from NOEUX and proceeded to billets in BARLIN, with headquarters about K.27.c.4.9. (SHEET 44.B.)	K.M.
BARLIN.	11th/19th		The battn. in BARLIN — platoon training	K.M.
	19th		The battn. marched to K.38.a.5.2.; entrained and proceeded to HISBOURG via HOUDAIN — DIVION — PERNES — TIERS — FONTAINES-LES-BOULANS	K.M.
HISBOURG	19th/31st		The battn. in HISBOURG F.19 (SHEET 44.C.) — platoon training — company training — battn. training	
	31st			

K.M.
LIEUT. COLONEL
Commanding, 1st Bn. The Black Watch

WAR DIARY
or
INTELLIGENCE SUMMARY.
(Erase heading not required.)

Army Form C. 2118.

HONOURS AND AWARDS — No 2799 SGT J ROBERTSON M.M.
— MERITORIOUS SERVICE MEDAL

OFFICERS JOINED — CAPT P.H.L.C. COLQUHOUN M.C. — Joined 6.8.18.
2/LIEUT S.L. DAVIE — JOINED 6.8.18; 2/LIEUT W.H. GRANT 12.8.18.
2/LIEUT. H.G. GREGORY-SMITH — 8.8.18; 2/LIEUT A.F.W. ROBERTSON — 12.8.18
2/LIEUT F.J. ANDERSON — 25.8.18; 2/LT A.T.H. DEMPSTER — 25.8.18

OFFICERS STRUCK OFF STRENGTH —
LIEUT J. BROWN — to INDIAN ARMY. 2.8.18; LIEUT J.W. LANG (A & S.H.) to R.A.F. 3.8.18
LIEUT T.C. JACOBS — to 1/TMB 15.8.18; LIEUT D.C. DALY to U.K. 22.8.18

REINFORCEMENTS JOINED — AUG 5TH — 14 OTHER RANKS; AUG 16TH — 3 O.R.

CASUALTIES — 1 O.R. WOUNDED — 2.8.18; 1 O.R. Wounded (at duty) 4.8.18
1 O.R. KILLED, 2 O.R. WOUNDED — 4.8.18; 1 O.R. DIED of wounds 7.8.18
1 O.R. accidentally wounded — 16.8.18

[signature]
LIEUT. COLONEL
Commanding, 1st Bn. The Black Watch

APPENDIX "A" Attached.
1 Relay 5/1 or vol 50

WAR DIARY
or
INTELLIGENCE SUMMARY
(Erase heading not required.)

Army Form C. 2118.

REF. MAP SHEET 51B 1/40,000

Commanding, 1st Bn. The Black Watch

Place	Date	Hour	Summary of Events and Information	Remarks and references to Appendices
	31st/1st	1 AM	The batln. entrained at ANVIN and detrained in ARRAS about 9.30 A.M. and marched in the area of the QUARRIES. The Commanding Officer and Coys. were immediately reconnoitred an assembly position near GUEMAPPE with a view to forming up in rear of the 14th CANADIAN DIVISION prior to the attack on the DROCOURT – QUÉANT SWITCH. This Bde. of Brigade Reserve had been allotted.	A.A.
	1st	8 PM	The batln. moved off from ARRAS and proceeded by march route to its assembly position near GUEMAPPE, on O.19.a. South of the River SENSÉE. The assembly was uneventful, and without medical spirit from the fact that the casualties were sustained as a result of an number of bomb shells with airplanes by a night-bombing enemy machine near the assembly position. Battn. Headquarters was established in the sunken road at O.19.a & 9.	A.A.
	2nd	3 PM	Artillery formation was chosen. The Battn. was drawn out in Artillery formation on a frontage of about 800 yards. A and B Coys. were in front – "A" on the LEFT "B" on the RIGHT. Followed by "C" and "D" Coys. respectively. No hostile artillery fire was encountered but came the Batln. little in the valley S.W. of ETERPIGNY and came in following was	A.F.

E. A. Atcheson LIEUT. COLONEL

WAR DIARY or INTELLIGENCE SUMMARY.

Army Form C. 2118.

REF MAP SHEET 51B 1/40,000.

Place	Date	Hour	Summary of Events and Information	Remarks and references to Appendices
	3RD		the dispositions — "C" Coy about P19.a.67, facing NORTH, responsible for the defence of the left flank; "D" Coy about P19.a.72 on the RIGHT; "A" and "B" Coy about P19.a.1.5 in SUPPORT. Batt. Headquarters was established at P19.c.35	
		3 PM	Instructions had been received to relieve the 2ND SEAFORTHS of the 4TH BRITISH DIVISION in the line, incl. RECOURT WOOD, and the battalion again advanced in artillery formation. Some hostile artillery fire was encountered on the high ground NORTH of DURY, but generally the advance proceeded without much interference. About 10 P.M. the battalion was established in its new position. C Coy was on the LEFT from RECOURT (exclusive) to P19.b.09; D Coy on the RIGHT from P19.b.09 to P19.b.80; A Coy was in support on the LEFT about P19.c.48; "B" Coy in support on the RIGHT about P19.a.99. A line of forward posts was established by B Coy in RECOURT WOOD at P19.c.73	S.A.
	4TH		Batt. HQrs was at RECOURT WOOD at P19.c.73. B Coy, together with B Coy 'CAMERON HIGHLANDERS' relieved 3 companies of 44TH CANADIAN BATT'N on the line from P19.d.80 to Q.13.central. Coy HQrs were established in each case in RECOURT QUARRY Q.13.a.O.O	S.A.

Commanding 1st Bn ? ? LIEUT. COLONEL

WAR DIARY
or
INTELLIGENCE SUMMARY.
(Erase heading not required.)

Army Form C. 2118.

REF MAP SHEET 51B /40,000

Place	Date	Hour	Summary of Events and Information	Remarks and references to Appendices
	10th		The following new dispositions were assumed to make good the right bank of the River Sensée, and is posted the left flank of the Canadian Corps which had pushed forward to Ecourt-St-Quentin. — D Coy Right Front Coy — HDQRS. at Q7d 4.0.; 2 platoons in sunken road at Q7 d 4.0.; 1 platoon in old trench Q8c 4.8.; 1 platoon in sunken road at Q14 b 5.7. 8 hours battn. was withdrawn to right of Q8 b 6.8 and at Q9 b 6.5. C Coy Left Front Coy — HDQRS. at P12a 8.1.; 3 platoons in sunken road P6 d 6.0.; 1 platoon at P12 b 2.3.; 1 platoon at P6 d 4.3. B Coy Right Support Coy — HDQRS in Saucepit Q13 a 0.0.; 4 platoons in sunken trench from P12 d 6.6. to Q13 centre. A Coy Left Support Coy — HDQRS and 4 platoons in trenches at Q13 a 5.5. Coy Canine Highlanders — HDQRS and 4 platoons about P18 a 0.8. — Counter-attack Company. Battn Hdqrs. at P12 c 7.3 Recourt Wood; Battn Hdqrs on Right in Recourt Chateau; Battn Hdqrs on left — P.11 a 8.1.	ref
30/8th			The battalion in the line. During the night there was much activity.	ref

J. A. de Moleur LIEUT. COLONEL
Commanding 1st Bn The Black ...

Army Form C. 2118.

WAR DIARY
or
INTELLIGENCE SUMMARY.
(Erase heading not required.)

REF. MAP SHEET 51B 1/40,000
SHEET 62C 1/40,000

Instructions regarding War Diaries and Intelligence Summaries are contained in F. S. Regs., Part II. and the Staff Manual respectively. Title pages will be prepared in manuscript.

Place	Date	Hour	Summary of Events and Information	Remarks and references to Appendices
			batalion On 7th Sept 2/Lt C.I.SUTHERLAND crossed RIVER SENSEE and carried out a close reconnaissance of HAMEL.	
	8TH/9TH		The battn. was relieved in the line by 2/LONDONS; bivouaced on the ARRAS-CAMBRAI ROAD WEST of VIS-EN-ARTOIS; and went back to be in accommodated in "Y" Huts on the ARRAS-ST POL ROAD near MARŒUIL	Att
	9TH		The battn. in "Y" HUTS	Att
	10TH	8AM	The battn. entrained at MARŒUIL; detrained at MARCELCAVE, and marched to the MORCOURT AREA Battn Hdqrs was established in the valley about ½ Kilomtr S.W. of MORCOURT CHURCH.	Att
	11TH/12TH		The battn. at MORCOURT	Att
	13TH		The battn. embraced on the MORCOURT - PROYART ROAD at 7.30A.M. and proceeded to an area near MONTECOURT. about ½ central Battn Hdqrs was established at the NORTHERN end of FOX COPSE On the evening of the 13th, BRIG-GEN H.P.EVANS V.C. D.S.O. commanding 114TH Infantry Brigade, visited the battalion	Att
	14TH	10AM	The battn. moved forwards to an area EAST of TERTRY. "A" Coy was disposed about Q33 d.1.4.; "B" Coy about Q34 d.3.5.; "C" Coy about Q33 a.6.2.; "D" Coy about Q34 central. Battn. Headquarters was established at Q33 d.5.8.	Att
	15TH		In consequence of a further advance on the part of the troops in the line	Att

J. Anderson LIEUT. COLONEL
Commanding, 1st Bn, The Black Watch

WAR DIARY
or
INTELLIGENCE SUMMARY.

(Erase heading not required.)

Army Form C. 2118.

Ref. MAP SHEET 62cSW 1/20,000

Place	Date	Hour	Summary of Events and Information	Remarks and references to Appendices
	16TH		resulting in the capture of MAISSEMY, the battn. again advanced to an area SOUTH-WEST of VERMAND. "A" and "C" Coys. were disposed in the valley in R.32.c; "B" and "D" Coys in the valley in X.1.b; Battn. Headquarters was established at R.32.c.0.0. A reconnaissance of the ground was carried out as far as the WESTERN outskirts of HOLNON WOOD, with a view to consolidating at batth in bogus reasons for an attack which was to be launched at a later date. At 6 p.m. the batth. moved up from VERMAND and occupied the old trenches in X.3.b and X.4.a east C. Batth. Hdqrs. was established at X.10.a.9.4.	diff.
	17TH		The battn. remained in same position. The day was fairly quiet with the exception of some scattered shelling which inflicted a few casualties.	diff.
	18TH		At 6 A.M. Battn. Hdqrs. moved up to X.4.a.2.8. At 9.30 A.M. the battn. advanced in artillery formation and at 11 A.M. deployed, digging in as follows: — "A" Coy - R.35.a; "B" Coy - R.30.a; "C" Coy - R.29.c; D Coy - R.29.c and R.35.a.; Battn. Hdqrs. was established in old British trench at R.29.a.3.5. At 8 P.M. A Coy was sent up to reinforce CAMERON HIGHLANDERS in VILLEMAY TRENCH about M.30.8.7.6.; D Coy followed A Coy at 11 P.M.	L.P.

L. Anderson LIEUT. COLONEL
Commanding, 1st Bn. The Black Watch

WAR DIARY
or
INTELLIGENCE SUMMARY.
(Erase heading not required.)

Army Form C. 2118.

REF. MAP SHEET MAISSEMY 1/20,000

Place	Date	Hour	Summary of Events and Information	Remarks and references to Appendices
	19TH		"B" Coy and "C" Coys advanced to positions on the sunken road in R.25.d and R.30.a, and at 6.15 p.m. Battn Hdqrs moved up to ESSLING ALLEY at R.24.c.3.0.	
			At 6 am the battalion less "A" and "D" Companies moved up to assembly positions in FOURMOY ALLEY, M.11.d. and M.13.c. with a view to capturing SAMPSON TRENCH from its junction with BRIENT TRENCH at M.16.a & 7. to M.18.c. & the trench junction at M.16.a.4.7. while "D" Coy was allotted the task of securing and holding the trench junction at M.21.b. & 8. The RIGHT bombed its way up ESSLING ALLEY to secure the trench junction at M.21.b. & 8. An hour later "C" Coy was detailed to go through "B" Coy to secure and to take the trench junctions at M.16.c.75.65 and M.16.c.5.5. It was understood from information received that the enemy was disorganized and was not holding these positions in strength. The operation was unsuccessful seen in its opening phases. Capt P.H.K. COLQUHOUN M.C. Comdg "B" Coy was killed by a sniper as he was forming out the objective on the ground to his platoon commanders. Lieut: R.G. GALBRAITH assumed command, and at 9 am "B" Coy attempted again the sunken road at M.15.c.2.9 along the trench towards MUGUET WOOD. Almost immediately the enemy counterattacked in considerable strength from MUGUET WOOD, and from the trench about M.15 central inte.	

J. Anderson LIEUT. COLONEL
Commanding 1st Bn. The Black Watch

WAR DIARY or INTELLIGENCE SUMMARY

Army Form C. 2118.

REF. MAP SHEET. 62B S.W. 1/20,000

Place	Date	Hour	Summary of Events and Information	Remarks and references to Appendices
			bombed "B" Coy from in front and from the flank. At this particular point, FOURMOY ALLEY was about 8 feet deep, and there was no firestep, so that "B" Coy was at a serious disadvantage, but the situation was saved by the keen sense of "C" Coy which broke the enemy counterattack and enabled "B" Coy to withdraw. In the first instance six wounded including LIEUT R.G. GALBRAITH were left in the trench beyond the road, but 2/Lt H.H. Smith immediately organised a rescue party, which succeeded in bringing in all the wounded. Unfortunately 2/Lieut SMITH was killed in the attempt. Meanwhile "D" Coy on the RIGHT had advanced up to M.15.c.5.0, but in view of the strength of the enemy instructions were issued to withdraw and to establish a bombing block at M.21.a.0.8. Later information proved that the enemy had been reinforced opposite our front, by two fresh divisions.	
19/20th			A line of forward posts was established from M.15.c.3.9 through M.15.c.0.3 to M.21.a.0.8. While the posts were being established, a 77mm anti-tank gun, well camouflaged, was discovered at M.15.c.0.3.	dd.
20/21st			The front was extended to the RIGHT, and posts were established at M.20.B.6.4	dd.

J.R. Clement COLONEL

Commanding 1st Bn, The Black Watch

WAR DIARY
or
INTELLIGENCE SUMMARY.
(Erase heading not required.)

Army Form C. 2118.

2nd B.S.W. 62

Ref. Map Sheet 62B.S.W. 1/20,000.

Place	Date	Hour	Summary of Events and Information	Remarks and references to Appendices
			at M20 b 8 1 and at M20 d 7 4, in order to cover the valley in M20 c and d. Battn. Hdqrs. was established at M14 c 6 2; C Coy at M14 d 3 3; D Coy at M20 b 8 7; "A" Coy at M20 b 6 9 while B. Coy remained in support with Coy HDQRs at M14 d 2 3	A.A.
	20/23RD		The battn. in the line. The front was fairly quiet with the exception that the enemy appears to be very nervous of attack, and carried out a heavy counter- preparation bombardment of all valley and possible assembly positions in the area, daily at "stand-to" morning and evening	
	24TH	4 A.M	The 2/ROYAL SUSSEX. REGT. assembled for an attack and the battn was withdrawn to VERMAND with the exception of certain forward posts detailed to cover the assembly. Very heavy fire was encountered in the valley in M19 b during the withdrawal, and fortunately only twelve casualties were sustained. The garrisons of the forward posts joined the battn. in VERMAND about 6 A.M.	A.A.
	24/26TH		The battn. at VERMAND. "A" Coy at R31 b 6 0; "B" Coy at R31 b 9 2; "C" Coy at R31 b 5 3; "D" Coy at R31 b 3 5; Battn. Hdqrs at R31 b 6 4.	d.t.
	26TH	6PM	The battn. moved off from VERMAND to relieve the 8TH Battn. SHERWOOD FORESTERS in the line in front of PONTRUET On completion of relief on	A.A.

J. Anderson LIEUT. COLONEL
Commanding 2nd The Royal Welch.

WAR DIARY
or
INTELLIGENCE SUMMARY. Ref. Map Sheet. 62BSW 1/20000

Army Form C. 2118.

Place	Date	Hour	Summary of Events and Information	Remarks and references to Appendices
	26/11		our dispositions were as follows :— "A" Coy HDQRS near "T" of BERTHAUCOURT; 2 Platoons near Coy HDQRS; 1 Platoon in HEDUC TRENCH; "D" Coy HDQRS and 3 Platoons in BEUX TRENCH; 1 Platoon at M.9.a.3.2.; C. Coy. in M.13.d.; B. Coy. and Battn HDQRS in M.13.b. Patrols that returned from 8/SHERWOODS. showed that PONTRUET was strongly held by the enemy.	2.A.
			As a result of our observation during the night 26th/27th it was decided that	A.B.
	27/11		PONTRUET VILLAGE was not held in strength by the enemy, and it was determined to occupy the village by peaceful penetration. At 2pm 2/LIEUT W.B. WEBSTER with Sgt J DAVIE and 2 battn scouts moved forward from M.9.a.3.4. through M.9. central to the CEMETERY and the CRUCIFIX thence along PALARIC TRENCH to road at M.9.b.9.1. The patrol was turned by heavy guns and sniper in HEDUC TRENCH. The village was found to be unoccupied and one platoon of D Coy moved up to trenches PALARIC TRENCH N.W. of M.9.b.9.1. while one platoon of A Coy occupied PALARIC TRENCH from M.9.b.9.1. to its junction with BRIENT TRENCH where touch was established with 1/NORTHAMPTONS. One wounded prisoner remained in our hands.	

J. Antide
LIEUT. COLONEL.
Commanding 1st Bn Black Watch.

WAR DIARY
or
INTELLIGENCE SUMMARY.
(Erase heading not required.)

Army Form C. 2118.

Place	Date	Hour	Summary of Events and Information	Remarks and references to Appendices
	28TH	5AM	Forward posts were established at M10.a.2.8, M10.a.5.5 and M10 central. Strong line of posts with M16.b.8.5 and M13.d.8.6 already established.	A.A.
	29TH	5AM	The Bath. attacked with the object of forming a defensive flank to the 118TH DIV. which was covering the ST QUENTIN CANAL, NORTH of BELLENGLISE. 1/4 NORTH LANCS co-operated on the left; 1/5 WELSH BORDERERS co-operated on the RIGHT. The attack was to be launched on a 3-company front — A Coy on the RIGHT, D Coy in the CENTRE, C Coy on the LEFT. "B" Coy remained in support in M13.b. Each company was to attack with 2 platoons in the line and 2 platoons in support and assaulting platoons was to be assembled along the line of the advanced posts from M10.d.3.3. to M13.b.4.0. by 4.30AM. Objectives and boundaries were as shown on attached map. Owing to the concentration of our artillery on the area NORTH of the canal, the GREEN objective had to be secured with the assistance of STOKES MORTARS and M.G. fire only. At ZERO hour, 5AM, each company pushed forward 2 LEWIS GUNS to cover the advance of the assaulting platoons, and at 4.30AM the latter moved forward. There was a dense mist which was intensified by smoke shell on the high ground SOUTH of the canal.	A.A.

J. Anderson LIEUT. COLONEL
Commanding 1st Bn. The Black Watch.

WAR DIARY or INTELLIGENCE SUMMARY

Army Form C. 2118.

(Erase heading not required.)

that owing it impossible to see more than a few yards. The assaulting troops reached the first objective in spite of bursts of MG fire which had to be met by hand but they were confronted by the mud and in many cases the flanks of the assaulting platoons were in the air. No 16 Platoon seemed to press on in the war the whole party was completed to withdraw and reformed on the assembly positions

At 11.30 A.M. the second attack and the attack on the GREEN OBJECTIVE was apparently resumed. FORGAN'S TRENCH was captured with about 50 prisoners, and the attack was carried to the RED objective, which yielded another 50 prisoners. About 2.30 P.M. the final objective (BROWN) was reached and companies consolidated along the line of the road in M30a. 9 M12 a.

Meantime the enemy was still holding out in FAUCILLE TRENCH on the right of our attack. About 5 P.M. the leading companies again attacked with the object of securing the line of the HINACOURT — THORIGNY ROAD from N.7. c. 8.0. to the CANAL. The attack was carried out by "C" and "D" Coys along the low ground SOUTH of the CANAL, while A Coy advanced on the BROWN objective to protect the right flank. During the attack, very many M.G. fire was brought to bear on the attacking troops from the high ground to the SOUTH, which was still strongly held by the enemy.

L. A. Henderson LIEUT: COLONEL
Commanding 1st Bn. The Black Watch

WAR DIARY
or
INTELLIGENCE SUMMARY.
(Erase heading not required.)

Army Form C 2118.

Place	Date	Hour	Summary of Events and Information	Remarks and references to Appendices
	29TH		and the attempt was abandoned for the time being "A" "D" and "C" Companies were established on their original position on the BROWN OBJECTIVE with an advanced post at M12.a.7.4. "B" COY was in support in FOREATS TRENCH which Battn H.Q were established at M15.d.5.1. During the day the battalion captured 2 Officers and approximately 150 other ranks. Our casualties amounted to Lieut J.B.STEWART wounded and about 50 other ranks.	J.A.
	30TH	8 AM	The batln again attacked with the object of securing the high ground from TALANA HILL (inclusive) to the CANAL. The advance was covered by an artillery barrage. The operation was entirely successful and by 8.35 A.M. the 1st OBJECTIVE — * BLUE — running NORTH from N7.c.8.0. to the CANAL — had been secured together with 1 Officer * 80 other ranks prisoners — and the attacking troops were pressing on to the final objective * The final objective was also secured with many more prisoners and consolidation began. Touch was established with the H.L.I. of 32ND DIVN on the left at the TUNNEL EXIT at N8.b.3.2. and with the 3RD Bde on the right at TALANA HILL.	* BLUE * YELLOW
	89/30TH		During the course of these operations many prisoners and much material was	J.A.

L. Mc..... LIEUT. COLONEL
Commanding, 1st. c... The *Black Watch*.

WAR DIARY
or
INTELLIGENCE SUMMARY.
(Erase heading not required.)

Army Form C. 2118.

Place	Date	Hour	Summary of Events and Information	Remarks and references to Appendices

captured. Putts first instance at FORGAN'S TRENCH, the enemy offered a very stiff

resistance to our advance, and it was not until he was outmanoeuvred and

recaptured the situation that our troops that he began to surrender.

During the period of 48 hours, the following personnel and material was captured:—

Six Officers.   9 FIELD GUNS.   2 ANTI-TANK GUNS.   20 H.M.Gs.

420 Other ranks.   1 H.V. Gun.   100 L.M.G.s.   4 T.M.s

Together with many rifles, 2 anti-tank rifles, ammunition, equipment, &c.

CASUALTIES

OFFICERS

KILLED — CAPT. P.H. & C. COLQUHOUN. M.C.   19.9.18.
        2/LIEUT. H.H. SMITH   19.9.18.
        LIEUT. W. WHYTE   28.9.18.

WOUNDED — CAPT. R. COOK   3.9.18.
         LIEUT. R.G. GALBRAITH   19.9.18.
         2/LIEUT. L. CLARKE M.C.   19.9.18.
         LIEUT. J.G. STEWART   29.9.18.

Sr. M. Roberson
LIEUT. COLONEL
Commanding, 1st/4th The Black Watch.

Army Form C. 2118.

WAR DIARY
or
INTELLIGENCE SUMMARY.
(Erase heading not required.)

Place	Date	Hour	Summary of Events and Information	Remarks and references to Appendices
			OTHER RANKS — ARRAS FRONT —	
			KILLED WOUNDED DIED OF WOUNDS MISSING	
			ARRAS FRONT. 1 67 3 1	
			ST. QUENTIN FRONT (29TH) 15. 113 6 13	
			ST. QUENTIN FRONT (24/30) 5. 65 1 6	
			TOTAL. 21 245 9 19.	
			REINFORCEMENTS.	
			Officers Lieut A MARSHALL M.C. — 8.9.18	
			Lieut I K HIGGINBOTHAM — 8.9.18	
			2/Lieut A MACNEILL — 29.9.18	
			Other Ranks — 32	
			HONOURS AND AWARDS	
			MILITARY MEDAL — No 3049 SGT J DAVIE (signature)	
			LIEUT. COLONEL	
			Commanding 1st Bn. The Black Watch.	

Headquarters,
1st Infantry Brigade.

The attached map
passed to you for disposal
please.

It should have
been attached to the original
copy of the WAR DIARY
for OCTOBER submitted to
you in the first week of
November.

The omission is
regretted.

L. Anderson
Lieut Col.
Cmdg. 1st Bn. The Black Watch

3.²/18.

HEADQUARTERS 1st BRIGADE
Date 4/12/18

1st R. Highlanders
Appx VC 51

H.Q.,
1st Div. "Q"

Forwarded

H. Darlington Capt
for Brig. Genl.
4/12/18. Commanding 1st Inf. Bde.

HEADQUARTERS
No.
Date
9313

D.a.6.

Forwarded

[signature]

Major General
Commanding
1st Div.

8/12/18

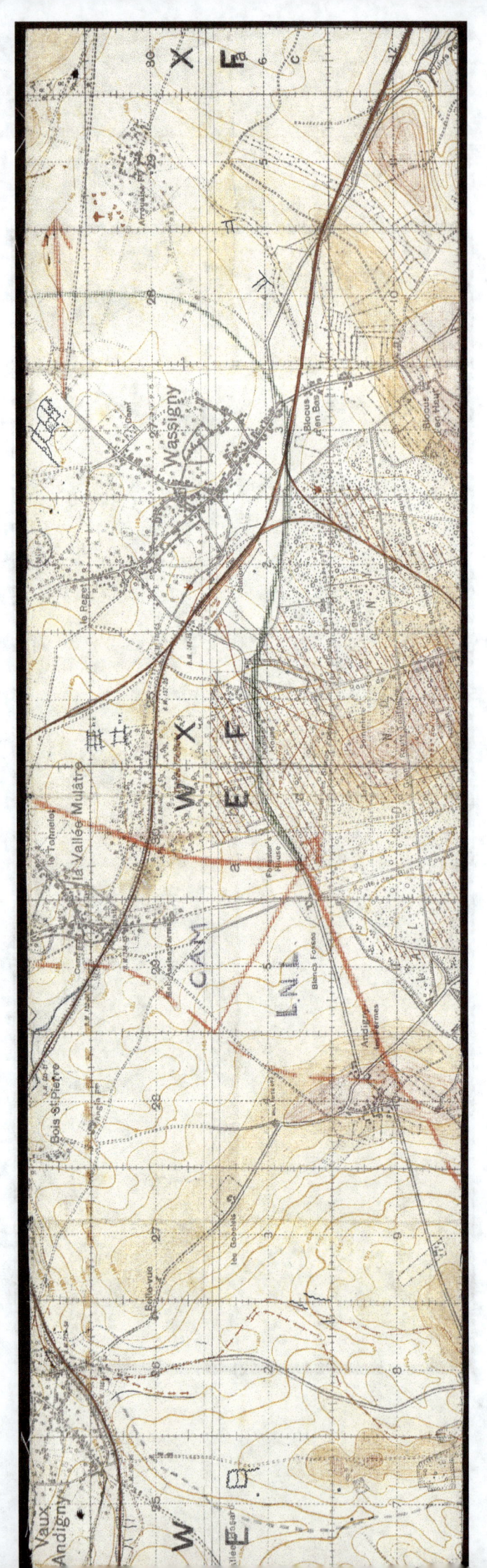

1st THE BLACK WATCH.   APPENDIX "A"

OPERATIONS from 17th to 24th September 1918.

On 17th Sept. 1918 the Battalion was accommodated in system of trenches about 1,500 yards North of ATTILLY with Headquarters about 500 yards North of this place.

The Valley between Headquarters and the Battalion was occupied by many 60 Pdrs. but except for a certain amount of Gas shells necessitating masks being worn, and one unlucky shell which killed a cook and damaged a cooker the Battalion enjoyed a peaceful time.

About midnight 16/17th there was a heavy thunderstorm which interfered with rest.

On the morning of the 17th Company Commanders, Battalion Scouts and Observers carried out reconnaissance.

On 18th September Battalion H.Q. moved to X.4.a.2.8.

At 9-0 a.m. Battalion moved forward in Artillery formation according to orders to the Area R.29. where Companies dug in and Headquarters were established at R.29.a.3.5.

At 2-0 p.m. two Companies were ordered to establish positions on MAISSEMY Road about 1,000 yards South of MAISSEMY.

At 2-0 p.m. the C.O. reported at Brigade H.Q. and received instructions to send forward 1 Company with orders to report to 1st Cameron Hrs Headquarters at the junction of FOURMOY ALLEY and VILLEMAY Trench.

A Company was detailed for this purpose and was moving forward at 2-45 p.m. being led by an Officer who had been forward to reconnoitre and establish liaison with 1st Cameron Hrs.

At 2-15 p.m. a further Company was ordered to report to 1st Cameron Hrs.

A Company was therefore ordered to move forward.

At 5-0 p.m. orders were received detailing Battalion Headquarters to be established on the MAISSEMY - HOLNON Road which was immediately complied with, and Headquarters were established at R.24.c.2.0.

At about 8-0 p.m. the C.O. was ordered to attend a Conference at Brigade Headquarters, at which arrangements and plans were made for the capture of the RED Objective which had not been reached on the 18th.

The method of attack can be briefly described as follows:-

'B' Coy. to advance along FOURMOY ALLEY and capture system of trenches in R.16.a. which would be bombarded from 9-0 a.m. till 10-0 a.m.

'C' Coy. would follow 'A' Coy and capture system of trenches in R.16.c. which would be bombarded from 10-0 a.m. till 11-0 a.m.

'D' Coy would assemble in ESSLING ALLEY and capture junction of trenches in R.21.b. this place being bombarded from 9-0 a.m. till 10-0 a.m.

O.C. 1st Cameron Hrs. undertook to issue verbal instructions to 'D' Coy. which had been attached to him.

Instructions were given verbally to O.C. 'B' and 'C' Coys. at 11-0 p.m.

Casualties amounted to six due to shell fire on the 18th.
The night of 18th/19th was again wet.

19th Sept.   At 6-0 a.m. the Battalion, less 'A' and 'D' Coys., moved forward from the Sunken Road S.E. of MAISSEMY in the order 'B' Coy., 'C' Coy., Battalion Hd. Qrs., through MAISSEMY and along the Sunken Road running N.E. through that Village to FOURMOY ALLEY at M.14.c.4.2

Battalion H.Q. was established in conjunction with the Headquarters of the 1st Cameron Hrs. at M.14.c.4.4.   The 2 Coys. filed up FOURMOY ALLEY to the assembly positions in M.15.c.

The Commanding Officer went forward with Captain COLQUHOUN, M.C., Commanding 'B' Coy to point out on the ground the objectives of the attack, then returned to 'C' Coy. to point out the objectives to Captain DUNCAN.

Almost immediately it was reported from 'B' Coy. that Captain COLQUHOUN had been sniped through the head. Lieut. R.G. GALBRAITH assumed command of 'B' Coy. and at 8-0 a.m. the advance was continued across the Sunken Road in M.15.c.

It had been reported that the enemy was very weak, and little or no opposition was anticipated, but as soon as the leading Company had passed the Sunken Road described above the enemy Counter-attacked in considerable strength from the direction of MUGUET Wood and up the Sunken Road.

'B' Coy. was at a serious disadvantage as the trench was 7 to 8 feet deep at the point where it was attacked, and there were no firesteps.

The Company was bombed from in front and from the rear, but 'C' Coy. Lewis Guns saved the situation and broke the counter-attacking party, and enabled 'B' Coy. to withdraw.

There were approximately 50 casualties, and in the first instance six wounded, including Lieut. R.G. GALBRAITH, were left West of the Sunken Road.

2nd Lieut. H.H. SMITH immediately organised rescue party, which succeeded in bringing in all the wounded. The rescue party was bombed and 2nd Lt. SMITH was killed.

Meantime, 'D' Coy. was bombing its way down ESSLING ALLEY and reached a point about M.15.c.4.0.

In view of the strength of the enemy instructions were issued not to continue the advance, and to establish a bombing block at M.21.a.0.7.

On the night of the 19th and 20th a line of forward posts was established from M.21.a.0.7. through M.15.c.0.3. to M.15.c.0.5. to M.15.c.2.7. and M.15.c.2.9.

On the night of the 20th/21st, the 1st L.North Lancs. were withdrawn and our Line was extended to the right, to the Brigade boundary about M.20.d.5.3.

Three forward posts were established covering the Valley, at M.20.d.5.3., M.20.d.5.8. and M.20.b.6.4. respectively.

Throughout the 21st, 22nd and 23rd there was nothing worthy of record beyond the fact that the enemy appeared to be very nervous of an attack, and bombarded all assembly positions and Valleys in the Battalion Area, throughout the hours of darkness and particularly at dawn.

At 4-0 a.m. on the 24th the Battalion was withdrawn to VERMAND with the exception of certain posts established to cover the assembly of Battalions on 2nd Brigade.

During the withdrawal the Valley in M.19.b. was heavily shelled and 12 casualties were sustained by 'B' Coy.

The posts mentioned above were withdrawn at 4-30 a.m. and rejoined the Battalion in VERMAND about 9-30 a.m.

The total casualties for the period amounted to:-

<u>OFFICERS</u>   Killed = Captain P.H.L.C. COLQUHOUN, M.C.
                         2nd Lt. H.H. SMITH.

            Wounded = Lt. R.G. GALBRAITH.
                         2nd Lt. L. CLARKE, M.C.

<u>OTHER RANKS</u>.Killed = 14. Died of Wounds = 5.
               Wounded = 113. Missing = 15.

****

CONFIDENTIAL

Army Form C.2118.

WAR DIARY
INTELLIGENCE SUMMARY.

(Erase heading not required.)

Instructions regarding War Diaries and Intelligence Summaries are contained in F.S. Regs., Part II. and the Staff Manual respectively. Title pages will be prepared in manuscript.

1R. W. Fus. Vol 51 Oct 5/

Place	Date	Hour	Summary of Events and Information	Remarks and references to Appendices
	SEPT. 30TH	6.30PM	The battn. was relieved in the line by the 2nd Bn. The WELCH REGIMENT and withdrew. The following dispositions was assumed :- "A" Coy. M12 B 5.0; "B" Coy. TRENCH at M12 B.9.9; "C" Coy. FOURTIER TRENCH; "D" Coy - FILET TRENCH; Battn. Hdqrs. moved at M12 B.3.0 where they had been established during the afternoon.	2A
	OCTOBER 1ST.	14.00	The battn. moved EAST of the CANAL into BRIGADE RESERVE. After the move was completed our dispositions were as follows :- Battn. Hdqrs. in the TUNNEL EXIT at N.2.C.95.35 with the personnel of Battn. Hdqrs. in dug-out bays in the TUNNEL. "A" Coy. round the limit sails in N.2.d.; "B" Coy. in the TUNNEL about the Bn. Hdqrs. at N.2.d.5.9; "C" Coy. in the gun pits about N.2.b.2.2; "D" Coy. in dug-outs along the CANAL BANK about N.2.d.6.6. The men were carried on without interference from enemy artillery, and in all cases the accommodation was good.	
	2ND		On relief 15 mitre were fd. the accommodation of a Battalion Hdqrs. of the FRENCH DIVISION on our RIGHT. It was found necessary to move "A" Coy. HDQRS and 1 platoon to the system of trenches about N.2.c.50. Otherwise our dispositions remain unchanged	2A 5E 2A 5E

2 Lieutenant M.A.

WAR DIARY
INTELLIGENCE SUMMARY
(Erase heading not required.)

Army Form C 2118.

Place	Date	Hour	Summary of Events and Information	Remarks and references to Appendices
	3RD		Orders were received to relieve the 1st Bn. Cameron Highlanders and the 1st Bn. 4. North hants. in the line, and at 18.00 hours the Battn. marched to their relief. The work had been previously reconnoitred by an officer and 2 runners per company, and the relief proceeded quickly. Very heavy hostile fire, including H.E. and gas, was encountered in the valley N.W. of FLECHE WOOD. but fortunately only 9 casualties were sustained including 8 gas casualties. At 22.10 hours the relief was complete and our dispositions were as follows. — "B" Coy — RIGHT FRONT COMPANY.— 1 platoon about N5.a.0.4., 1 platoon about N4.b.8.9.; "D" Coy. — LEFT FRONT COMPANY — 1 platoon round the copse about N5.a.0.5.; 1 platoon about H35.c.65.50; 1 platoon about H35.c.0.5.; 1 platoon about H34.d.75.65. "B" Coy. and "D" Coy. HDQRS. were established together at H34.d.30.05. "C" Coy was in support along the line of the sunken road from N4.a.7.3. to H34.c.8.0.; "A" Coy was in reserve in ECURIE TRENCH WEST. of the sunken road in N4.a. Battn. HDQRS. was established at N3.b.45.7.x.	

J. Atherton
Lt.

WAR DIARY

INTELLIGENCE SUMMARY.

(Erase heading not required.)

Army Form C. 2118.

Place	Date	Hour	Summary of Events and Information	Remarks and references to Appendices
	4TH		Whilst the above relief was in progress, instructions were received that the battalion would be relieved in the course of the night by a battalion of FRENCH infantry. At 01.00 hrs the relief began. There was some delay but at 06.10 hrs the relief was complete and the battalion withdrew to the area previously occupied on the 30/31st in M.13 a, b and c. At 14.00 the battalion again moved back and was finally accommodated in the ORCHARD S.W of the CEMETERY in VERMAND at 17.00 hours.	S.A. S.A.
	7TH		The Divnl. COMMANDER addressed the battalion on parade, and expressed his appreciation of the work which had been carried out by the battalion during the trying phase of operations, and of the month which had been achieved by this relation, and the duration is duty of all ranks.	S.A. S.A.
	5TH/9TH		The battalion at VERMAND — company training was carried out daily.	S.A.
	9TH		At 12.00 hours the battalion paraded and marched to an area about 300 yards North of ST HELENE near PONTRUET, via BIHÉCOURT and VADENCOURT.	S.A.
	9TH/10TH		The battn. remained in the area near ST HELENE. During the period	S.A.

WAR DIARY
INTELLIGENCE SUMMARY

Army Form C. 2118.

Place	Date	Hour	Summary of Events and Information	Remarks and references to Appendices
			Finning was carried out to the first of the battles which were fought by the Battalion the with such success East of PONTRUET on the 29TH and 30TH days of September, and the various phases of the battle was re-enacted. Nearly 200 reinforcements from SALONIKA, from the 10TH Batt. had been received during the first days of October, and this training both met valuable first in succeeding operations.	
	16TH		The battn. marched to BOHAIN via BELLENGLISE, BEVERGIES, SEBOURG HART, FRESNOY and occupied billets in the WESTERN outskirts of the town.	2.A.
	17TH		At 0.3.00 hrs. the Battalion moved off in the following order from BOHAIN — "A" "B" "C" "D" "Bn. HQRs." — the road to the assembly position was carefully policed by scouts — there was no traffic which interfered with the approach march and the assembly formed without a hitch. The ASSEMBLY AREA was EAST of BECQUIGNY, about V.29.c. (Ry Map Sheet MASSIGNY 1/40,000) The Assembly was complete at 05.15. hours. The advance in ARTILLERY FORMATION to the area round W.86.c. was commenced at 05.40 which was 10 minutes after ZERO, thus	2.A.

J Anderson Lt/C

WAR DIARY
INTELLIGENCE SUMMARY.
(Erase heading not required.)

Army Form C. 2118.

allowed the Leading Battalions of the BRIGADE, "Camron Highlanders on the WEST, and "Royal North" hence on the RIGHT to get forward. Fog and smoke rendered the advance very difficult and the use of the compass by some platoon commanders enabled the advance to be carried out promptly and with rapidity. The road running through W.25 central was used as an intermediate assembly position. The advance from W.25's central to W.26 a was rendered difficult owing to heavy shell fire and M.G. fire from BELLE VUE W.26.b.8.0. (Ry. Map Sheet ANDIGNY FOREST 1/20,000). This position which was strongly held was reached the attention of the 6TH DIVN which were the leading DIVN of the CORPS, and was responsible for capturing and holding the RED DOTTED OBJECTIVE. (See attached map). At 11.30 hrs the Battn moved forward to the area immediately EAST of ANGIN FARM, Inspired which no further advance was carried out, and Battn HDQRS. was established at the cross-tracks, 200 yards WEST of ANGIN FARM, W.28 a.3.9.
During the running instructions were received that the battalion would attack S.E.

J.J. Anderson Lt Col.

WAR DIARY
of
INTELLIGENCE SUMMARY.
(Erase heading not required.)

Army Form C. 2118.

Place	Date	Hour	Summary of Events and Information	Remarks and references to Appendices
	18TH		on the following day in conjunction with the 1st Cameron Highlanders on the RIGHT, and the 3RD INF. BDE. on the LEFT, with the object of capturing WASSIGNY. ZERO hour was fixed at 11.30 hours and the attack was entirely successful.	
			OBJECTIVES and BOUNDARIES was as shown on the attached map.	
			"A" Coy was ordered to cross the railway at LA VALLEE MULATRE and to advance with their right on the railway as far as X25.b.80. They then becoming responsible for capturing the NORTHERN portion of WASSIGNY.	
			"D" Coy was ordered to follow the line of the railway as far as X25.b.8.0. which found the railway was to be crossed and then continuing the advance with their right on the railway, they were held responsible for the capture of the SOUTHERN portion of WASSIGNY.	
			"B" Coy was ordered to move in close support to "A" and "D" Coys. with the additional object of forming a defensive flank, facing SOUTH, along the railway from X26c to F3d., finding touch being established with the FRENCH at BLOCUS D'EN BAS.	2ft
				J Alderson 1st

Army Form C. 2118.

WAR DIARY
or
INTELLIGENCE SUMMARY.
(Erase heading not required.)

Instructions regarding War Diaries and Intelligence Summaries are contained in F. S. Regs., Part II. and the Staff Manual respectively. Title pages will be prepared in manuscript.

Place	Date	Hour	Summary of Events and Information	Remarks and references to Appendices
			"C" Coy was held in RESERVE and was instructed not to move forward without orders, but to hold itself in readiness to move to the area round MAL-ASSISE FARM.	
			At 11.00 hours "A" and "D" Coys commenced their advance in artillery formation, in order to follow close behind our Barrage, which was arranged to fall immediately beyond the RED line through W.30 and E.6a.	
			At 11.45 hours our troops were advancing rapidly, overcoming all opposition. Several prisoners were captured, and one machine-gun with which offered some resistance yielded up FIVE Officers and 18 other ranks.	
			At 18.15 hours it was observed that the assaulting companies were still vigorously pressing their attack, advancing close under our artillery barrage, and indeed materially supported by the concentration of M.G. fire on strong points of resistance. They had reached the WESTERN outskirts of the village and were in close touch with the 2ND WALES REGT on their LEFT.	
			The enemy made a vain effort to stay our advance on the enemy Left.	

J Roberson Lt Col.

Army Form C. 2118.

WAR DIARY
or
INTELLIGENCE SUMMARY.
(Erase heading not required.)

Instructions regarding War Diaries and Intelligence Summaries are contained in F. S. Regs., Part II. and the Staff Manual respectively. Title pages will be prepared in manuscript.

Place	Date	Hour	Summary of Events and Information	Remarks and references to Appendices
			of the railway West of the village, and again at the STATION and the WESTERN outskirts of the village itself, but the resistance that was offered was quickly overwhelmed and an advance proceeded almost without interruption to the village itself, little resistance was encountered. In one cellar alone 5 officers and 78 other ranks were captured by a drummer Boy. The general had no trouble but the firing of a drum down the slope of the cellar proved equally effective in forcing the surrender of the occupants. D Coy discovered FIVE GERMAN officers at lunch in a cellar. This capture was also commenced. Consolidation on the EASTERN outskirts of the village was established with the immediately and at 17.30 hours, which was established with the FRENCH at BLOCOS D'EN BAS.	
			Batn. Hdqrs and "C" Coy moved forward to MAI-ASSISE F.M. as soon as the enemy held was reported within WASSIGNY. At 17.30 hrs Batn Hdqrs again moved forward with the RESERVE Coy to a system of trenches in X 25 a.	

J. Anderson Lt. Col.

Army Form C. 2118.

WAR DIARY
or
INTELLIGENCE SUMMARY.
(Erase heading not required.)

Instructions regarding War Diaries and Intelligence Summaries are contained in F. S. Regs., Part II. and the Staff Manual respectively. Title pages will be prepared in manuscript.

Place	Date	Hour	Summary of Events and Information	Remarks and references to Appendices
	19th		In accordance with instructions, 'C' Coy carried out an advance in conjunction with the FRENCH on our RIGHT and the 2ND WELCH on our LEFT — the advance commenced at 05.30 h.s.	
			Fog rendered liaison between attacking platoons a matter of extreme difficulty, had the enemy had withdrawn during the night and ARROUAISE FME was occupied without opposition.	
			This completed the operations carried out by the battalion and showed an advance of over 5000 yards in the two days' fighting. The total number of prisoners captured amounted to 30 officers 350 other ranks. The material captured included 1 Field Gun, 5 T.M.s. 13 Lght M.Gs & Heavy M.Gs.	
			Our casualties during the period from 17th to 19th inclusive amounted to :— OFFICERS — Killed – 3 ; WOUNDED – 4. Other ranks — Killed – 12 ; Wounded – 79 ; Missing – 9	
		16.00 hrs	the battalion was withdrawn and was billeted in the village of WASSIGNY. Battn Hdqrs was established at X.26.d.8.2. Int. J Robson Lt Col	

WAR DIARY or INTELLIGENCE SUMMARY

Army Form C. 2118.

Place	Date	Hour	Summary of Events and Information	Remarks and references to Appendices
	20/23rd		The Bn at WASSIGNY:— The Bn indulged in a much needed rest during this period, huts of the line being allotted to the use of men & ammunition.	AA
	23rd		At 16.30 hrs the Bn moved off in the following order from WASSIGNY, Bn HDQRS, C. D. A. & B Coys. The Bn relieved the 2nd Royal Sussex Regt (2nd Bde) in the line, taking over a line of posts which ran — R.17.c.5.1 — 23.a.6.3 — 23.e.6.5 — 29.b.11 — 30.b.2.9 — 35.b.7.1. On the 5/b 35 ½ 20/20
			DISPOSITIONS C + B Coys in the front line from R.17.c.5.1. — 29.a.9.4. D Coy " " " " LA LOUVIÈRE F.M. — 35.b.7.1. B Coy in support around LA LOUVIÈRE F.M. A " Reserve in front of LA HALE TONNOILE F.M.	
			This period in the line was generally quiet. An endeavour was made to ascertain the line by pushing men forward in open fashion but the enemy was found to be about at most points for much progress to be made by this method, however the advance right posts were advanced to points R.28.b.7.4. + R.23.b.8.8. and the right posts to R.36.a.5.9 + R.36.a.6.1. Our patrols was very active and carried out several daring reconnaissances which resulted in much valuable information being obtained with regard to enemy.	AA

L. Roberton Lt Col

Army Form C. 2118.

WAR DIARY
or
INTELLIGENCE SUMMARY.
(Erase heading not required.)

Instructions regarding War Diaries and Intelligence Summaries are contained in F. S. Regs., Part II. and the Staff Manual respectively. Title pages will be prepared in manuscript.

Place	Date	Hour	Summary of Events and Information	Remarks and references to Appendices
	27th		dispositions and strength. On the night of the 27th the Bn was relieved by the 2ND SUSSEX and the 1/NORTHAMPTON Regts (2ND Bde) and withdrew to bivouis at LA VALLÉE MULÂTRE without casualties.	
	28th/31st		The Bn at LA VALLÉE MULÂTRE. — Company and Platoon training carried out. The following casualties occured during the month. Officers Killed. Lt H.H. JALLAND 2/Lt D. SMITH. M.C. D.C.M. } 18-10-18 2/Lt E.W. GYLE. " Wounded. Lt. G.S.M. BURTON M.C. } 17-10-18 " 2/Lt E.R. WILSON M.C. " 2/Lt P.R. FYALL } 18-10-18 " Lt A. MARSHALL M.C. " 2/Lt J.S. CHRISTIE } 25-10-18	

J.R. Jerda Lt.Col.

WAR DIARY
or
INTELLIGENCE SUMMARY.

Army Form C. 2118.

Casualties on 19:
OR. Killed, 19 Wounded 146. Missing 2

The following reinforcements joined the Bn. during the month.
Officers 16.
O.R. 407.

J. Anderson Lt.Col.
Comg. 12th Bn. The Black Watch.

WAR DIARY
or
INTELLIGENCE SUMMARY.

Army Form C. 2118.

(Erase heading not required.)

Crossing of R. OISE - SAMBRE CANAL

Place	Date	Hour	Summary of Events and Information	Remarks and references to Appendices
LA VALLEE - MULATRE	1ST/3RD		The battn. in billets with the Brigade in DIVISIONAL RESERVE	2d
	3RD	20.00	The battn. marched off from LA VALLEE MULÂTRE and arrived in the assembly positions about 23.30 hrs. Digging in was commenced immediately. The route to the assembly positions had been tapped, which was followed by main roads, and then across country to RIBEAUCOURT, near which place, FME. DU MOULIN and FME. DE LA HOUVIERE. were reconnoitred and river guide and company lamps used as follows:—	
			ASSEMBLY POSITIONS — BATTN. HDQRS. in Northern house of LA HOUVIERE. A. COY. — R.35.a.0.0. B. COY. — R.35.b.0.5. C. COY. — R.35.b.1.2. D. COY. — R.35.b.8.0. Attached to the Battalion were:- 1 Section M.G.s. 1 Section of No.1. T.M.B.	
	4TH	04.00	The enemy commenced many counter preparation fire.	
		06.45	At ZERO hour the brigade advanced in the assault. The 23RD Field Coy R.E. quickly constructed bridges, and	

J. Anderson Lt Col
CMDG 1st Bn. The Black Watch

WAR DIARY
or
INTELLIGENCE SUMMARY.

Army Form C. 2118.

(Erase heading not required.)

Place	Date	Hour	Summary of Events and Information	Remarks and references to Appendices

—and the 1st Bn. Cameron Highlanders with the 1st Bn. N. Staff. having crossed the OISE – SAMBRE CANAL, and continued the attack.

At 07.30 hours, "B" and "C" Companies advanced across the CANAL, followed by "D" Coy., Batn HDQRS. and "A" Coy. to the 2ND ASSEMBLY POSITION along the HAUTREVE – CATILLON ROAD. "B" Coy., in the process of their advance, mopped up 10 of the enemy in the house at M.36.d.4.4.; "C" Coy was compelled to organise an attack in order to capture the house at M.37.a.4.0. which was strongly held. The position was rapidly taken, but 3 officers and 50 other ranks were captured. LIEUT H. Nilsson, D.C.M. Commanding "C" Coy. was wounded by a M.G. during the advance. Companies were formed up ready to attack from the 2ND Assembly Position at the following hours.

"D" COMPANY on RIGHT at 08.35 hours.
"E" COMPANY in CENTRE at 09.20 hours.
"B" COMPANY on LEFT at 09.30 hours.

"B" COMPANY on LEFT at 09.30 hours advanced beyond the BLUE DOTTED line and drew fire at 09.32 and was enveloped at first but later it became ragged, and stood with the result that many finish – Masters AA

J. Anderson LIEUT. COL.
C.O./D/G. 1st. Bn. The Black Watch

WAR DIARY
or
INTELLIGENCE SUMMARY

Army Form C. 2118.

prisoners who would otherwise have been captured, were unable to walk
about the swamp. "D" Coy on the right in touch with the CAMERON HIGHLANDERS, passed on through the Southern houses of BOYAU DE HEU and advanced on PETIT GALOP the other difficulties the FARMS of GRAND GALOP and PETIT GALOP the only difficulty the experience was H.G. fire from the Right flank, from the overhead of as the men around M.G. at 5' A platoon was detached from "B" [Coy?] to deal with (this was situated on the flank. As the advance was continued forward from GD GALOP FERME) In chasing were observed "running" from the farm they were fired on when some also issued than fell when were observed "running" from the garrison field of GD GALOP. The defenders had retreated behind the first position of PETIT FARM were captured Our troops reached the position, others had been killed battery and the 11/38 hours and two officers and ten other ranks had the remaining garrison of Our Officer, and ten other ranks had the remainder of the garrison of the HILLMAN HOUSE and THE IRON CROSS by when they attempted to retaliate. PETIT GALOP FERME, would not second it had been detached to assist FIRE by second of the enemy at the 4/7 mm guns were taken
completion after a short fight.
W.L. Read Tony Prisoners and war

J. Anderson LIEUT COL

CMDG. 1st Bn. The Black Watch

WAR DIARY
or
INTELLIGENCE SUMMARY.

(Erase heading not required.)

Army Form C. 2118.

Place	Date	Hour	Summary of Events and Information	Remarks and references to Appendices
			A resolute party of the enemy still held out about M29c.7.9 and efforts to dislodge them failed; later a T.M. was brought up and 50 rounds were fired. The enemy was thrown back, but he took up a second position which had been previously constructed, and he continued to snipe and fire with M.G.s along the road leading in a North-Westerly direction to GRAND GALOP FME. 2 VICKERS GUNS were then brought up to protect our Right flank and 2 platoons of the Reserve Company carried out a reconnaissance and manned in readiness to counter attack in this direction, if necessary. As soon as GD GALOP FME was captured, Riflemen were cut off and fired at the enemy whenever they attempted, as they advanced to new positions. Efforts were also made to cut off our breaks in the line. One NCO and another were captured by the enemy reconnoitring patrol, but our others made good their escape. Our old civilian was found returning to GD GALOP FME, "C" COMPANY advanced on BOYAU DE NEU, from SWAN NORTHWARDS with its LEFT on the LA GROISE – LANDRECIES ROAD. Very little opposition was encountered till the horses about M.22 contg. where the enemy offered a stiff resistance and backed. At this point the many efforts and all honours to	

12.15 hours

L. Aderon Lieut. Col.
1st Bn. The Black Watch.
C.M.B.G.

Army Form C. 2118.

WAR DIARY
or
INTELLIGENCE SUMMARY.
(Erase heading not required.)

Instructions regarding War Diaries and Intelligence Summaries are contained in F. S. Regs., Part II. and the Staff Manual respectively. Title pages will be prepared in manuscript.

Place	Date	Hour	Summary of Events and Information	Remarks and references to Appendices
			with finally in our hands. Beyond this however, the enemy continued to hold the line of the stream astride the main road, and he poured an accurate and heavy fire from MGs on all forward exits from the village. The 32ND. DIVN. was attacking on our LEFT. No signs of it could be observed, so further attempts to advance to the road junction at M 22.b.9.9. were abandoned. "B" Coy. on the LEFT, in touch with "C" Coy. on their RIGHT, advanced behind the barrage, and encountered little resistance until reaching MEZIERES. Her, the enemy made a show of resistance, but he was caught by surprise; many were killed including 2 officers who tried to escape on horseback; 50 prisoners were taken; 12 horses were captured, while the teams of two limbers were shot down at the road junction M 22.b.9.9. "C" Coy. attempted to capture some guns about M 22.b & 2.; indeed the gunners held up a white flag; but as the party advanced the enemy opened rifle fire. 2/LT. W. H. GRANT was wounded in the arm and in the leg. Two guns remained in the hands of "C" Company	

J. Anderson LIEUT - COL.
CMDG. 1st. Bn. The Black Watch

WAR DIARY
or
INTELLIGENCE SUMMARY.

(Erase heading not required.)

Army Form C. 2118.

Place	Date	Hour	Summary of Events and Information	Remarks and references to Appendices
	4TH/5TH		"B" Coy established touch with L.N. Lancs. at M.23.b.0.5. at 11.40 hours, and consolidated, to await the advance of the 14TH Infantry Brigade, commanded by BRIG-GENL. L.P. EVANS V.C. D.S.O. Such was established with ROYAL SCOTS at M.15.b. and a joint post was established at the MALASSISE BRIDGE just NORTH of MEZIERES. At 14.15 hours. On the night of 4TH/5TH the Battn. was relieved in the line by the 5TH LINCOLNS, 46TH DIVN, and withdrew to billets in MAZINGHIEN. The total number of prisoners captured by the Battn. during the operations on the 4TH amounted to 5 officers, and 128 other ranks. In addition 5. 77mm guns. 11 horses, and much material was captured. On casualties amounted to 3 officers WOUNDED; 4 other ranks KILLED, and 30 other ranks wounded.	2A.
	5TH		The Battn. marched from MAZINGHIEN to billets in VAUX ANDIGNY.	3A.
	6TH		The Battn. marched from VAUX ANDIGNY to billets in FRESNOY-LE-GRAND.	3A.
FRESNOY-LE-GRAND	6TH/12TH		The Battn. in these billets. Much instructional training was carried out during the period.	2A.

J. Anderson LIEUT-COL.
CMDG. 1st. Bn. The Black Watch

WAR DIARY or INTELLIGENCE SUMMARY.

Army Form C. 2118.

Place	Date	Hour	Summary of Events and Information	Remarks and references to Appendices
	11TH		SIGNATURE OF THE ARMISTICE TERMS	
	13TH	07.00	The battn. entrained on the FRESNOY-LE-GRAND — BOHAIN ROAD and proceeded via CATILLON and LANDRECIES to billets in LA BASSE MAROILLES.	
	13TH/14TH		The battn. in LA BASSE MAROILLES.	
	15TH	08.00	The battn. marched to billets in SARS POTERIES. Route MAROILLES — MARBAIX — DOMPIERRE — ST. AUBIN — DOURLERS — MONT. DOURLERS — SARS. POTERIES.	
	16TH	09.00	The battn. marched out from SARS POTERIES — LE — CHATEAU and returned to SOLRE — LE — CHATEAU via a SOUTH AFRICAN battn. of the 66TH — HESTRUD — GRANDRIEU.	
			DIVN in GRANDRIEU.	
	19TH	10.00	The battn. marched from GRANDRIEU under the orders of C.R.E. 1ST DIVN. and proceeded to SILENRIEUX via BEAUMONT — BARBENÇON. — BOUSSU — LEZ — WALCOURT.	
			The battn. marched to HANZINELLE via WALCOURT — TARBOIS — CHASTRES — FRAIRE — DONVEAU. Battn. HDQRS. was established in the CHATEAU 1 KILOMETRE NORTH of DONVEAU X-ROADS.	
	18TH	09.40	The battn. in billets at HANZINELLE	
	19/22ND		The battn. marched out from HANZINELLE and proceeded via MORIALME — FLORENNES. — CORENNE. — FLAVION, to billets in ANTHEE. Battn. HDQRS. was established in the CHATEAU DU VTE. DE JONGHE.	
	23RD	09.30	HDQRS. of the ex-GERMAN ex-CROWN PRINCE	

L. Anderson LIEUT-COL.
CMDG. 1st. Bn. The Black Watch

WAR DIARY
or
INTELLIGENCE SUMMARY.

(Erase heading not required.)

Army Form C. 2118.

Place	Date	Hour	Summary of Events and Information	Remarks and references to Appendices
	24th	11.00	The battn. marched to billets in SOMMIERE via ONHAYE - WEILLEN.	A.A.
	24th/30th		The battn. occupied billets in SOMMIERE. Training consisted of company and battalion drill.	
			HONOURS AND REWARDS:-	
			BAR TO DISTINGUISHED SERVICE ORDER — LIEUT-COL F. ANDERSON D.S.O. M.C.	
			BAR TO MILITARY CROSS — CAPT. N.D. MAXWELL M.C.	
			MILITARY CROSS — LT (A/CAPT) D.I. STEWART ; LIEUT A.F. RITCHIE.	
			2/LT A.J.H. DEMPSTER ; 2/LT N.A. MACNAUGHTON.	
			2/LT W.B. WEBSTER (A & S H); 2/LT C.I. SUTHERLAND (A & S H)	
			DISTINGUISHED CONDUCT MEDAL:-	
			No 7675 CPL. W. HUTCHISON M.M.	
			No 821 CPL. R. RITCHIE	
			No 43594 PTE (L/CPL) J. McDOUGALL	2.A.
			BAR TO MILITARY MEDAL :-	
			No 292499 PTE (A/CPL) J. NICHOLSON M.M.	

J. Anderson Lieut-Col.
CMDG. 1st Bn. The Black Watch

1st Royal [Regt?]

Army Form C. 2118.

WAR DIARY
or
INTELLIGENCE SUMMARY.
(Erase heading not required.)

REFERENCE MAP SHEET MARCHE 9 1/100,000

Place	Date	Hour	Summary of Events and Information	Remarks and references to Appendices
	1st		The battn. marched to billets near CELLES. Accommodation was found in the CHATEAU about 400 yards SOUTH of the village. ROUTE — ROSTENNE — BOUVIGNES — DINANT — CELLES.	2.A.
	2nd		The battn. resumed the march and proceeded via PAYENNE — SANZINNE — MONT GAUTHIER — CHEVETOGNE. Battn. HQrs, A Coy and B Coy were accommodated at ENHET. C. Coy. and D. Coy. were accommodated at RONVAUX.	2.A.
	3rd / 8th		The battn. rested at RONVAUX and ENHET. Ceremonial parades were held on two occasions, and in the Bois de SOMMON, in the form of wild boar hunting was carried out.	2.A.
	6th		The Colour Escort, comprising Capt D.I. STEWART M.C., Lieut A.C. TARBUTT M.C., No 9413 C.S.M. W REID D.C.M. and No 6330 No 2102 R.Q.M.S E. ROBERTSON M.M.; Sgt G. FOOTE M.M., who had been sent to SCOTLAND to bring out the REGIMENTAL COLOURS, rejoined the battalion with the COLOURS.	2.A.
	8th		The COLOURS were formally received by the battalion on parade. The battn. resumed the march, and proceeded via CHEVETOGNE — HAVERSIN — NETTINE to billets in HEURE.	2.A.
	9th		The march was continued via BAILLONVILLE — NOISEUX — PETIT HAN to BARVAUX.	2.A.
	10th		The battn. marched via TOUR to billets in HEYD.	2.A.
	11th / 13th		The battn. rested at HEYD	2.A.
	13th		The march was resumed via LES ARNAIS — GRANDMENIL — MANHAY to billets in MALEMPRE.	2.A.

J. Anderson. Lieut-Col.
Comdg. 1st The Black Watch

Army Form C. 2118.

WAR DIARY
or
INTELLIGENCE SUMMARY.

Ref. MAP SHEET. — GERMANY. 1M — 1/100,000

(Erase heading not required.)

Instructions regarding War Diaries and Intelligence Summaries are contained in F. S. Regs., Part II. and the Staff Manual respectively. Title pages will be prepared in manuscript.

Place	Date	Hour	Summary of Events and Information	Remarks and references to Appendices
	14th		The battalion continued the march, and proceeded via the road junction at the 89 Km. Stone on the MANHAY – HOUFFALIZE ROAD – REGNÉ to JOUBIEVAL and JOUBIEVAL. Battn. Hdqrs. C Coy and D Coy were accommodated in HEBRONVAL; A Coy, B Coy and the Regtl Transport were accommodated in JOUBIEVAL.	
	15th		The march was continued via SALMCHATEAU to BEHO.	
	16th		The march was again continued, and at 10.00 hours, the battalion crossed the GERMAN FRONTIER. The Regimental Colours were un-cased. The battalion marched past the Divisional Commander at a point about 300 yards East of the International Boundary, reached about 14.00 hours, via SCHIRM – ST. VITH. Battn. Hdqrs, B Coy, C Coy and D Coy were accommodated in BREITFELD. A Coy and the Transport station in NEIDINGEN; A Coy and the Transport station in	
	17th		The march was continued via ST. VITH – SCHONBERG to billets in MANDERFELD and KREWINKEL. Battn. HDQRS, C Coy and D Coy were accommodated in MANDERFELD; A Coy, B Coy and the Transport station in KREWINKEL.	

G. Anderson Lieut-Col.
Comdg. 1st Bn. The Black Watch

Army Form C. 2118.

WAR DIARY
or
INTELLIGENCE SUMMARY.
(Erase heading not required.)

Instructions regarding War Diaries and Intelligence Summaries are contained in F. S. Regs., Part II. and the Staff Manual respectively. Title pages will be prepared in manuscript.

Place	Date	Hour	Summary of Events and Information	Remarks and references to Appendices
	18TH		The march was continued via HALLSCHLAG — KNONENBURG — billets in DAHLEM.	AA
	19TH		The battn. marched from DAHLEM to billets in BLANKENHEIM.	AA
	19TH/21ST		The battn. rested in BLANKENHEIM.	AA
	21ST		The march was resumed via TONDORF — HOLZMULHEIM — MUNSTEREIFEL to billets in IVERSHEIM.	
	22ND		The march was continued via RHEDER — STOTZHEIM — KUCHENHEIM — WEIDESHEIM. Battn. Hdqrs. A.Coy. and C.Coy. and D.Coy were billeted in WEIDESHEIM; B.Coy. was billeted in ESCH.	gA AA
	23RD		The battn. marched into its final destination in ROISDORF via OLLHEIM — HEIMERZHEIM — BORNHEIM.	
ROISDORF.	23RD/31ST		During this period, the battn. remained in billets in ROISDORF. Some platoon and company training was carried out, and proper bands joined the battn. On 29TH, the Regimental band with Educational training.	aA

G. Anderson Lieut.- Col.
Cmdg. 1st Bn. The Black Watch

WAR DIARY
or
INTELLIGENCE SUMMARY
(Erase heading not required.)

Army Form C.2118

Place	Date	Hour	Summary of Events and Information	Remarks and references to Appendices
	4TH		MILITARY MEDAL:- No 2102. C.S.M. (A/R.S.M.S) E. ROBERTSON; No 350191 SGT G. BERRY; No 5776 SGT J. HISLOP; No 5290 SGT J. GRAY; No 40625 SGT R. MILLAR; No 5265 SGT R. ANDERSON; No 35962 PTE W. STEPHEN; No 19961 PTE W. LONGMUIR; No 1122. PTE D. FERNIE; No 2432. PTE P. SPENCE; No 40246 CPL J. MURDOCH; No 1806 CPL W. URE; No 19365 PTE J. HOPE; No 1838 PTE W. JOHNSTONE; No 8633. PTE W. MEEK; No 9145 PTE J. McGINN; No 14318. PTE A. McGOWAN; No 3707 PTE. J. DONNELLY; No 14312 PTE D. DUFF; No 3789 PTE (L/CPL) M. REEKIE; No 6080 PTE (L/CPL) W. HANSON; No 1363. PTE (A/CPL) F. EASEDALE; No 290688 PTE A. BROWN; No 24239 PTE A. HAY; No 266062 PTE C. SPRATT; No 12537 PTE J. PURDIE; No 40204 PTE W. WHITECROSS; No 268326 PTE H. SPALDING; LIEUT B. G. VALENTINE M.C. LIEUT W. WILSON D.C.M. 2/LIEUT W. H. GRANT. LIEUT I. K. HIGGINBOTHAM (13TH). CASUALTIES - OFFICERS - WOUNDED - OTHER RANKS - KILLED - 4 ; WOUNDED - 36. 2/LIEUT R. B. MAVER (16"/15); 2/LT G. W. FERGUSON M.2 M.M. (28"/15) 2/LIEUT H. DRURY (27"/15) REINFORCEMENTS - OFFICERS - 2/LIEUT - 19.11.18. OTHER RANKS - 109 - 16.11.18 ; 6 - 19.11.18 ; 36 - 10.11.18 ; TOTAL - 238. 84 - 4.11.18 ;	

J. Anderson LIEUT-COL
C.H.D.G. 1st Bn. Black Watch

Army Form C. 2118.

WAR DIARY
or
INTELLIGENCE SUMMARY.
(Erase heading not required.)

Instructions regarding War Diaries and Intelligence Summaries are contained in F.S. Regs., Part II. and the Staff Manual respectively. Title pages will be prepared in manuscript.

Place	Date	Hour	Summary of Events and Information	Remarks and references to Appendices
	December 1918		HONOURS AND REWARDS.	
			MILITARY CROSS — Lieut W. Wilson D.C.M. } IX Corps. H.R/416.	
			Lieut W.F. Bushe } a. 11.12.18.	
			T/Capt P.B. Hepburn — IX Corps H.R/717 a. 16.12.18.	
			DISTINGUISHED CONDUCT MEDAL —	
			No 777 Cpl (Lce/Sgt). R. Dunbar. IX Corps. H.R/917 a. 16.12.18.	
			REINFORCEMENTS —	
			Other ranks — 41 — 6.12.18 ; 52 (Regtl band) — 29.12.18 ; 38 — 29.12.18.	
			Officers — 2/Lt R.J. Prescott — 12.12.18 ; 2/Lt H.G. Gregory-Smith 29.12.18.	
			Lt A. Ferrier-Kerr — 30.11.18.	
			Lt A. Ferrier-Kerr — invalided to U.K. 9.12.18	
			2/Lt A.F.W. Robertson — Medical board in U.K. — 29.11.18.	
			Struck off Strength —	
				L. Anderson. Lieut-Col.
				Cmdg 1st Bn. The Black Watch

W —

A.O.O.
1 Rhyl Forts

Army Form C. 2118.

WAR DIARY
or
INTELLIGENCE SUMMARY.

(Erase heading not required.)

Ref. Map Sheet. GERMANY 2L 1/100000 of C 54

Place	Date	Hour	Summary of Events and Information	Remarks and references to Appendices
ROISDORF, GERMANY.	1919 Jan. 1/31.	—	Throughout the month the Battalion remained in billets in ROISDORF. Billets were good and large halls were available for meeting, indoor training and recreation.	KJM
			As hitherto since entering GERMANY, each company maintained an outpost guard of 1 N.C.O. and 6 men, mounted 1 hr 24 hours of one platoon which found 2 day sentries on fault and patrolled their respective company areas by night sentries were placed.	KJM
			Training was carried out during the month as follows:— (a) Educational training was given priority over other training and consisted of Company training 8 hrs in the morning, and Voluntary training in the afternoon or evening. Company devoted one day a week to Compulsory training which was composed mainly of Reading, Writing and Arithmetic and lectures on History and Citizenship. all men being divided into three Standards. Voluntary training consisted of classes in accordance with Company subjects. Voluntary training and lectures by civilian and ex-officers given. German and Book-keeping, and lectures by civilians and still returned, who visited the Battalion.	KJM
			(b) Military training was carried out to the extent of about two hours daily on the mornings and consisted of Platoon and Company training, including Physical training. Rifle Drill and Ceremonial. Battalion or Company Route Marches took place twice a week. A 100 yards Range was improvised, where Musketry and Lewis Gun training was carried out.	KJM
			(3) Recreational training included inter-Platoon Company & Battalion A number of Cross country Runs & Paper chases were held — Brigade Cross Country Team Run on Jr 31." A Boxing Team was training but Brigade orders cancelled it — Dancing Classes were held nightly in the ROISDORF Hall, where Training and Dancing	KJM 5HE SAS R. Willis Major Commanding 1st Bn The Royal War Cap

A8001) D. D. & L., London, E.C. Wt. W 17711/M 2931 750,000 5/17 Sch. 52 Forms/C2118/14

Army Form C. 2118.

WAR DIARY
or
INTELLIGENCE SUMMARY.

REF. MAP SHEET - GERMANY 2LY
(Erase heading not required.)

Place	Date	Hour	Summary of Events and Information	Remarks and references to Appendices
ROISDORF, GERMANY	1919 Jan 1/31.	—	Demobilisation :- During the month 6 officers and 162 other ranks were despatched for dispersal, including all the miners who were previously serving in the Battalion.	[initials]
			Leave facilities having been greatly increased, 11 officers and 305 other ranks have proceeded on leave to U.K. during the month.	[initials]
			Re-enlistment :- Under Army Order IV of 10th Dec. 1918, 10 men have re-enlisted for four years and 1 man for three years.	[initials]

R.Q. Miles Major
Comdg
1st Bn. R.D. Fusiliers Black Watch

Army Form C. 2118.

WAR DIARY
or
INTELLIGENCE SUMMARY.
(Erase heading not required.)

Instructions regarding War Diaries and Intelligence Summaries are contained in F. S. Regs., Part II. and the Staff Manual respectively. Title pages will be prepared in manuscript.

Place	Date	Hour	Summary of Events and Information	Remarks and references to Appendices
	January 1919		HONOURS & REWARDS:-	
			MILITARY CROSS:-	
			Capt. J.S. Young	New Year Honours List 1919.
			Lieut. M.H. Na Noble	
			PROMOTION:-	
			Capt. & Quarter-Master W. Fowler	
			to be Major	
			M.S. MEDAL:-	London Gazette 17th, 18th Jan 1919 (Published 20.1.19)
			7957. Sgt J. Dunjanson	
			2260 L/Sgt L. Hobbs	
			REINFORCEMENTS:-	
			OTHER RANKS +7. — 7.1.19. 20.-11.1.19. 17-13.1.19	
			OFFICERS:- Capt. D. Lumsden, M.C. 14.1.19. 2/Lt. T.B. Jones - 17.1.19	
			2/Lieut. A. M.C. Blair - 7.1.19	
			STRUCK OFF STRENGTH:- Capt. J.S. Young M.C. — Proceeded for Demobilization 22.1.19	
			Lieut. S. Arthur " 26.1.19	
			" W.V. Thomson. " 27.1.19	
			" J. Walker " 21.1.19	
			2/Lieut D. Baxter M.C. " 26.1.11	
			" E.A. Smith. " 15.1.19	
			" U. Stewart	

WAR DIARY
or
INTELLIGENCE SUMMARY.

Army Form C. 2118.

1 B/W Vol 5-5

Place	Date	Hour	Summary of Events and Information	Remarks and references to Appendices
ROISDORF, GERMANY. REF. MAP SHEET, GERMANY 2L 1/100,000	1919 FEB. 1 / 28		Throughout the month, the Battalion remained in billets at ROISDORF. The comfort of the troops was considerably increased through the completion of latrines & ablution accommodation. An O.R.R. Detour is being constructed to take the place of the SERBIAN B'talia which have been condemned by the A.D.M.S. During its reduction in strength through Demobilisation the four Company Guards were on 31st January, cut down to two, alternately found by 'A' 'B' and 'C' 'B' and 'D' Companies. The Guards as before each found double sentries by night who patrolled the Battalion area to prevent the circulation of civilians. Orders were received on 15th Feb. to hold in readiness a party of 3 Officers 7.100 other ranks to proceed to ROTTERDAM on Guard Duties. The party marched off to the 16 under command of Captain P.B. Hepburn, M.C. Training was continued, as in January, as follows:- (1) Educational Training consisted of Compulsory Instruction in elementary subjects carried out by each Company one day a week, and Voluntary Instruction in French, German Shorthand, Bookkeeping in the evening a number of instructors lectures were given by detainees visiting the Battalion. Four candidates underwent examination for Certificates of Education on the 2nd. (2) Military Training was continued for two hours daily, consisting of Platoon & Company training, which included Physical Training, Close Order Drill & Ceremonial. The 100 yards Range was allotted to each Coy once a week & Lewis Gun practice & Musketry were carried out. Elementary Lewis Gun Classes were instituted to replace trained Lewis Gunners who had been Demobilised.	26. 2A. 2A. 2A.

J.A. Anderson Lt.Col.
1 Bn The Black Watch

Army Form C. 2118.

WAR DIARY
or
INTELLIGENCE SUMMARY.
(Erase heading not required.)

Instructions regarding War Diaries and Intelligence Summaries are contained in F.S. Regs., Part II. and the Staff Manual respectively. Title pages will be prepared in manuscript.

Place	Date	Hour	Summary of Events and Information	Remarks and references to Appendices
ROISDORF GERMANY. REF. MAP SHEET GERMANY, 2L 1:100,000	1919 FEB. 1/28.		**Training (cont)** Recreational training was continued on the same lines as last month. An inter-company Athletic Championship Competition was held, including football, boxing, tug of war & cross country running. This was won by "D" Company. In the Brigade Championship which is not course of being completed, the Battalion has won the Cross Country Run and the Boxing. 9946 C.S.M.S. Wainwright, 4092 Sgt Morgan, 9-25334/ Pte Ward representing the 1st Brigade in the 1st Divisional Championship, held at BONN, on the 27th, as Heavy, Light & Feather weights respectively.	2A.
			Demobilisation:- During the month 4 Officers and 13 other Ranks were despatched for dispersal.	2A.
			Departure of Major Fowler, M.C. On the 24th Maj. & Q.M. Mr W Fowler M.C., left the Battalion to proceed for duty at Blighty, after over 35 years service in the Regiment, and continuous service, without a break, with the Battalion throughout the war. His departure was a matter of great regret to everyone and the high esteem in which he was held by all was expressed by the voluntary turn out of the Battalion to escort him to the station. Both the Pipe & Brass Bands were in attendance. In reaching the station, the Brass Band played "Auld Lang Syne," after which Major FOWLER addressed the Battalion and said good-bye. As the train moved out of the station, the pipers played "Scotland the Brave," accompanied by much cheering.	2A.

J. Anderson Lt.Col.

Army Form C. 2118.

WAR DIARY
or
INTELLIGENCE SUMMARY.
(Erase heading not required.)

Place	Date	Hour	Summary of Events and Information	Remarks and references to Appendices
FEBRUARY	1919.		HONOURS & REWARDS:-	
			MENTIONED IN DESPATCHES:- LIEUT. W.F. BUSHE. AUTHORITY, LONDON GAZETTE. 30.1.19.	
			" G.E.B. HONEYMAN " " " 28.12.18.	
			366 CPL. J. CORMACK " " " 30.1.19.	
			S/5773 PTE. G. GRAY. " " " 28.12.18.	
			R.A. 10099. W. WISSON. " " " 28.12.18.	
			265,200 L/CPL. J. HUTCHISON. " " " 30.1.19.	
			MILITARY MEDAL:- S/43344 PTE. A. REID. " " " 11.12.18.	2A.
			REINFORCEMENTS:-	
			OTHER RANKS:- 6 on 14.2.19. OFFICERS:- NIL	
			STRUCK OFF STRENGTH:-	
			CAPT. J.A. SMITH, M.C., LIEUT. W.F. BUSHE, M.C., 2/LIEUT. J. McNEILL - PROCEEDED FOR DEMOBILIATION 10.2.19.	
			CAPT. N.D. MACLEOD, M.C., LIEUT. D.I. STEWART, M.C. - TO U.K. AUTH. A.G. 8568(a) 12.2.19. (dated 21.1.19.)	
			CAPT. A.G. DUNCAN, M.C., 2/LIEUT. H.G. GREGORY SMITH - Do. - 13.2.19. - Do.	
			2/LIEUT. J.G. JONES, 2/LIEUT. W.M.C. BLAIR - Do. - 14.2.19 - Do.	
			MAJOR & QR. MR. W. FOWLER, M.C. - 24.2.19	
			2/LIEUT. W.B. MAVER - 16.2.19 DEMOBILISED.	2A.

J. Anderson Lt.Col.
1 Bn: The Black Watch.

WAR DIARY
or
INTELLIGENCE SUMMARY.
(Erase heading not required.)

Army Form C.2118.

1/Black Watch

Vol 56

Place	Date	Hour	Summary of Events and Information	Remarks and references to Appendices
RONSDORF. GERMANY. REF. MAP SHEET GERMANY 1/100,000 2L	1919. MARCH 1st /17th		During this period, the Battalion remained in the same billets in RONSDORF, the daily programme being the same as that of the previous two months. Two company Guards were mounted at ROSDORF daily, which found armed sentries at night who patrolled the Battalion area. Training was carried on as before, consisting of 1 day's Educational Training for Company per week, Military training, 1 day's Platoon training, 1 day's Company training, 1 day on the Rifle and Maxim. Standing orders to Battalion Patrols and Route Marches. Recreational training was continued on the same lines as during the previous month, comprising among others, a five-a-side Platoon football Competition which was won by No. 8 Platoon. The finals of the 2nd Army Boxing Tournament took place in COLOGNE on 21st, 22nd, 23rd, 1st the month, in which 5379/4 Pte F. WARD represented the 1st Division as feather Wright. He was however defeated in the semi-final on the 23rd. On the 29th the Final of the forthcoming Competition for the Army Commanders Cup was played at CO----GNE between 1st Cameron Highlanders IX Corps and 8 B.W. The Black Watch VI Corps. After an evenly contested match the Cameron won by 2 goals to 1.	

J Anderson Lt Col

Bde 56E 6Sheet

Army Form C. 2118.

WAR DIARY
or
INTELLIGENCE SUMMARY.
(Erase heading not required.)

Place	Date	Hour	Summary of Events and Information	Remarks and references to Appendices
ROISDORF, GERMANY.	1919 MARCH		After the 17th the Battalion became too weak in numbers, on account of demobilisation, to carry on ordinary training & the 2 Coys. Group had to be reduced for furnishing to a single piquet which was responsible for patrolling the area.	2A
	19.		On this date orders were received to expect reinf. by the 1/4th Cheshire Regiment on the 23rd & to prepare to billet a draft of 15 officers & 210 O.R. of the 1st K.S.L.I. who were arriving on the 20th to reinforce the Cheshires.	2A
	20.		Arrival of K.S.L.I. Draft.	2A
	23rd		1/4th Cheshire Regiment arrived & took over the area & duties.	2A
	25.		The Transport & Mobilization Stores were handed over to the 51st (Young Soldiers) Bn. Bedfordshire Regiment. Special Order by the Brig. by Brig. Gen. L.L. WHEATLEY, C.M.G., R.S.O. Comdg. 1st Inf. Brigade. was received, copy of which (with copy of reply) are attached.	A. 2A.
	30.		The Battalion paraded on A Coy's Dining Hall to receive an answer delivered by Maj. Gen. E.P. STRICKLAND, CB, CMG, DSO, who impressed great regret that the time had come when the 1st Bn. The Black Watch should leave the 1st Division (now called "Western Division")	2A.

J. Anderson Lt.Col.

Army Form C. 2118.

WAR DIARY
or
INTELLIGENCE SUMMARY.
(Erase heading not required.)

Place	Date	Hour	Summary of Events and Information	Remarks and references to Appendices
ROISDORF, GERMANY.	1919. MARCH 31st		Demobilisation:- A party of 124 O.R. were despatched for demobilisation, which practically completes the despatch of all the releasable men in the Battalion, and on the departure of the "Reinforce Men" who proceed to the 6th M. Black Watch on 1st April, the Battalion will be reduced to cadre establishment. Band: Throughout the month the Band were in great demand in the IX Corps Area. They played at Corps H.Q. Gen. EUSKIRCHEN, several times. A-M Murray receiving much congratulation on the fine performances he made.	20.

J. Anderson Lt.Col.

Army Form C. 2118.

WAR DIARY
or
INTELLIGENCE SUMMARY.
(Erase heading not required.)

Place	Date	Hour	Summary of Events and Information	Remarks and references to Appendices

	MARCH 1919.		REINFORCEMENTS :-
			 OTHER RANKS :- NIL. OFFICERS :- 2/Lt. W.P.BARCLAY 14.3.19
			 2/Lt. T.D. CRAVEN 25.3.19
			
			 STRUCK OFF STRENGTH :-
			 CAPT. D. LUMSDEN, M.C. 15.3.19 (2 months furlough) LIEUT-M.C. JOHNSTONE, 7.3.19 (Demobilised)
			 LIEUT. W. ADDISON, M.C., D.C.M., 7.3.19 (Demob) G.W. FERGUSON, M.O., M.M. 27.3.19 (Demob)
			 " G.E.B. HONEYMAN, 28.3.19 (2 months furlough) R.J. MASTERTON, 14.19 (2 " T.M.O. furlough)
			 " C.F. SUTHERLAND, M.C., 14.19 -do.-
			
			 CAPT. P.B. HEPBURN, M.C. CAPT. J.W.H. ROBERTSON, M.C. ⎫ Transferred to
			 LIEUT. A.C. TARRUTT. LIEUT. W. HARROP ⎬ Reserve of
			 " S.L. DAVIE J.R. HOUSTON ⎭ Officers
			 2/LIEUT. J. PENNINGTON 2/LIEUT. H. DRURY Retained under
			 " R.J. PRESCOTT A.O. XIV of Jan.
			                                                                                      1919, to 1/6 th B".
			                                                                                      The Black Watch.
			
			 J. Anderson Lt.Col.	

APPENDIX 'A'.

The Black Watch thank Brigadier General L.L. WHEATLEY, C.M.G., D.S.O. for his very kind farewell message, and hope that the time will again come when they will have the privilege of serving under his command.

SPECIAL ORDER OF THE DAY
by
Brigadier General L.L. WHEATLEY, C.M.G., D.S.O.,
Commanding 1st Infantry Brigade.

25th March, 1919.

To Brigade Headquarters, 1st Bn. The Black Watch, 1st Bn. Loyal North Lancashire Regiment, 1st Bn. The Cameron Highlanders, and the 1st Trench Mortar Battery.

The Brigade is about to break up.   For your loyalty in the past I thank you, for the present I say Good-bye, and for the future I wish you good luck.

It has been the proudest six months of my military service to have had the honour to command you.

***   ***   ***

www.ingramcontent.com/pod-product-compliance
Lightning Source LLC
Chambersburg PA
CBHW080852010526
44117CB00014B/2235